RAINBOW ROCK

Books by Dan Jorgensen

Rainbow Rock
And the Wind Whispered
Killer Blizzard
Andrea's Best Shot
Dawn's Diamond Defense
Kelli's Choice
Sky Hook
Jargon, The Book
Family Hiking Trails in South Dakota (co-authored with Roger Brandt)
The First Day (play)

SPEAKING VOLUMES, LLC
NAPLES, FLORIDA
2022

Rainbow Rock

Copyright © 2021 by Dan Jorgensen

All rights reserved. No part of this book may be reproduced or transmitted in any form or by any means without written permission.

ISBN 978-1-64540-705-8

Rainbow Rock

Dan Jorgensen

Dedicated to my wife Susan and to our children and grandchildren: Kari, Obie, Theodore & Cyrus Diener and Becky, Evan, Joshua & Nolan Yeager. May you always have great books to read and share.

This is a work of fiction, but some of the locations and people in the story are based on real individuals and places in the Black Hills, its surrounding prairielands, and communities depicted during the mid-1950s. More about factual and fictional events, people and places in the story are expanded upon in the book's "*Afterword*" section.

Foreword

Frank held out the photo picturing Elizabeth, Gene and their parents standing on a flat rock overlooking a small river below. A rainbow caused by the rising mist arced off the water behind them, both filling the low sky and seeming to embrace them within its brightly colored bands.

*****

"Have you ever wondered why a rainbow doesn't have a shadow?" he asked, picking the photo up again and turning it toward Maria. "No matter how hard you look, you can't see a rainbow's shadow, can you? I'll bet finding a pot of gold at the end of a rainbow would be easier than trying to figure out where a rainbow's shadow begins or ends."

Chapter One

Monday, January 31, 1955
Evening of the first day

The Rock Pile at Rainbow Rock
(Iya Iyupah ekta Iya Wigmuke)

"Gene! Gene! Get up! Come on man, get up!"

Frank Silver Shore grabbed his friend by the shoulders and struggled to pull him from where he lay sprawled on the ground. He tried shaking him, an action that only succeeded in eliciting a huge groan in response.

Gene Darveaux's eyes flickered open. He was fighting for each breath and sweating profusely despite the near-zero temperature. Frank had found him semi-conscious on the frozen ground, half-hidden amid the hardened skiffs of snow and clumps of western wheatgrass growing between the grain bins where he had fallen.

"Gene, listen to me! You've got to get up and let me help you." Frank shook his friend again.

Darveaux groaned even louder, moved his right arm and half sat. It was only then that Frank saw the dark stain on the front left corner of his friend's coat. Now that Gene was sitting, it was clear to see that his entire left side was bloody. He swung his gaze back to Gene's face and swallowed hard. Struggling to keep from vomiting as he dropped onto both knees, Frank reached across and tried to support his friend's back. Gene rocked sideways but remained in his half-seated position.

"Gene, who did this to you?" Frank was surprised at the tone his voice was taking—almost a rasping whisper. He cleared his throat hoping that might help him speak more clearly. "What happened?" he finally croaked.

Darveaux grabbed at Frank's arm. "I . . ." he gasped the word and stopped, breathing harder. "There are some men . . . some men . . ." he looked back over his shoulder. "Still after me. You-you . . . better get away . . . get away from here. Go! Hurry!" He slipped back into semi-consciousness and sagged against Frank's arms.

"Gene! Man! Come on, please get up." Frank half-sobbed the admonition, renewing his efforts to raise his friend's body from the ground. Darveaux coughed and re-opened his eyes, fighting against Frank's efforts.

"No! Just . . . you leave me! You . . . get away. It's . . ." he shuddered. "It's too late for me."

"Don't talk like that man! It's not too late. Let me help you get over to the café. We'll call for help. My car's over there. I'll get you to a doctor or something."

Gene pushed away, pulling free from Frank's grasp before falling heavily back to his original spot. He spoke again, sounding angry now. "Go on! Get . . . away Frank! Those men will find us . . . kill me. You too! Run! Get away!"

Frank looked around. He was frustrated and feeling helpless. But now he also felt afraid. He and Gene were partly concealed in the shadow of one of the large bins on the fringe of the Sandman Elevator complex out on the prairie east of the Black Hills. Frank had found Gene after first looking for him inside the nearby Railway Café, a place he'd been drawn to after getting a frantic phone call about an hour earlier from his now fallen friend.

*****

Frank had been settling into his room for the night, listening to the fabulous Bill Haley and His Comets singing "Rock Around The Clock" on KOMA, the rapidly rising "Teen Fave" clear channel radio station out of Oklahoma City. Singing along while he started getting ready for bed, he reached over and turned the radio's volume up just as his father banged on the door. "Sorry dad!" he called, turning the volume back to where it had been before.

"The phone's for you. It's that damn Darveaux kid." His father's voice was angry, as usual these days. "You tell that kid I don't want him disturbing us in the middle of the damn night!" his father grouched as they walked up a flight of stairs and down a hallway leading toward the living room. "And quit playin' that shitty rock music so damn loud. A man can't hear himself think with that crap filling up the air!"

The elder Silver Shore strode past the phone, which was anchored on the hallway wall, and dropped down into a shabby overstuffed chair. He turned up the volume on his flickering black and white TV set as Frank reached for the phone's receiver draped down across a small table directly beneath the wall-mounted phone.

"Middle of the . . . come on, dad, it's only 9:30!" Frank glared at his father. "And I barely had the sound up on the radio until just when you got there, and you know it!" He tried a more lighthearted response. "It was 'Rock Around The Clock!' Gotta have the sound up for that one." Roy Silver Shore ignored him, opened a bottle of beer and took a huge swig.

Frank grabbed the phone's receiver and twisted the cord so he could turn his back on his dad as he talked. "Hey man, what's up?" he asked casually as he cupped a hand near his mouth to try to keep their conversation even more private.

"Frank, I'm in trouble . . . really bad trouble!" Gene gasped. "I need you . . . to come . . . and meet me. I'm out by the Railway." He stopped as if trying to catch his breath. "But you gotta be careful!" The Railway was one of the few area cafés that served Indians, so Gene calling from there was not a surprise. The tone of his voice, however, was.

"What? Why?" Silver Shore turned further away from his dad and tried to muffle his voice. "What do you mean you're in trouble? What's going on?" His father twisted part way toward him, still angry but also curious.

"You tell that kid you can't come out this time of night!" Frank's dad exclaimed. He sat forward, arms folded with the half-empty beer bottle tucked close to his belly, glaring as Frank listened to Gene's raspy voice coming over the line.

"Just come. Quick!" Darveaux sounded like he was having trouble formulating his words. "Please!" Darveaux begged. He said the last word so loudly that Frank had to hold the phone out away from his ear. "I really need your help!" An operator interrupted, asking for more money to keep the conversation going.

He heard the operator say, “You have one minute remaining. Please deposit another 10 cents to continue your call.”

“Frank,” his friend gasped again. “Please! I need you to come. And be careful! Don’t trust anybody. Okay?”

Frank cradled the receiver on his shoulder trying to ignore his father’s angry gaze. “Okay. Just hang on buddy. I’m on my way. I’ll try to be there in 45, hour at the latest.” The phone clicked and he heard a dial tone. Frank re-cradled the receiver onto the phone. “Gene needs me to come and get him. I’ll be back as soon as I can.” He started back down the hall leading to the stairway that went to his room. He stopped and looked back over his shoulder. “Unless he needs me to take him home, or something. I might end up at his place for the rest of the night if he needs me to drive him.”

“Fucking hell!” his dad grumbled, sitting back in the chair. “You need to find your own place. You’re almost 20 years old and I’m tired of this shit. Phone calls in the middle of the night; radio blasting; running off to God knows where?”

“I need to go help my friend!” Frank whirled back toward his father, his face contorted in anger. “Something’s wrong and he needs my help. And don’t worry,” he added, “I’m looking for my own place. Gene and I are talking about finding someplace together soon. You can count on it!”

“Good,” his father muttered. “ ’Cause I’m sick of it.”

Frank started to retort that that made two of them, thought better of it, and continued on toward his room.

“It’s 1955 Dad!” He shouted at his father as he came back upstairs and headed for the door, keys in hand and pulling on his coat. “People help each other these days!” He saw his dad start to get out of the chair, quickly slammed the door shut and jogged over to his car so he couldn’t hear his father’s response.

*****

Frank located Gene's car at the far edge of the Railway Café's parking lot, and pulled up alongside a small shed owned by the Sandman Elevator Company—the grain shipping company that co-shared the sprawling gravel-covered parking space with the café. Frank cruised past, pulled up closer to the back side of the café, and walked back across the lot to where Gene's car was sitting. It only took a few seconds to see that the driver's side window was shattered and there was blood on the door. After making sure Gene wasn't inside or lying on the ground nearby, he hurried back to the café's front door, which faced out toward the rail line that ran between the building and the many rows of the Sandman's steel grain bins and its elevator complex operations office.

Pushing the door halfway open, Frank waited for its overhead bell to stop jingling and spoke to a tired-looking mid-thirties-aged man cleaning off the counter. "I'm looking for a friend of mine," he called to the man. "He's an Indian kid like me." Frank looked around. "He called me from a pay phone a while back and said he was out here waiting for me to give him a ride home."

"Yeah, I saw someone—I think it was a young guy or a teenager maybe—at that booth outside," the clerk replied, nodding toward the far left window where the edge of a phone booth could be seen. "But he hung up and left. It was half hour, 45 minutes ago, maybe." He shrugged. "Didn't see where he went. Thought he might've been drinking or something. Seemed to be having a hell of a time staying on his feet."

Frank nodded as if to confirm the man's assumption and stepped back outside. Eyeing the blue and grey phone booth at the corner of the building, he walked over to check it out. A smear of blood on the outside of the booth's door immediately caught his eye. He reached out to pull the door open, stopped, and looked it over more carefully. Slipping on his gloves, he slowly opened it. There was more blood splattered around inside. He checked the receiver. Blood there, too.

He pushed the folding door back shut and knelt down, listening for any unusual noises in the cold night air. Then he stared back toward Gene's car. There were so many footprints it was hard to tell which direction his friend might have gone after making the call. He cautiously started back along the east edge of the parking lot where the railroad tracks separated the café from the adjacent grain bin complex.

Kneeling to study some of the footprints, he looked up and down the rail line, brushing cautiously at a couple of the prints just as a trio of vehicles—two coming from the north, the third from the south—met briefly at the parking lot entrance. After what seemed to be some sort of meeting among the drivers, they all drove slowly off the road and into the far end of the parking lot. Caravanning along the lot's roadside edge, the vehicles stopped momentarily beside each other again and then split into three directions.

The first one—a dark colored pickup truck with a custom split rail style box—moved across toward Frank's side of the lot, and drove past the café's small storage building and on up toward the parking lot area beside it. After disappearing briefly the truck re-emerged near the corner of the building where Frank had parked his own car. It stopped for a few seconds and a flashlight swept out from the vehicle's window illuminating Frank's old jalopy. The driver shut the light off, pulled ahead and slowly turned around, this time shining the flashlight out across the gravel parking lot as if looking for the empty car's driver.

The middle vehicle drove up closer to the café's entrance and stopped, while across the gravel lot by the little shed where Gene's car stood abandoned, the third car pulled up just short of the shot-up vehicle. After driving back and forth past it a couple times, the car stopped a few car lengths behind the other vehicle, turned kitty-corner in their direction. Its headlights flashed up on high beam, went back to low, and then re-flashed on high. After several more seconds the driver eased up alongside the trunk end of the damaged car, its position seemingly setting up a roadblock on the vehicle in case the driver was still inside and might try to move it.

Frank watched as the blocking car's interior lights came on and the driver got out. It looked like he was holding a gun in one hand and a large flashlight in the other. He approached the abandoned car and pointed the light inside the rear window. He walked alongside the car continuing to shine his light inside then swung the light around in their direction and flashed it off-and-on in a rapid rhythmic progression. Whoever was holding it then made a sweeping circular motion with the light as if signaling to come and join him.

The pickup truck, which had been inching forward from Frank's car, swung away from the back of the café and rapidly drove across the gravel lot. A few seconds later the car that had stopped by the café's entrance followed. As it moved away from him, Frank could see an exterior bubble shaped light on the roof and some sort of official insignia featuring the words Prairie City on its side.

"A cop car! What the hell is that all about?" Frank muttered as he watched it go. He debated whether to stand up and signal to them, but remembered his friend's admonition to "Be careful."

Crouching back low to the ground, he crept further away from where the three vehicles were now stopped and effectively blocking off both the front and rear ends of Gene's car. Frank flattened down, slipped across the railroad tracks and edged down the embankment and away from the parking lot, keeping the rails between himself and whoever those men were. It was there, at eye-level with the rails, that he spotted a bloody footprint in the middle of a dirty patch of snow and halfway between two of the railroad ties.

The print's toe end was pointed south as if whoever made it was trying to walk toward a small driving path that crossed the tracks several yards beyond. From there the path headed out into the rows of steel grain bins that were lined up behind him.

Frank brushed away the print and slipped further down the embankment on his side of the tracks. Still half-crouched, he crab stepped his way along the cinders that were shoring up the railroad ties until he reached the driving path. Although it was narrow, it was built up and packed hard to handle the traffic of grain trucks and wagons transporting grain and other supplies over to the bins.

A small snowdrift had formed where the path turned downward on his side of the tracks and there a sharp bloody image of a second footprint was clearly visible alongside the drift's outside edge. "Shit," Frank muttered as he examined the print. He had a bad feeling that it might be Gene's. Several drops of bright red blood were spattered alongside the print.

Shifting into a seated position so he could get a closer look, he took off his glove and felt at the drops. The blood was starting to freeze but it was still wet. "Shit, shit, shit!" he hissed. He brushed both the blood spots and the second print away and scooted further down the east side of the rail line embankment. Continuing to crouch as low as possible, he started to follow the path.

After half a dozen paces, he was completely below any sight lines from most of the west side parking lot. Coughing softly, he stood back up and walked over to a point where the path split. One lane led off toward the rows of bins on his left, the other went toward the grain company's small office building and loading dock on the right. That's when he first heard a groaning sound coming from in among the bins.

And it was there that he had found his friend.

Chapter Two

Frank gently lowered Gene's head and peered about. There was no sound of anyone moving their way. Half standing, he stayed low and edged deeper into the shadows. Flattening himself against one of the metal bins, he slid sideways and looked down the alleyway formed by two long rows of the bins, all filled with grain and stretching out for maybe a quarter mile.

It was a nearly starless night; clouds building for a possible snowfall. He started to move forward, but quickly jerked back as some sort of movement a couple dozen bins further down the row caught his eye. He crouched down and stayed still, staring intently at the spot. Finally, a shadowy figure emerged; then two more. The three shadows stood clustered together before turning and starting toward the railroad tracks. Frank jumped to his feet and hurried back to Gene's side.

"Somebody's out there all right," he whispered. "I think it's those men you're worried about. Who are they Gene? I saw someone over by your car? Are they cops? What should we do?" The questions poured out of him as he looked quickly around, surveying his surroundings. Beyond the bins to the east stretched a broad open field of dried grass. Not a good choice to make a run for it. The best thing would be to go back to the café, just as he had been urging Gene to do. But that would probably expose them to the three men as they crossed over the tracks.

A low rumbling noise filled the air and he jerked up at the sound. A train was coming. It was still out of sight but it would be entering from the southeast side, coming right between the café and the grain bin complex, cutting off that line of escape. Intermittent blasts from the train's whistle suddenly pierced the night air as the train reached a gravel roadway that ran across the tracks about half a mile further south.

"Gene, we've got to move. The train's coming and the headlight's gonna give us away. Gene! Damn it! Can you hear me?"

Darveaux's eyes opened wide. He made a gurgling sound as he reached into his coat pocket and pulled out a small, ornately carved and painted wooden box. He thrust it at Frank. "Take this!" Gene ordered, suddenly very lucid. He coughed and shook violently but still kept the box elevated toward his friend's face. "Take it and give it . . . to Marshal Twocrow . . . in Hot Springs . . . and tell him there's a man . . . a man named Sarge. He's the one. Sarge did this."

He grabbed Frank's coat with his other hand and roughly pulled him down. "Take the box . . . it's the red fox . . . in the . . ." he stopped talking and coughed. "On the box . . . give it to Twocrow. Do you understand?"

Frank leaned in closer trying to figure out what his friend was saying? Finally he gulped and nodded hard. "The red what? What do you mean? A fox or do you mean the box? Gene, what?" He felt Gene's fingers dig deeper into his arm as if willing him to understand. "Yeah. Okay, I got it." He held out the box. "Get this box to Twocrow."

"Remember about Sarge!"

"And tell him it was a guy named Sarge. He shot you. Right?"

"And, tell Elizabeth . . . there's money in a big leather bag. Go get it and take it to Twocrow . . . I hid it." He swallowed hard and whispered something that sounded like rock. He gasped and spoke louder. "Wihg, Frank, it's at the wihg . . . the rock pile . . . Iya Wigmuke." He coughed and pulled Frank toward him so that his friend's face was very close to his own.

"Gene," Frank said. "I don't understand Lakota. I don't know any Ee-yah Wee-gmue-kay."

"Rainbow, rain . . . the rock pile. It's on the rock pile." Gene stopped as if unable to speak any more, then he cried out. "Frank, you gotta tell Elizabeth I'm so, so sorry! Tell her I love her."

Another piercing blast came from the train's whistle. "On the rock pile? What rock pile? Gene, talk to me! What the hell's the rock pile?"

Gene loosened his grip and seemed to be looking at something over Frank's shoulder. A peaceful smile came to his face, replacing his anguish. "Mother," he whispered. "I'm coming to you now."

Frank turned his head to look just as a puff of wind, emitting a tiny whistling sound, blew across them. He looked back to Gene. His friend's arms had dropped limply to the ground and his head was now twisted to one side. Frank leaned in, his ear close to Gene's face, but there was no breath; no further movement. As quickly as it had come, the little breeze subsided, as if it had come to take his friend's spirit away.

He shivered, both from the cold and the eeriness of it as tears filled his eyes. He carefully laid Gene's upper body back on the frozen grass while grasping tightly onto the small, carved box. Now the train's noise seemed to completely surround them, and as the huge engine twisted around a bend and came into view its bright yellow-white headlamp illuminated the trio of men who were standing and looking toward the glare of its oncoming light. Frank watched in horror as the light bounced across the black void to completely filled up the space between the two rows of bins. There would be no hiding once it reached them.

One of the trio—a heavyset man—was standing at an angle, displaying a large white swatch of hair below his hat on the right side of his head. The patch of hair acted like a reflector for the train's headlamp, seeming to further bounce the light in Frank's direction. The man swung one arm up and waved it toward the area where Frank was waiting, obviously telling the others to watch the space being lit by the train's light beam.

Frank watched as all three men turned to follow the beam as it went past them and continued bouncing toward him. Then he lost sight of them as the powerful light flooded the area where he was kneeling alongside his friend's body.

His first instinct was to duck, then realizing how fruitless that would be, he shook his head at his own stupidity and stood up. No sense trying to hide now. They could spot him easily. The train's engineer laid on his whistle, an obvious warning to that first group standing so near the track. He probably hadn't seen Frank yet, but the three men would have, and he was certain they'd soon be moving toward him.

Frank gave Gene one last glance, slipped the little box into his coat pocket and dodged away, moving rapidly from bin-to-bin for cover. He circled around until he was back to a point almost directly in line with the doorway to the café. The train engine's roar was deafening as he stepped out from behind the shelter of the bin and into the glare of its approaching headlight.

Still unsure what to do next, Frank looked back up between the rows of bins and was startled to see the three men rapidly leapfrogging toward Gene's body. They were setting up as if to cover one another as they moved forward. Despite his fear, Frank laughed. They obviously thought he either had a gun or that he was Gene. He stared over toward where Gene's body lay on the grass. Did Gene have a gun? Maybe he should go back and check?

"Oh, come off it, Silver Shore?" he said under his breath. "Even if you had a gun, you wouldn't know what the hell to do with it." He flattened back up against the bin and edged around it to where he could see across to the other side of the tracks. The train engine was less than a couple hundred yards away now. His heart was beating fast and hard and he thought the men surely could hear its thumping even over the din created by the train cars crossing over the switching connection across the main road.

Staying low, he started forward at a crouch and on line toward the café. If he timed it right he could jump up and over the tracks just before the train came through and then use the train cars for cover. He snuck a look back toward the spot where he had left Gene's side and was stunned to see that the men had already arrived there and were gathered around his friend's body.

The big, heavyset man was kneeling next to Gene and gesturing again, pointing back toward the approaching train engine. As the man stood up his cowboy hat blew off exposing an even larger patch of his bright-white hair. The man's hair reflected even more of the train's powerful headlamp the light rapidly filled up the open space between them and the tracks. Facing Frank's direction, the big man dropped down onto one knee to snatch his hat from the snow and put it back in place.

As he adjusted the hat he looked up directly toward Frank just as the open area between them brightened further before being completely lit by the headlamp. He shouted something. Jumping to his feet, he pointed and quickly raised his other arm. Frank saw the flash of a gunshot, followed by another.

A small pile of snow near his feet erupted as one of the bullets struck beside him, and a whistling sound near his head caused him to drop to his knees as a second bullet flew past. "Holy maloley and rat crap pie!" Frank yelled aloud to no one but himself since the noise from the train was easily drowning out both the gunshots and anything he or anyone else said. Or did for that matter. Any gunshots would definitely NOT be heard if the men continued shooting at him.

Frank scooted around and prepared to get up and run toward the rails. He checked back on his pursuers and saw the big man move closer toward him, stop and plant his feet at shoulder width, bracing himself as he raised the gun again and took aim to fire once more in Frank's direction.

"Shit!" Frank dropped flat to the ground, and then pulled himself into a classic sprinter's stance. He had been a track standout in high school and now, he thought, was definitely a good time to utilize all of those running skills and make his final move toward the rails. "Okay asshole!" he shouted over his shoulder. "It's time for me to make like a tree and leaf! See you later alligator!" He gave the man a little two-fingered salute off the corner of his right eye and leaped forward just as the man fired again.

The train's whistle erupted, drowning out any sound of the bullet, as the engineer caught sight of an obvious lunatic about to run across the tracks in front of his 150-ton engine. The din created by the combination of the whistle, the train cars banging along, and the roar of the big steam engine sent shock waves coursing through Frank's body as he raced up to the east side cinder embankment. He threw his body forward and swan dived headfirst across the tracks, instinctively tucking in his upper body in mid-air. He hit the ground hard on his right side and grunted in pain as he rolled down the west side of the embankment almost directly on line with the café's front door.

As the train thundered past, Frank grimaced again as he rolled over and brushed himself off. He sat up and began checking to make sure he hadn't broken anything. The engineer leaned out the window and yelled something in his direction, an angry expression filling his face. Although Frank could not hear a single word, he was pretty sure none of them were a concerned, "Hey kid, how you doin' down there?"

He sat still for a few more seconds, now positive that he could hear each and every beat of his heart. And even if he couldn't, he for sure could feel all the beats because it felt like his heart was about to jump out of his chest.

The images of Gene's bloody left side and lifeless body drew him out of his momentary stupor. He sharply sucked in a deep breath and got back to his feet. His right shoulder ached but there was no time to check it further. Car after car of the long freighter kept rolling past, picking up speed as the train started moving away from the elevator complex and on toward Rapid City. He had to move quickly again because once the last car went by he was pretty sure the three men would be waiting to follow him across.

Running to the corner of the café, Frank paused to collect himself, catch his breath and figure out what to do next. Should he go inside and report Gene's death? Even if he did, would anybody believe him? Too often he had seen Indians arrested for killing other Indians even if there was no proof that they were guilty.

Despite what he'd yelled earlier at his dad about this being the progressive year of 1955 and people helping each other, he also knew that as an Indian he might just as easily be charged with killing his best friend. He didn't want to risk getting himself tossed into a jail cell with no way out.

As he leaned up against the building gulping big mouthfuls of air, he was startled by the sudden opening of the café's front door. The man from the counter who he'd talked to before stepped out, looked at Frank and shook a fist in his direction. "What the hell, man!" the counterman yelled, pointing to a broken window alongside the door. "Why you throwing rocks at my windows? What the fuck you doing? Get the hell away from my building. I'm calling the cops!"

"Yes!" Frank yelled back. "Call them! Call them!" But as the train continued going past, rapidly picking up even more speed, he realized the man probably just thought he meant he HAD been throwing rocks at his café windows and not that he wanted him to call the police. "What the hell!" he half-sobbed it in frustration. He turned back toward the door as he heard it slam. The counterman was probably locking it up to guard against any attempt Frank might make to enter.

He eyed the train again. There were only about a dozen cars left to go on by. He had to get away from there before the last one passed. He raced around behind the café to where his beat-up 1941 Plymouth coupe was parked and jerked open the door. Fighting to get the key into the ignition, he finally got it inserted, cranked the engine and prayed. It sputtered twice, caught and started.

"Thank you! Thank you!" He shouted his thanks aloud while looking skyward. Shifting into gear, he released the handbrake and headed away from the backside of the café and out onto the gravel parking lot. Keeping the lights off he cut diagonally toward the parking lot's exit onto Highway 79.

Reaching the exit, he slapped at the sun visor that was dropped down like a big eye patch over the top part of the passenger side of his windshield, trying to move it out of his line of sight. The visor had been broken for several months and usually wasn't a problem hanging halfway down. But tonight, with no moon, it made it much more difficult to see the right side of the road, especially without his headlights, and the last thing he needed was getting into an accident.

Skidding to a stop at the lot entrance, Frank glanced back toward the café where just a few train cars remained to go past. The closest way to get out of sight would be to turn south from the lot and head up and over a small hill toward Hermosa. That might be just opposite of what the men who were chasing him would expect him to do, thinking he'd turn north toward Rapid City instead. If he could get beyond the hilltop before the men could make their way across the tracks, he'd be out of their sight by the time they made it around to the back side—his side—of the café.

Almost simultaneously with the last train car's passing, he shifted into low gear, turned left and urged his car up the hill, hoping the engine wouldn't throw a rod or simply stop running in protest. Growling loudly, the old car crept steadily upward, reaching the crest of the hill and picking up speed as he shifted to second gear and headed back down and out of sight from the café and elevator complex's double entryway.

Had the men seen him or not? Frank drove on, shifting into higher gears and continuing further south past the small town of Hermosa, which seemed almost abandoned on this cold winter night. The bitter cold also seemed to be keeping traffic off the road. Good and bad, he thought. There might be no one to flag down for help if needed, but there also would be no one to turn him in. He decided to keep his lights off to avoid being spotted.

After another mile and no sign of anyone following him, he pulled over to the side of the road, took the car out of gear and sat with his foot on the brake. What now? Go on to Hot Springs? Turn around and go back into Rapid City? He nervously drummed his fingers on the steering wheel. Had they seen his car? Did they have his license plate? Too many unanswered questions.

Maybe the best thing would be to drive to Hot Springs right now, park his car out of sight and go talk to Gene's best friend, his sister Elizabeth. He hadn't seen either of them for well over a month, not since he had moved in with his Dad at the end of December. Would she welcome him or throw him out?

He grimaced at the thought of their last meeting when she'd called him a bad influence because he was a high school dropout without a job.

Elizabeth had vowed that Gene was going to make something of himself and she had been pushing her brother to find a good job and settle down—and to stay away from Rapid City where Frank was living. What Elizabeth didn't know was that the two of them had still been making housing plans together behind her back.

While Frank hadn't seen Gene personally, they'd had several phone calls, talking strategy and planning for a time to get together to start looking for an apartment that they could share. Frank was excited about the possibilities, especially if it meant moving out of his Dad's house and into some kind of place of his own.

What in the world had Gene been doing up here? Why were those men looking for him? He reached into his pocket and pulled out the carved wooden box. And what the hell was this, anyway? More questions without answers.

"Gene said give it to Twocrow," Frank said aloud. That was easy. Alvin Twocrow was the best-known Indian lawman in the region, trained by the great Seth Bullock himself and now a grizzled old Deputy Marshal living in Hot Springs.

When they were high school juniors, he and Gene had interviewed Twocrow for a story in the school newspaper. It was Elizabeth's idea, and at first the two boys didn't want to do it. But after meeting Twocrow and hearing about some of his many escapades, they had been glad they did it. And on top of that they got one of their best English writing grades ever—a B+ for each of them. Since then they had maintained off-and-on contact with the old man.

"Okay, so I gotta drive to Hot Springs, find Elizabeth and then Marshal Twocrow," Frank reassured himself while still drumming his fingers on the steering wheel. He stopped and reached over to shift back into low gear. Checking the road even though it was still clear, he eased the old coupe back out onto the highway, flipped on the lights and turned the heater knob as high as it would go.

The Plymouth's temperamental heater wheezed in response. While it seemed to be only partially working, he figured his heart was pumping so hard there wouldn't be any problem keeping warm, or alert, on the 40-mile drive to Hot Springs.

Chapter Three

Al "Sarge" Tollefson punched his revolver back into the holster he kept at his side, turned and scanned the nearly vacant parking lot. He had just looked for the second time inside Darveaux's abandoned car, searching it more carefully than before. But it was still empty, and there was not a sign of the leather satchel filled with their cash and papers. A ray of light from the headlights of a passing car reflected off his badge for just an instant. He turned to where the other two men—Batch Hillman and Pete Delaney—stood waiting for instructions.

Tollefson's men were remarkably different from each other. Hillman, who wore a Prairie City police uniform like his boss, was very handsome and trim, about 5-foot-11 with an athletic build. Delaney was several inches taller, heavy-set and dumpy with huge jowls. He wore a nondescript, partially wrinkled brown work uniform with grease spots on the pants. While Hillman was shifting around as if trying to keep his feet warm in the cold night air, Delaney was standing stoically neither speaking nor moving. He held his hat in both hands, displaying the large thatch of bright-white hair that was covering the entire right side of his head.

Like the two police officers, Delaney had a sidearm attached to his belt, but it was the only indication that he might also be "official."

"No new tracks by the café? Nothing?" Tollefson queried.

"No, not from the edge of the café on," Hillman replied. "A lot of people been walking in and out of there, and when I asked the guy behind the counter he said he chased an Indian kid away from the front steps while the train was going past. Said he didn't know who he was, but he threatened to call the cops on him because the kid broke one of the windows alongside the front door."

"What? Broke his window? What the hell would that be all about?" Tollefson looked back over at the café. "And, for sure, he said he didn't know who the kid was?"

"Naw, he didn't know him. But he said the same kid had come inside earlier—just before we pulled in—looking for another Indian kid."

"Did he know that other one?"

"He said he didn't talk to that one, or anyone else, since around 7:30. Cold night, so pretty quiet, I guess. Just said that he saw what looked like another Indian kid using the pay phone around an hour or hour-and-a-half ago. He said that first kid never came inside; just used the phone. Said he looked like he might be drunk or something because he seemed to be having trouble standing up straight."

Tollefson nodded and grunted. "Sounds like the Darveaux kid. Probably calling the other kid to come and get him because he'd been shot."

"Anyway," Hillman continued, "he said that second Indian kid—the one who came inside earlier and then got chased away—he drove up and peeled out of here in a beat-up old car. He came in and asked about a friend, and then went back outside just a little before we pulled in and started looking for Darveaux."

Delaney finally spoke up as Tollefson stood staring out toward Highway 79. "You know, I saw an old beater parked out back of the café when we got here, but I figured it belonged to somebody working inside. It was a late '30s, early '40s. Plymouth or Dodge I think. Might've been that second kid's car. I got a look at him when he was in the train's headlight, and he was definitely a teenager or younger man. If I see him again, I think I could I.D. him."

Tollefson muttered something under his breath and glared at the others. "Well, whoever it was, let's hope he found Darveaux's corpse and not a source of information, or worse—our cash. If he was just an

Indian kid, maybe he's scared shitless and heading back out to the Rez as quick as he can."

"You want me to put in a request to the Rapid cops or the Highway Patrol to watch for the kid's car?" Hillman said. "We can take a stab at it being a late '30s or early '40s Plymouth, like Pete was thinking he saw."

"No. Too many side roads he could'a turned off on by now. Be a waste of time, especially since we can't positively verify what kind of car he was driving." He paused as if re-thinking the question. "That counter guy didn't say what the make of that kid's car might be, did he? I mean, when he was chasing him away?" The other man shook his head. Tollefson looked around. "All right, look, you go back in there and check with him again, then do a quick look up-and-down the highway for a mile or two each way. Maybe two to the South and one North. Let me know before you head back to the shop, and I'll write down a few things here while I'm waiting."

He blew out an exasperated breath in frustration, pulled off his hat and shook off the light snow that had accumulated on it while they were standing in the lot. "Well, at least on a dark night like this whoever that kid was, he isn't likely to have seen who WE are either, unless Darveaux was still alive and told him something."

"Darveaux wouldn't have known our names anyway," Hillman said quickly. "We've never identified ourselves to him, right Delaney?" The heavy man nodded vigorously to affirm what his partner was saying. "And he's never even met you. I mean, I guess he might've heard me call you Sarge, but that's about . . ."

"What?" Tollefson's face reddened as he cut Hillman off in mid-sentence. "How the hell did he find out you call me Sarge?"

"It was an accident boss," Delaney inserted, coming to Hillman's defense. "Besides, we didn't think it would make any difference. We only talked about you that one time and neither of us ever mentioned your name again." He shrugged as if reassuring himself that everything was going to be fine.

"You two get more idiotic by the day. The two stooges!" Tollefson stormed. "I don't care if he was a high school kid or a government agent. I told you before you don't use real names OR nicknames. Ever! You understand?"

They both nodded sheepishly.

"Let's just hope the hell my name never went any further."

Tollefson stared back toward the spot where they had left Darveaux's body. "I didn't find anything on him, but I'm not surprised. He probably stashed our money someplace along the route out here . . . and now we got nothing." He kicked angrily at a small pile of snow and looked satisfied when it exploded into bits and pieces. "How could a young KID trick us like that?"

Not waiting for a response, he went on. "All right, look, I'm going to write this up and send a report over to the Rapid police and the Highway Patrol. Maybe get a copy out to the Pennington and Custer County cops, too. I'll list it as a routine shooting—you know, another Indian getting liquored up and shot by one of his pals over a bottle. I'll go over and dump some liquor in him and then leave the bottle alongside. Something like that. You two check again with the counterman, then hit the roads, then check back here before you head over to the shop."

The two men started moving away as Tollefson tugged at his coat and cursed softly to himself.

"Batch!" The handsome Hillman turned back while gesturing for his partner to keep on going.

"After I get my report filed, I want to put together something for the *Black Hills News*. So, when you do get back to the shop, start digging to find out anything you can about who that second kid might be. If he was out there with Darveaux, there's a good chance they knew each other, especially since he stopped inside first and told the counter guy he was looking for his friend.

"Check any records, files, whatever you might be able to find. See if you can get something more about the Darveaux kid's background. And, I want you and Delaney to plan on driving down to Hot Springs tomorrow morning. Earlier the better. Talk to the locals and see if you can find a picture of Darveaux. If you do, stop back here and show it around inside the café. Even if nobody recognizes his name, they might know something else about him—especially if he comes here very often. Who knows? Maybe somebody'll know who that other kid might be, too." He nodded more to reassure himself than Hillman.

"We need to get a jump on anyone else who starts looking into this kid's death before the Coroner does his thing and makes things more formal. If we get going now and get down to Hot Springs early tomorrow that ought to give us a half day's head start or maybe even more on whatever investigation the Sheriff, or the Rapid cops, or Feds might do."

"Feds?" Batch asked, startled by that idea.

"Well, he's Indian ain't he? That means they'll probably send somebody in for a quick look; maybe from the U.S. Marshal's office. It's pretty routine."

He waved back toward the café. "Okay, get moving. Talk to that counterman again, and do a quick check on the roads and report back to me. Then I want you to head on back to the office and start digging. Shit, I know I'm just repeating myself but this has got me really worried." Batch nodded and started away. "And have Delaney pick up a couple of maps of the area," he called out. "See if he can map out any of the roads Darveaux might've driven between the time he left the Prairie City area and when we caught up with him out here."

Batch gave him a thumbs up and walked on to join Delaney, who had already reached where his Prairie City police car was parked alongside Darveaux's abandoned vehicle. The heavyset man had methodically started brushing the light snow from the car's back window until Hillman reached his side. Together they finished clearing all the windows, then got in and drove back to the front of the café where Delaney got out, repeated the snow-brushing procedure with his pickup and got in.

Tollefson stood watching them for a few more seconds before opening the door on his own Prairie City police cruiser and sliding inside. He started the engine and flipped on the windshield wipers to clear off the light snow that had continued falling. Coughing a couple times, he removed a pack of cigarettes from his pocket and lit one while his car's heater kicked in. After taking a deep drag and blowing out the smoke, he slammed his open palm against the top of the steering wheel.

"Why?" he shouted at the windshield. "Why in holy hell did this have to happen just when everything was going so good?" He cranked the heater higher, pulled a clipboard out from under his seat, then shouted again. "Damn it anyway!"

*****

Sarge Tollefson, Batch Hillman and Pete Delaney had first arrived in the Black Hills in 1944 while still serving in the Army Air Corps. All three had been assigned to the Army Air Base—just recently renamed Ellsworth Air Force Base—located out along Highway 16 about 15 miles east of Rapid City. When the war ended, the three buddies mustered out but stayed on, impressed by both the Black Hills' rugged beauty and a lucrative drug trade they'd gotten started through their work with the Air Base pharmacy.

Tollefson and Delaney were Military Police officers assigned to provide security for drug shipments that Hillman was transporting as part of his job at the Base motor pool. The trio had found themselves responsible for dozens of drug shipments that moved monthly both onto the Base and being dispersed out to satellite locations around the sprawling military complex.

They quickly realized that there were a lot of people who were being mustered out of the service who were still in desperate need of special "help" that only their prescriptions could provide. And there were others seeking the not-so-easy-to-obtain drugs that the military had readily provided for them. Especially the "miracle" drug methamphetamine. Ex-GIs were more than willing to pay more than a little extra in order to keep obtaining the drug they had come to regularly rely upon.

Before long the trio had developed a system of skimming some of the drug freight off the top of almost every base delivery. They rapidly built a nice sideline business re-distributing these contraband drugs to both their on base "clients" as well as to their former military customers who had stayed in the region.

When the war ended in August 1945, all three men mustered out of the Army Air Corps to take on jobs at the nearby and rapidly growing community of Prairie City. It was a town anchored by its newly constructed regional airport—one the city fathers hoped might eventually challenge the much bigger Rapid City airport to the west.

Tollefson and Hillman had signed on to help develop a quickly expanding Prairie City Police Department, while Delaney had taken on a position as a "do-everything" airport logistics director. There, he was in charge of a fleet of trucks and other equipment required for the airport's ever-growing cargo and private aircraft needs, set up to serve West River area ranchers, farmers and small businesses.

By mid-1946 Tollefson had moved into the main leadership position for the Prairie City police force, and within just a few more months he had taken over as safety coordinator for the airport, too. He quickly earned the nickname "Sarge," both for his past Army rank and for his crew cut, button down, and no nonsense appearance.

Hillman, whose movie star good looks and friendly demeanor attracted a wide range of friends and hangers-on, soon earned a nickname of his own. Everyone called him "Batch" because of his self-proclaimed determination to maintain his bachelorhood as long as possible, and for his proclamation that he was planning to continue "playing the field."

With Delaney in place as their "logistics man," overseeing all the airport's equipment and its outlying buildings and hangars, they had a natural number of locations where their shipments could be taken, stored and re-packaged for deliveries. And within a year they were able to quickly expand their black market drug operations, reaching an ever-widening circle of clientele.

But then, early in 1947, the whole operation had almost come apart at the seams.

Working at a refueling site for the fleet of city transport vehicles, Delaney was nearly killed by a nitrogen hydroxide explosion. After spending six months in the hospital and three more months in rehabilitation, he had finally recovered from the blast but had been left with two longstanding reminders: a mangled ear and nearly half his head permanently bleached a bright white where the chemicals had burned deep into the right side of his skull.

He was proud of his self designated "white badge of courage," gained from surviving the explosion. And even his grotesquely wrinkled right ear didn't bother him that much. Following a full recovery, he was grateful to have Tollefson lobby on his behalf to become the Airport's "general duties officer" as well as special liaison to the Police Department. He also got Delaney a nice cash payment that covered all his hospital expenses and more.

While Tollefson said he had made the suggestion to city management as a way to be sure Delaney didn't sue anyone for his injuries, the old Sarge also was looking at the promotion and payout as a way to insure that his former Army buddy would remain loyal to both him and their growing "business."

With their positions fully cemented in place by late that same year, the three men now had free rein across Prairie City and several other nearby properties that the city was managing for the regional airport. There, they were able to set up special rendezvous' times with a flotilla of private aircraft that could land and take off virtually unnoticed during late night and early morning hours when commercial traffic was not flying into their location.

Thus, by the end of 1948 they not only had established a regular schedule for their own Black Hills carriers, but also had reached out to contacts who could bring in their black market drugs from new suppliers operating as far away as Omaha, Kansas City and Minneapolis.

Shipments had regularly arrived to be sorted and divided into "special delivery packages" after first being moved over into one of Delaney's specially designated warehouses. From those preparation points, the packages were carefully re-distributed throughout the region, transported by a group of drivers recruited mostly from down-on-their-luck ex-Veterans to high school and college-age kids looking to make some easy money.

Drivers were recruited for their willingness to drive any place at any time, taking the packages to out-of-the-way locations, no questions asked. Payments to the drivers were always in cash—tax-free—so long as they did the driving without complaint for whatever hours they needed to make their deliveries.

But, when Tollefson, Hillman and Delaney moved to expand their operation to the Pine Ridge and Cheyenne River Indian Reservations as well as other communities with large numbers of Indian customers, Tollefson decided they needed to hire some Indian drivers too; drivers who would "know the territory" into which they made those deliveries.

One of their newest drivers was a quiet, efficient teenager from Hot Springs named Gene Darveaux.

Darveaux had soon become one of their most dependable delivery men, not only on trips out to the "Rez" but also for taking on additional delivery assignments on short notice while never asking questions. He would just make his package drops and bring back sealed envelopes filled with cash payments. Thus, tonight's assignment seemed like a perfect fit for their willing and "trustworthy" kid.

They'd have him meet Batch, who would be picking up a satchel with $50,000, money they were getting from a "silent" partner on Rapid City's west side. Once Batch had transferred the satchel to Darveaux, they'd have him take it out to the Prairie City airport where he would drop the satchel with Pete. Pete would be meeting a private plane bringing in one of the largest drug shipments they'd ever ordered, and he would hand off the cash to the pilot.

Darveaux would be paid for his driving by Delaney before the plane arrived and then sent on his way. It would be a simple Point A to Point B to Point C operation with their faithful young driver moving the money for them during the first two legs of the transfer. And if something went wrong along the way, he would be clueless and they would be in the clear.

Batch would drive out and meet with Delaney after he had met the plane, paid the pilot and picked up the drug shipment. Then, together, they would drive the drugs to a new warehouse location Delaney had found in the small town of Fairburn where he lived. As their operation continued to grow, the Fairburn locale seemed like a much safer, out-of-the-way place. The warehouse there was spacious, once used to store timber being shipped by the railroad to building sites back East.

It would be simple as A-B-C. Nothing to it and lots of profits waiting on the back end. At least that's how the night's events had been planned before everything had started falling apart.

Chapter Four

For Gene Darveaux, the fateful night had actually started in mid-afternoon with a call from his driving job contact to his and his sister Elizabeth's home telephone. It was late notice, the man said, but if Gene could come up to Rapid City right away, he was needed that night to help make a delivery and it would be double his usual pay. And, his contact caller reassured him, he'd be home by 10; no problem. So he'd left Hot Springs by 5 p.m. and arrived at his regular meet up point just south of Rapid City a little before 6.

This was the first time he'd be making a delivery on a night other than the weekend, but his contact caller had made out like it was really important for him to come. Plus there was that promise that by coming on short notice like this it would mean a big bonus payment for his effort.

But when he arrived at the spot where he normally stopped to pick up the packages he had to deliver, a man he'd never seen before walked up, rapped on his window and handed him a small, tightly folded scrap of paper. Without speaking, he quickly turned and walked away.

Gene unfolded the note and stared at the message: "Come to the Holiday Motel on Mount Rushmore Road by 6:30 for delivery instructions," read the note.

He stared at the message and frowned, rubbing his hands back-and-forth across the top of his lap. Debating with himself over whether to continue with this job, or not, he finally rolled down the window, started to call to the man, then stopped and shook his head. "Just go do it, Darveaux. What have you got to be scared of?"

He rolled the window back up and refolded the note. Shaking his head again and muttering to himself, he reached into his coat pocket and pulled out a small, brightly painted carved box. The box was covered with tiny intricately detailed wildlife and nature carvings.

Running his fingertips over several of the birds, trees and animal heads that graced the box's sides, he stopped on the face of a red fox defiantly looking out from a dark spot directly beneath the center of a rainbow. He had always wondered whether the spot was supposed to be the fox's den or he was instead emerging from under the rainbow's shadow.

Holding it at a slight angle to take advantage of a nearby street light, he took a pencil from his shirt pocket and pushed a tiny dot that was located on the inside corner of the fox's left eye. The action caused the end of the box to pop open revealing a hidden compartment. "Better safe than sorry," he mumbled.

Gene took the message, folded it down as tightly as possible and then scribbled the date and his name on the paper's corner. He crammed it inside the compartment alongside another note he'd placed there two weeks before. That first note contained his Rapid City contact person's phone number written alongside a name he had heard on one other night when he was driving—"Sarge." Together the two notes barely fit into the little space, and Gene had to use the pencil's point to tuck them snuggly down inside before snapping it shut.

As he always did when opening the little box, he paused to marvel at its intricate workmanship. The fox eye's tiny "trigger" was virtually invisible, as was the compartment—unless you knew they were there. It had been a birthday gift from his mother two years before, shortly before she and his father had been killed in a car accident, broadsided by a man high on amphetamines and half asleep as he hot-rodded his way through a four-way stop sign at the intersection of the highway leading out to the Pine Ridge Reservation.

"This box is for keeping your secrets safe," his mother had told him with a hug and a smile after showing him the tiny hidden compartment. "Use it wisely."

He slipped the box back into his jacket pocket and put the pencil back into his shirt pocket. Easing out onto St. Joseph Street, he merged into traffic and headed past the School of Mines, merging onto the one-way Main Street headed west as he crossed over Steele Avenue en route to the downtown Rapid City area. Reaching Highway 16—also recently labeled as Mount Rushmore Road—he made a left turn and headed southwest toward the Holiday Motel.

Tonight, this "short notice" job had come at a perfect time. Gene wasn't sure what he might be delivering, but he and his sister really were getting desperate for more money. Elizabeth had been sick for nearly a week and had been unable to fight off whatever it was that was affecting her. With the extra cash he would earn tonight, maybe she could buy whatever medicines she needed and take a few days off to finally get well.

On top of that, he thought, maybe his willingness to take on such a short-notice assignment would lead to even more lucrative driving jobs and the chance to move up in the organization. Maybe tonight's job would be his big break, ultimately leading to a bunch of better things for both him and his sister.

Gene had been driving now for about 3 months. His payments always were envelopes with cash—no questions asked, nothing else shared. He had met a couple of his employers before, but didn't know their names. Only one time had they talked about anyone by name, mentioning that man named Sarge; asking what time Sarge had called for Gene to come and drive?

He realized immediately that they were flustered about using the contact man's name, especially when Gene had shrugged and said he didn't know anybody named "Sarge." After that evening's work was finished, he had decided to write down both his contact's phone number and the name Sarge and stash them in his box's secret compartment—a little "job security" if ever the need arose.

Arriving at the Holiday Motel a few minutes early, he parallel parked in front of the office, turned off the engine and glanced around. Movement at the motel's office door caught his eye and he sat up straighter as one of his regular contacts—a very good-looking guy who he often dealt with—came out from the lobby carrying a bulky leather satchel. The man looked in as if verifying this was his driver, then gave a little wave to Gene and opened the back door. He tossed the satchel onto the seat and waved at Gene again.

"Hi-ya kid," This time he gave the young man a cordial nod, shut the door and opened the front passenger side door. The usual routine was that a package would be put inside, Gene would be handed an address, and then he'd drive out and make his delivery, getting a sealed envelope in return. After that he'd bring that sealed envelope back, pick up another envelope with his pay and head back home. A satchel like this was something new.

The man handed him a large white envelope with the name Prairie City Airfield written on it in block letters. "You know it?" he asked. Gene nodded. "Okay, when you get there, drive over to the east side of the new runway. You'll see a man waiting there in a dark red Chevy pickup truck. It's got one of those fancy, split-rail boxes," the man said. "Give him this envelope and that satchel in back."

Gene was confused by the change in his usual routine. "Will I get an envelope to bring back? And where do you want me to bring it? Should I come back out here?"

"No. There's nothing to bring back tonight. Once you drop off the envelope and the satchel, you'll be done for the night and you can go back to Hot Springs." Seeing the confusion on Gene's face, he leaned in. "Don't worry kid, you'll get your pay as usual; when you make this drop you'll get paid." With a reassuring sound in his voice, he added, "Just make the delivery and then head on out."

"So, I give this bag to the guy in that red truck and he'll have my money?"

The handsome man laughed. "Yeah, that's it. Simple as that. And the guy waiting is a guy you've met before. It's the big man; white hair on his right side. He'll be waiting for you out there."

"Okay." Gene was still a little confused, but tried not to show it. He turned and started the car as the handsome man shut the door and stepped back just as another man came running from the motel lobby toward the car. He reached the handsome man's side and urgently grabbed at his arm, pointed at the car and said something. The handsome man shook his head and turned back toward the car just as Gene started to shift into gear. He banged hard on the window and Gene jerked to a stop as the man pulled open the door.

"Hang on! Kill the engine." His contact person held up his hand for Gene to wait and turned back to the other man. They continued their conversation for another minute or two and then the handsome man patted the newcomer on the shoulder and handed him a set of keys. He pointed at a car parked in front of the motel. The second man hurried over to that car, jumped in and quickly drove away. His contact waited until the car had gone out of the parking lot and watched as it headed up the street before he turned and climbed into Gene's car.

"Change of plans," he said, puffing slightly. "Looks like I'm going to be riding along out to the Prairie City Airfield with you." The handsome man glanced over his shoulder at the satchel before settling back in the passenger seat. "I know this is different, but my man here needs my car for an emergency. And I'm going to need to get out to that airport sometime tonight too. So, I might as well make it now." He chuckled. "Free taxi, right?"

Gene eyed him nervously. He'd never had someone ride along before.

Seeing Gene's hesitation, he said, "You said you know how to get there, right? Just pretend I'm not riding along." The passenger pointed out the front window in the direction of downtown Rapid City. "Fastest route is back through the downtown area, cross over past the School of Mines and then head south from there. It's actually south, then east, on out a ways past the Regional Airport. Or you could drive further down 79 and head east when you reach Hermosa. Prairie City's pretty much straight north of the Fairburn agate fields."

Gene nodded. "Yeah, okay. I know Prairie City and I'm pretty sure I know where the airfield is. But since you're riding along with me, I'm not worried. You can just direct me, I suppose?" He re-started the car and shifted into gear. "This IS kind of weird, you know? What's going on, anyway?"

"It's not weird at all. I'm riding out with you and you'll drop me there. We'll meet my friend out there and drop off this delivery together," the man answered. "Then I'll just stay there with my friend."

"And then you'll pay me and I'll go?"

"Mmmmm hmmm. Right."

Gene licked his lips and nodded, pulling away from the front of the motel and looking back at the satchel in the process. What was he carrying in there? The last thing he wanted to be delivering was something that might get him in trouble with the cops. He turned his gaze back toward the front and pretended to adjust the rear view mirror, eyeing the satchel again in the process. Jeez, what had he gotten himself into? He started moving, glanced over at his passenger then back to the mirror. A reflection in the mirror caused him to make a little gasping sound.

"What?" The man looked at him with concern in his voice.

"Oh, nothing; nothing. Just thought that car pulling up behind us might be getting a little too close. That's all." He gestured toward a car that had just pulled into the motel parking lot. "Sort of scared me, I guess," Gene said. He turned the steering wheel to the left and moved forward past another car that had been parked near them.

The man looked back at the first car, now pulled up to the motel office and waved his arm impatiently toward the street. "Come on then, let's go!"

Gene looked back into the mirror again and shook his head. When he'd looked before he had been startled to see the eyes of someone staring at him with a look of disapproval. And while he knew that it couldn't be true, he still thought they looked like the eyes of his dead mother.

Chapter Five

They drove in silence for 15 minutes before reaching their first turnoff. Then it was another 15 before they hit a sign reading Black Hills Regional Airport. From there, they drove east and south, following signs for Prairie City before finally turning at a smaller sign designating a roadway that led off straight south toward the newest runway of the Prairie City Airfield.

Half-mile down from the main road they reached a protective barbed wire fence that also was defining the outer edges of the runway. Gene began cruising alongside and looked across to where a shadowy series of hangars and storage buildings lined the runway's far west boundary. About half-mile further to the south he could see the airfield's main terminal building, accented by several steel-sided Quonset huts. Aside from a rotating, flashing red light atop the main building, the complex was dark, shut down for the night.

"Take that gravel road," the man said, pointing to Gene's right. It was the opposite direction from the way most traffic would go. "Drive all the way out to the south end of the runway and then turn back around and up to the northeast side. The meeting spot is going to be over there and my friend, the one you've met before—the big man with the bad ear and white hair—he should already be at the meeting location. Just pull in and park alongside him when you see his truck."

Gene nodded and turned his car along the bumpy, lane-and-a-half wide side road. Finally driving up along the far edge of the runway, he spotted the other vehicle—a dark red pickup truck with a split rail box. He pulled in alongside it and stopped. A big man wearing a heavy sheepskin coat and cowboy hat was seated inside the other vehicle staring intently toward the runway. He made no move or reaction to their arrival even after getting a little wave of acknowledgement from the man sitting next to Gene.

The big man was definitely the same guy Gene had seen from some of his earlier contacts. And while Gene didn't know the man's name, the bright white hair along the right side of his head was a dead giveaway to his identity. The man finally looked in their direction and gave them a small wave as he opened his door and the interior dome light in his truck popped on. As he emerged from the driver's side and turned partway back in their direction, the dome light reflected off some sort of insignia on a patch above the right side pocket of his shirt.

Gene eyed the patch, trying to read it to himself. "Prairie City Wat . . ." The big man pulled the coat tight around his chest and backed away from the open door. His actions effectively covered the insignia just seconds before he slammed the door shut, extinguishing the dome light in the process.

"I'm going to keep the car running. Keep things warm," Gene said, glancing over at his companion, who was buttoning up his own coat as if he might be preparing to exit. "So you'll stay here with him and I can take off now, right? I mean, after he pays me?"

"Sure, don't worry kid, you're gonna get paid. But just hang in here for a few more," his passenger said. "I want to see if we might need you to help unload a few boxes."

Gene glanced around. "You mean from that pickup?"

His passenger chuckled. "No. We've got a plane coming in and we'll need to get a few things unloaded from it after it lands."

"Umm," Gene started to explain that he had to get going, then decided a few more minutes would probably be okay. "So . . . I'll just cut the lights. Is that okay?" he asked, making it sound as if that's what he had intended to say all along. His companion just grunted in response as he looked across the hood of Gene's car to where the shadowy figure of the other man was now moving around the front end of the neighboring vehicle.

"Roll down your window," his passenger said. "I'll just check with my buddy and see if he needs you to stay or not." Gene complied and then reached over to turn up the car's heater to counteract the sharp influx of cold air rushing in from the open window at his side.

Suddenly a hard buzzing sound filled the air and a small, single engine airplane dropped out of the low clouds and bounced to a quick landing almost directly in front of them. The plane roared on past them and up the dark runway to the north, skipping along for several hundred yards as its wheels finally settled down onto the hard surface. After about a minute, the plane slowed and began a wide turn before banking around and taxiing back in their direction.

Darveaux's passenger pulled some papers from inside his coat pocket and checked them over, settling his finger along a row of letters and numbers. He grunted an approving noise, stretched and reached across the top of the seat to snag the bulky satchel still lying behind them. He pulled the large bag forward until it fell heavily onto the seat in between them. Setting it up on end, he unsnapped the main clasp that was holding it shut. He gave Gene a lopsided half-grin as the teenaged driver gaped at several large stacks of cash now exposed inside.

The man laid the papers down on top of the cash, took out a small notepad and wrote some things on it, tamped everything back into place and re-secured the bag's clasp.

"Okay," his passenger said—more to himself than to Gene as his sheepskin-coated partner moved from the front of his truck and turned toward their car. "You get the tail number?" he called across Gene through the open window as the heavyset man—now adjusting the leather cowboy hat atop his head—moved down to the passenger side of the pickup and walked over toward them.

"It was N-1213-B. It's a Piper Super Cub. I saw the pilot and the co-pilot. Didn't know he'd have someone along, did you?" the big man responded. "Does that match up with what you have on your manifest?"

"Yeah, that's it. And it's not his co-pilot. I'm betting he brought along some muscle. You know, just in case. Although, man, why worry about US, huh?" He laughed then pointed to where the plane had touched down. "Those Super Cubs are really slick ain't they? Man." He stared off toward where it was taxiing. "Hey, do you want the kid to stay and help unload and then move the packages into your truck before he goes?" He pointed at Gene as he spoke. "I asked him if he could stay around for a while just in case."

The heavyset man kept his hand on his coat and nodded. "Sure. I guess that'll work. We'll be getting a lot more boxes of drugs tonight . . ." he stopped as Darveaux's passenger gave him a warning glance. "I mean there's a shitload of *packages* that need to be taken off that plane, plus it'll take some time to get them all loaded up in my truck, you know?" He pointed at Gene. "Listen kid, you stay and help us unload the plane and load my truck. And that'll be it. After that you can take off."

He tapped his pocket where the end of an envelope was protruding. "And that's when you'll get your pay." He took out a twenty-dollar bill from his pants pocket and held it up. "And besides the double payment that's in the envelope, there'll be a little something extra for you when you're finished since we've got such a big load. Okay?"

Gene swallowed hard. "Did you say there were drugs?" He swiveled sideways toward his handsome passenger. "Did he say there were drugs? Hey, I didn't know we were doing anything with drugs. Look, I'm not so sure that's something I want to be part of." He was speaking rapidly, glancing around in fear. "My parents were killed by a driver high on drugs, so I don't think I want to do any . . ."

"Zip it!" His passenger glared angrily at him, reached between the open buttons on his jacket and extracted a gun from a shoulder holster underneath. Gene gulped and shrank back in his seat as the man pulled his coat back tighter around his shoulders and placed the gun on his lap. "Now listen to me kid. You just pretend you didn't hear anyone say anything about drugs and get ready to give us a hand. We don't have time for your game of twenty questions."

He gestured absently toward the runway where the plane continued taxiing in their direction. "I'm sorry about what might of happened to your parents, but this is something completely different. So just shut your trap and do your job."

"But, this ISN'T my job," Gene protested. "That guy who hired me said I was just going to be a driver."

"Just shut up! No more talking! Like I said, you didn't hear anything—especially about drugs," he forcefully instructed as he grasped the handle on his door. He pointed toward Gene. "Now look, I don't want to hear any more questions OR complaints. You got that?" Looking miserable, Gene just nodded.

The passenger looked across Gene toward the bigger man who nodded his approval and pulled back a flap on his own coat to display a wicked looking gun of his own. Gene sat very still on the seat, hoping the fear he was feeling inside wasn't showing on his face. His passenger picked up the gun from his lap, re-opened the top of his coat and slipped the weapon back into its holster.

Seemingly satisfied that their young driver was properly cowed by the weapons display, the handsome man half-shouted over the plane's ever-growing engine noise as he pointed toward the approaching Piper aircraft. "Okay! Guess it's time to go pay the piper, huh?" He laughed at his own joke, tapped Gene on the arm and made a "roll up the window" motion with his hand as the plane started to swing in nose first at the spot where they were parked.

Gene cranked up the window as his passenger pushed his own door open and slid his feet out, his left hand still resting on the satchel lying between them. As he started to stand, Gene suddenly reached across and ripped the bag from the man's grasp. "Hey!" the man shouted. "What the fuck you think you're doing?"

Slamming the car into reverse, Gene jerked the bag toward him while pulling the steering wheel hard to his left and stepping on the gas.

Already halfway out of the car, his surprised passenger was knocked toward the ground as the door hit him squarely on the side. He sprawled in the frozen dirt with a howl and scrambled sideways to get out of the way as Gene whipped the car back around in the man's direction. Caught off guard by Gene's actions, the big man still standing on the driver's side dived down into the shadow of the pickup truck, using his own vehicle for protection.

Gene shifted into first gear, spun his car in a tight right turn and hit the gas again as the passenger side door flopped wildly back and forth a couple more times before slamming shut. His actions brought the car completely around and turned back into a direct line facing where the men were both still on the ground. The big man alongside his truck fumbled for the gun inside his coat, finally pulling the weapon free from beneath his bulky sheepskin garment. He rose from his knees and pointed the barrel toward Gene's car as he stood.

Yelling and cursing but still out in the open, Gene's passenger rolled over again and ducked as his partner sighted in at the oncoming vehicle and started shooting at it as it raced past. The window beside him shattered and Gene cried out in pain as a bullet ripped into the front part of his left forearm that had been elevated to grasp the top of the steering wheel.

Gene dropped his wounded arm and looked in shock at a growing bloodstain forming around the hole in the forearm material of his coat. Before he could fully react to the wound, he heard a barrage of additional shots and cried out again as a searing pain coursed through his entire left side. The driver's side window glass, shattered by the bullets, dropped almost completely away, leaving just a few shards remaining in place.

He groaned and leaned forward between the steering wheel and gearshift, trying to avoid being struck by any more bullets. Stomping down hard on the gas pedal, he pulled the steering wheel back to his right and released it while struggling to shift into second gear, now using his uninjured right arm to do all the work.

Successfully making the shift, he re-grasped the wheel. "Okay," he said as he glanced into the rear view mirror to see muzzle flashes from both men's weapons as another volley of shots rang out. He swerved sharply to the right and heard at least one bullet strike the back of the car as he started accelerating down the bumpy narrow road. Pain wracked his left side and he groaned again, fighting to maintain control without exposing his head and shoulders. Both shooters were now on their feet and firing steadily at his fast-receding vehicle.

As the men strode after him, continuing to shoot as they moved, the small plane—which had nearly finished its maneuver into where their cars had been sitting—revved up its own engine, pulled back around toward the center of the runway and took off. As it lifted into the air, the plane flew for a few seconds alongside Gene's fast-retreating car before rising and disappearing back into the cloudbank as the young driver raced away.

Chapter Six

Gene was headed toward the Prairie City airfield's far northside crossover road, steadily accelerating his speed to put as much distance as he could between himself and the two men before they started to follow.

But when he reached a point where the protective fence alongside him stopped, he flipped off his lights and cranked the steering wheel hard left, cutting directly across the runway instead. As he reached the far side of the hard surface, he cut sharp left again, hoping that if they were behind him they had not seen his unorthodox maneuver.

Now following the westside service road going south, he headed down into a little valley, took a chance and flipped his lights back on, continuing along for another quarter mile on low beam as he kept advancing through the depression. As the road started back up, he turned the light switch back to off and moved into the center of the road.

Halfway up the incline with the hilltop still shielding his car, he pulled to a stop and turned on the interior light. His left arm and side were thoroughly soaked with blood. And, despite the fact that his entire left side felt like it was on fire from where the bullets had hit him, his right hand that he had been using to operate the steering wheel was half-frozen from the icy air pouring in through the shattered window.

He reached into his coat pocket and retrieved a pair of gloves, exclaiming in pain from his injuries as he struggled to put them on. Finally succeeding, he shivered violently, reached up and snapped off the dome light. Shifting back into low gear he started moving again. As he reached the next crest in the road he shifted up a gear as the car picked up speed on a long, gradual decline toward the airfield's southside entrance.

Reaching a point where a hard-surface highway intersected with the gravel road he was on, he eased to another stop and did a quick check for traffic. Seeing no other vehicles approaching, he pulled the steering wheel into a hard right turn, flipped the lights back on and saw a sign identifying the road as U.S. Highway 44. It was the primary hard surface road leading between Rapid City to the west and the Badlands and Pine Ridge Indian Reservation to the east.

He looked briefly back toward where he had been driving, caught a glimpse of car lights approaching on the horizon and hit the brakes. "Just wait! Wait! Think!" he admonished himself aloud. He pulled over to the shoulder of the road, set the hand brake and once again completely cut his own lights.

Sitting in the darkness, he painfully shifted his body in order to get a better look at where he had just been driving. From this angle he could see headlights fast approaching down the side road. He checked the rearview mirror and stared back ahead. The main highway remained clear of traffic in both directions.

Still in low gear, he released the brake, let up on the clutch and turned across the road, reversing his direction. Now he was heading east toward the Badlands and Pine Ridge Reservation and away from the lights of Rapid City and the Prairie City Airfield complex.

Picking up speed and shifting into higher gears, he sped past a second Airport Service Road intersection, crossed two small hills and took a chance to turn his lights back on again. Continuing over yet a third hill, he passed a road sign depicting a right-hand T-shaped intersection ahead and once more hit his brakes, jerking to a stop in front of a gravel road that was heading straight south from the point where it intersected with the main highway. The road was marked by a nondescript sign perched atop a slender corner post identifying the southbound gravel as "Creston/Deer Creek Road."

Gene re-checked his rear view mirror again, saw nothing, and once more turned the steering wheel hard right. He hit the gas but struggled to shift, the car jerking forward in the process. Spinning around from his actions, the car slid sideways as he hit a windrow of loose gravel that had been graded up to the road's edge.

His clumsy driving sent a wave of pain and nausea coursing through his body as he was forced to use both hands to fight the wheel to regain control. With his car clinging to the top edge of the right-hand ditch, Gene backed off on his speed and finally got straightened out. Sweating profusely, he drove back on a line toward the center of the narrow road, slid to a stop and killed the headlights yet again.

He sat there shaking, positive that someone would have seen his lights careening sideways and soon would come racing up with guns blazing. But again nothing happened. Finally, he shifted down to low, stepped gingerly on the gas pedal this time and slowly moved forward, creeping along at about 15 miles per hour with his lights still off. After two excruciating miles, he passed under a railroad trestle and began traversing a new series of rolling hills that headed steadily downward, as if leading toward a deep valley or river bottom.

At the top of the next hill, he stopped the car once more. He was confused about where he had been driving. He stared intently down the narrow road, which dropped off into shallow ditches on both sides. The pitch-blackness of the night made it almost impossible to see where the road ahead might be leading. He needed help.

"Nagi Tanka!" he suddenly cried out in Lakota, holding his good arm up and looking toward the sky. "Great Spirit! Help me! Omshima-la ye!" He groaned as the pain intensified in his left side. Taking a chance he turned on his headlights. He looked up one more time into the rearview mirror and for the second time that night could swear he saw his mother's eyes staring back at him.

"Maka, Mother?" he sobbed. He looked back to the mirror, but she was gone. "Mother? Hiyo wo. I need you here to show me. Show me the way."

He clicked the headlights up to bright, not only illuminating the road and ditches but also the nearby barbed wire fences that appeared to be held in place by fence posts that were made from cottonwood tree branches.

Also lit by his lights was the outline of a small rustic cabin tucked up tight against the gravel road. The cabin was built so that it looked like the right-hand ditch went partially underneath its closed-in porch. Maybe this was a place for help? He gunned his engine a bit, debating what to do.

His bright lights and sound of the revving engine caused a dog to begin barking and after a few seconds a light popped on inside the cabin. A doorway exiting onto the porch sprang open and Gene could see the figure of a man holding a rifle or a shotgun. The figure raised the gun through the porch's outside door and fired a warning shot into the air. "Private property! Get the hell away from here!" he shouted. The silhouette of his weapon was clearly accented by the back lighting shining from the doorway.

Gene sucked in sharply, his heart pounding, slid his foot off the brake and popped the clutch, nearly stalling the car as the dog's barking intensified. Steadily increasing his speed, he once more turned his lights off and strained to hold his car as close to the center of the road as possible while shifting up a gear.

He guided the vehicle up and over yet one more hilltop and the cabin disappeared from his rearview mirror. Taking advantage, he quickly turned his lights back on and yelped in surprise as a beat-up metal road sign pockmarked with rusting bullet holes reflected back into his face. He stepped on the brakes and slid to a stop. This was getting tiresome.

He glanced once more in the mirror to be sure there was nothing or no one behind him before backing up a few feet for a better look at the sign.

"Lower Spring Creek Road, 2 Miles," he recited aloud. Below the words was a T-shaped line indicating that the Creston and Deer Creek Road would be ending at this intersection with the Spring Creek Road.

He smiled ruefully and nodded skyward. Nagi Tanka had heard his cry for help. Even though he had never driven this far eastward on this particular roadway before, he knew all about Spring Creek Road. It had long served as "the" major trail, beginning near Keystone just below Mount Rushmore and crossing from west to east out of the Black Hills and running east then southeast toward the Cheyenne River. Ultimately it connected to the road headed out toward where his parents' family members lived on the Pine Ridge Indian Reservation.

Gene pressed on, still following the gravel road as it continued its meandering route to the south and southeast. The road made a big sweeping curve to the east, wrapped around a dense clump of pine trees, and then cut back toward the promised intersection, finally dead ending at the much wider and paved Spring Creek Road.

Three signs were stacked neatly atop a wood pole at the dead end intersection. Beginning at the top was the largest one with white letters printed inside a broad double-pointed arrow filled in with a black background. It read: Lower Spring Creek Road. Directly beneath it was a slightly smaller sign with an arrow pointing east reading: "Pine Ridge Reservation, 37 miles." And, under that about halfway up the pole, the third sign read: "S.D. Hwy. 79, 18 miles." This one had an arrow beneath the words and even though the arrow was partially broken loose it still clearly pointed to the west.

Highway 79 was the main highway Gene drove every time he went from Hot Springs to Rapid City and back.

“Pila Mita, Wakan Tanka,” he said reverently. “Thank you Great Spirit for hearing my voice.” Since his parents’ death a year-and-a-half before he had looked deeper into his Lakota heritage for both solace and support. Every week he was learning more and more about his native language—the words of his elders—and about the Spirit world that the Lakota believed governed their daily lives and history.

One reason his parents had chosen to live in Hot Springs was that it was just south of the sacred Wind Cave, the Source. He had learned that it was there that the Great Spirit resided. His mother once told him that her grandfather had been a spiritual leader for his people—a Pejula Wacasa; a medicine man. He had been a revered figure in his tribe back in the days of Crazy Horse and Sitting Bull.

Gene wanted to know more and his curiosity had led him to make regular visits back to the Reservation, seeking out elders from his family and his parents’ tribe who might be able to appease his growing appetite to learn. He ached to know more about his heritage and the stories they might have to share from his great-grandfather’s time.

And when he was back in Hot Springs, he had found himself drawn to both the pine-covered hillsides overlooking the entrance to Wind Cave, and to the white robed undulating lands of the Fairburn Agate Fields located between the Black Hills and the Pine Ridge Reservation. At both places, Gene felt a vivid presence. He could hear the voices from his people’s past. His great-grandfather, grandfather and his mother, all their voices were speaking to him, guiding him along a path that seemed to have been set for him even before he was born.

At Wind Cave, he had learned that the movement of the wind was the Great Spirit emerging from the cave each morning and returning each night. The Great Spirit was riding on the whispers of the wind and he felt a great sense of awe; a calling; whenever he was there.

His sister Elizabeth said he was being foolish, but Gene truly had felt it. He just knew that he was in the presence of not only his long-dead ancestors but also the Great Spirit at both of those sacred places. They had become equally sacred to him and his beliefs. But now? Were those beliefs being tested?

"Pila Mita," he whispered again, nearly sobbing it as another sharp pain wracked his body and drew him out of his reverie. He remained at the intersection for just a few seconds longer, turning his lights back down to dim while idling the car's engine. He could feel the strength leaving his body and wondered if he could even make the long drive home?

Finally, he pulled the satchel over closer, unsnapped it, and once more turned on the interior dome light. Inside the bag, there were those papers that his passenger had been reading, and beneath them was a large amount of cash; many thousands of dollars in neatly wrapped bundles.

He looked back at the sky. "What should I do? Wakan Tanka. Guide me!"

He tapped lightly on the steering wheel and leaned toward it trying to make the sick feeling in his stomach dissipate. "Twocrow," he said aloud. He needed to get back to Hot Springs and call the Marshal. Twocrow was an Elder he had grown to trust. Old Marshal Twocrow would know what to do. He sat back, turned off the dome light and turned the car's headlights back up to bright. He eased off the clutch and headed west.

Yet another wave of nausea washed across him and Gene nearly passed out. He pulled over. Reaching across his body with his right hand, he opened the door and vomited. Feeling a little better, he pulled the door shut and drove on, finally reaching a spot where the road brushed up against the banks of nearby Spring Creek, the small river from which the highway got its name.

Less than a quarter mile further the road started bending back north, away from the river. Right at that bend his lights illuminated another small signpost, this one announcing the Fairburn Agate Fields and an arrow pointing to the south. Just beyond the sign he reached the point where an unremarkable dirt road intersected with the much larger Spring Creek Road.

With this approach from the east, the intersection was mostly hidden, framed by a grove of giant old pine and cottonwood trees that now were surrounded by a tangle of leafless shrubs and underbrush. Sweeping southwest away from the grove, a flat rocky plateau stretched out toward a mish-mashed upheaval of large pieces of granite and shale stacked in a pile and overlooking the winding river below.

He exclaimed in recognition. "Rainbow Rock!" He had come to this place before, several times, but he always had approached from the other direction, driving west to east from Highway 79. He was surprised how much easier it was to see the intersection when you were approaching from the other direction.

"Yes!" He shouted as he looked up. "Iya Iyupah—the rock pile!" The name he and his sister had given it was Rainbow Rock, but his father always just called it the rock pile because of the formations that both surrounded it and were formed on top of it. Gene had learned the Lakota name and called it that whenever they were near.

"This is perfect!" He nodded skyward once more. He could stash the big leather bag here, just to be safe, before driving on toward Hot Springs. Hiding the bag here would be his negotiating guarantee if the men either caught back up with him or were able to track him down.

He pulled his car onto the dirt road and over onto a small turnoff near the edge of the rocky plateau. Pulling up next to a wooden cattle guard he was confronted by a scrawled handwritten sign in faded red letters: "No Trespassing!" The sign had been there as long as he had been coming here and he had never seen anyone come to enforce it. Tonight he almost hoped that they would.

Dragging the satchel along behind him, he half stumbled out of the car and grunted in pain as he lifted the leather bag off the seat. He struggled across the cattle guard and moved forward for about 50 yards, finally reaching the first of several rugged outcroppings. This one appeared to have been shaped by some giant hand taking layer after layer of granite pieces and piling them up to make a scenic, rainbow-banded rocky overlook.

Just below this almost natural diving spot was a broad circle of ice, the winter result of what became nature's nearly perfectly formed swimming hole during the summer months.

Gene labored onward across the flat surface of the rocky slabs until he reached the far side of the plateau. There, several smaller pieces of shale appeared to be interlaced like puzzle pieces into one another before locking into the roots of a very large cottonwood tree. The tree itself seemed to be defying gravity as it leaned out precariously over the open space above the ice. Gasping from the effort and the intense cold air, he dropped the satchel and knelt down until he was on his knees alongside the tree.

From this vantage point, behind the puzzle piece rocks and below the tangled tree roots, a large tumbleweed was snagged on top of a messy matte of dead grass and stringy weeds. He pushed the tumbleweed aside. The mass of weeds and grass had covered a mostly unseen opening, an opening that led into a hollowed out area beneath the large tree's anchoring root system. Grunting in pain as he worked, he pulled back at the matted tangle until he exposed a much larger open area beneath.

He glanced back toward the flat, rocky area he had just crossed. Years ago, he had begun his journeys to Rainbow Rock with his father. His dad would call their outings "Fishing and swimming expeditions to Iya Iyupah—the rock pile. It's our special place." And Gene always thought no one else in the whole world knew about it. On one of their earliest excursions, he had discovered this hollowed area beneath the tree roots.

At mid-afternoon the big tree's shadow would fall directly across Gene's treasure spot, stretching out toward the puzzle piece rock formation. It was, he thought, a sign that this was meant to be his special hiding spot.

So on another particularly lazy summer afternoon as his father napped nearby, he decided to expand upon nature's creation and make this natural hiding place into an even larger hideaway. He would call the old tree Wagichun Wagi—the "sacred tree"—and this hollowed out spot would become "his most sacred" hiding place. After what seemed like hours of digging and shaping, he thought it was the perfect place for any treasures—either found or brought with him. For anything he might ever want to have hidden here.

Now, he smiled as he looked into the hole. It was still here after all this time. He reached down and extracted a badly rusted red cookie tin. It was the first thing he had ever put into the hole—and it turned out to be the last thing, too. Until now. He lifted up the tin and banged the top edge of it against one of the roots, finally loosening the lid. He opened it and a piece of paper fluttered out —his version of a message in a bottle, but obviously never discovered. Now, so many years after he had hidden that message he couldn't even remember what he had written down.

He eyed the escaping paper with regret as it floated out across the now frozen stream before snagging on a leafless bush on the far side.

His smile turned to a grimace and he groaned again. Laying the tin container back down, he reached for the satchel.

After stuffing the bag into the hole, he pulled and pushed back on the grass and weeds he had just removed until they mostly re-covered the opening. Then, he grasped the tumbleweed by its woody stem and re-anchored it into its original spot on top. There, it whipped back and forth in the breeze but held firm.

Picking up the cookie tin with his good right arm, he threw it under-hand as far out onto the ice as he could, once more grunting in pain as he fought against an urge to double over and vomit once again.

The sound of the tin hitting the ice echoed, then died. The wind intensified for a few seconds, rustling the dead leaves that still clung to both the cottonwoods and a cluster of smaller chokecherry trees lining the frozen waterway's meandering path. Then he heard the scraping of the tin container across the surface of the ice as it skittered away, pushed onward by another gust of wind.

The wind's intensity increased and swirled, blowing a mix of snow and dust across the surface. "Good," he said aloud as he watched the wind's action already starting to obliterate the disturbances he had made to the ground and around the base of the tree. "Thank you Tah-tay," he reverently spoke aloud to the spirit of the mighty north wind.

"Good," a voice from the wind seemed to echo in reply. Gene jerked back against the tree trunk, startled. Then he saw something. It appeared to be the outline of a woman's figure, tangled in the dry rustling leaves amid the branches of the sacred tree towering above him and accented by the light snow swirling around him. It was Wonagi—spirit figure. A reddish glow seemed to fill the air around it. He looked down and blinked, then turned back. The glowing red figure remained.

"Wo-nah-gee. Come with me!" He called out, extending his hands. He gasped and leaned forward as the figure suddenly seemed to respond and become much clearer, emerging from the red mist toward him. "Inya! Mother?" he cried, stretching out his hands further in her direction.

"Wahi! Toksha ake wacinyuanktin ktelo—I see you. Mother." He sobbed. "I see you." A sudden shower of snow flurries, whipped by a new gust of the north wind, seemed to move the spirit figure back in among the tree's branches almost as if signaling him that now was time to leave; to move on to a safer place. Then, just as quickly as the spirit woman's figure had appeared, it started to dissolve. Gene struggled back to his feet, groaning in pain as he stood.

"Inya! Please! Don't leave me," he uttered, imploring his spirit mother to stay. "Mama," he softly sobbed as the figure continued to disintegrate and blow away, finally disappearing among the tree's shriveled leaves and the intensifying snowflakes. The red glow was gone as a gentler wind whispered through the branches. Just as quickly as they had appeared the snowflakes also were gone.

But in the dying wind and clearing sky he heard his mother's voice again, reassuring him. "The Great Spirit will watch over you my son. Ohlate Ista Wakatankan. This place is safe. It is beneath God's eyes. He will watch." The voice trailed away and a dead calm filled the air.

Gene swiped his good arm across his face, brushing at his tears. "Yes. I must go, too. I can't stay," he agreed. As if replying, the north wind now gusted again, even harder than before. Its earlier whispers were replaced by an achy, half-howling moan. Gene turned into the wind and labored his way back across the open space. Finally reaching the shelter of the lower shrubs and bushes, he stumbled over to his car.

Crying out in pain as he fought to get behind the wheel, he finally pulled the door shut and started the engine. Sweating profusely despite the cold, he backed out onto the dirt road, drove north toward Spring Creek Road and once again headed to the west.

At Highway 79, he turned south and soon reached the Sandman Elevator complex and the parking lot it shared with the nearby Railway Café. He remembered. They had a phone booth. He could call Frank for help. Together, they could go on to Hot Springs. Together, they could locate Marshal Twocrow and get help. He could call Frank so he could be safe. He cranked the wheel hard left and turned into the gravel parking lot.

Chapter Seven

Hillman, Tollefson and Delaney's initial search for Darveaux had been fruitless until Delaney suggested they check in with the Railway Café up north of Hermosa. Considered a "primo hangout" spot for Indians, it also was a place he liked to stop for coffee whenever he drove back to his new mobile trailer home in Fairburn. It wouldn't be unreasonable, he said, for Darveaux to go there for help.

They caravanned into the café's parking lot and almost immediately spotted Darveaux's abandoned and bloody car. In less than twenty minutes, they also had located the young Indian's body before encountering a mysterious second person running away.

Now, together in Delaney's new Chevrolet pickup truck, he and Hillman pulled up alongside Tollefson's police cruiser after taking a quick look up and down Highway 79 to double-check routes the missing man might have taken when he drove away. Hillman rolled down his window and leaned out toward his boss.

"We went out about a mile north and then two south like you said, but there wasn't any sign of anyone else or a car. Road's flat out empty," he said as Tollefson rolled his own window down in response. "Couldn't really see anything on the road either direction." He waved out the window toward Gene's shot-up car. "You think we should take the Darveaux kid's car back into the shop? Car keys are probably on his body."

Tollefson shook his head. "No, that wouldn't make any sense to anyone looking into the shooting. It'll have to be here for whatever kind of investigation gets done tomorrow, so just leave it where it is." He leaned back, scrunched his eyes shut and exhaled sharply. "Delaney, when that guy ran off and jumped in front of the train, are you positive he wasn't carrying anything?"

"Well, I'm pretty sure," Pete answered. "When I took those shots at him, he stopped and looked back, and I could see him when he jumped. I'm sure he wasn't carryin' anything. He didn't have nothin' in his hands, and I didn't see him throw anything either. He showed up pretty clear in that bright headlight."

He pointed past Hillman toward the café. "And that counterman inside said he didn't see nothin' in the kid's hands either when he came out and yelled at him for bustin' his window."

Tollefson nodded again. "Okay. So somewhere between the Prairie City Airfield and here, Darveaux must'a pulled over and stashed the satchel. Tomorrow, we need to start checking on all the possible routes and get out there and drive them. We gotta find that satchel and retrieve our money."

He pulled a file folder off the passenger side seat and took a phone number from a small red notepad inside. "I'm going to give our New York friends a call and find out where their pilot ended up. We need to get him back here with the drugs as soon as possible."

"Back out to our airfield?" Hillman asked. "You sure that'll work during the day?"

"Well," Tollefson pondered the question. "Maybe it's not so good to have him come back there. Maybe we should have him come in toward Fairburn and land out north or east of the agate fields? What do you think? That ground is pretty flat around there ain't it? There's gotta be some good spots to put down a small plane, right?"

Delaney nodded. "Yeah. What about Fitz's ranch out along the Cheyenne? Out by Red Shirt? His place might work, 'cause he's got a small landing strip out along the south side of his barn. That Piper ought'a be able to sit down there without any trouble."

"Yeah, I think that's right." Tollefson said. "He does have a spot, doesn't he?"

"For sure he does 'cause he and I landed out there last fall," Hillman agreed. "And it's right on line with Prairie City, too, so the pilot will have a reference point."

"That's good. Real good," Tollefson said. "I'll get ahold of Fitz and see if he'll be okay with us putting a private plane down out there. Just a quick in-and-out. Only needs to be an hour at the most. Batch, you can drive down and wait at the ranch to unload the plane, and Delaney can bring his truck over and pick up the shipment afterward. That work for you?" He directed the last question to Pete.

"Sure, no sweat," Delaney responded. "I can get set up over on the east side of the agate beds and direct him in from there. Once he's on the right flight path he should be able to spot Fitz's airstrip down in the Cheyenne River Bottoms without any problems. But if he does have to put down away from the strip, he can just make the drop anywhere across the river from Red Shirt. All of that is Fitz's land, too.

"Batch should probably carry a signal light of some sort with him, too, just to be safe?"

"Yeah. That should work. But, you know, if the pilot's not used to landing on grass and hard dirt, he'll probably want to do an early morning arrival to avoid any of those cross winds they get out in that direction later in the day," Hillman added. "I remember the wind was a son-of-a-bitch when I flew in there in the middle of the afternoon with Fitz. If he hadn't been the one flying, I don't know if we would've landed safely."

"For sure. He's right Sarge. Those winds can get really nasty mid-to-late day," Delaney agreed. "And you're right Batch, it's usually pretty calm along there in the early morning."

"Well, that would mean two mornings from now then, because I won't be able to check in with Fitz until tomorrow morning soonest. So, let's shoot for that. We'll have the pilot skip Prairie City completely." Tollefson said. He pointed to Delaney. "So, that means you're gonna have to get your butt out of the sack early that morning so you're out by the agate beds to flag that plane in safely. That's not going to be a problem, right?"

The heavy man nodded. "No, 'course not. It's just a few miles drive from where I've got my trailer parked anyway." He grinned. "I told you guys that living down in Fairburn would pay off."

Tollefson stroked his chin and rubbed the corners of his eyes. "You and that fucking ghost town. Who the hell lives in a ghost town?"

"It's NOT a ghost town Sarge, it's just a mostly *abandoned* town. It's officially called a 'semi' ghost town. We even got our own post office."

"That right? That would be a good point to drop things off for you if we ever get to that point."

"For sure. Like I was telling Batch. It's a straight in route to the town and the post office is right smack dab in the middle of it." He chuckled. "And, you know . . ."

Not really wanting a further explanation, Tollefson waved dismissively in Delaney's direction while muttering, "Yeah, yeah, I got it, okay?" He looked back and spoke again to Hillman. "We're going to need to go into the cash reserves to make the payment for this load until we can locate the satchel that the kid took. Like I said earlier, we really gotta find that bag."

"Don't worry boss, we'll get it back," Hillman answered. "Both the money and the papers."

"What papers?"

"Well, you know, the manifest and the plane I.D. are in the satchel, too."

"Are you out of your mind? You put the plane's I.D. INSIDE the cash bag? What if he handed off the bag to somebody else? Jesus H. Christ!"

Hillman gave his boss a chagrined look in return. "Sorry Sarge. I just tossed the papers in there on top of the cash so I could pull them out quick as soon as the pilot taxied up with the boxes." He shook his head. "Hey, I'm sure that kid didn't have a clue what he had—besides the cash I mean. I should'a never let him see I had so much money."

He held his hands wide. "And Boss, don't worry. I'm sure he just stashed that bag someplace before he tried to make a run for it. He didn't have time to give it to nobody. So, we're gonna find it and everything will be fine."

"You better hope," Tollefson said softly, now worrying more about the papers that listed the incoming plane's tail number and manifest than about the money itself. "I don't think our friends in New York are going to be very understanding about ANY of this if we don't." He waggled a hand in the general direction of the café, the bins, and Darveaux's car. Both Delaney and Hillman nodded in agreement.

They didn't think that Sarge's New York "friends" would be very understanding about any of this either.

*****

Elizabeth Darveaux coughed hard, the action deeply darkening her normally pretty face in a sour grimace of intense pain. "You need to do what Gene said. You need to go see Marshal Twocrow."

Frank nodded. "Yeah, I know. But I thought I better wait until morning." He glanced over at the clock. It was nearly one a.m. He had arrived at Elizabeth and Gene's apartment around midnight, almost simultaneously with Gene's older sister, who was returning from her cleaning job at the State Veterans Home. "Do you think I should go back up to Rapid and tell the police what I saw?"

Elizabeth shrugged. "That's another question for the Marshal, but I think it might be a big mistake. You'd probably find yourself in a jail cell so fast your head would be spinning—both for holding off reporting it . . . and maybe even getting yourself arrested as being the killer." She walked over to the table, sat down and began to cry. Frank moved over to join her, sitting in the next chair and draping an arm across her shoulders.

"I'm sorry Elizabeth. What was Gene doing up there tonight? Did he tell you why he was going up to Rapid?"

"No. I didn't even know he WAS going up to Rapid tonight. He was still here when I left to go do my shift at the State Home. That always goes until around midnight or 12:30, and he's usually in bed when I get back. I haven't 'checked' on him for at least a year, you know? He's been working off and on and doing a lot of driving for some company up there, so maybe it was something for them. He wouldn't tell me who he was driving for, so I just let it go. It's not like he's a little kid anymore. I mean for crying out loud, he's 18 years old!"

Frank swallowed hard. "Yeah, I know. He talked about getting me hooked up with that driving thing too." He swallowed once more, dropped his head to his chest and gave a deep, heaving sigh of his own. "And even though I'm a year older, we share a birthday you know? Well, shared."

"Oh, God, Frank I know. I know! I'm sorry for you, too. You lost your best friend and I've been kind of a bitch trying to get between the two of you for the past few months." She sobbed harder, again her pretty features presenting an anguished appearance as she cried. "I-I just wanted him to become something, you know? That's why I worked so hard to get you guys and Marshal Twocrow together. I thought seeing what could happen . . . if . . . if . . . well, you know?" She let the question trail off, coughed again and sobbed harder.

Frank leaned closer and hugged her and they both sat crying for a couple more minutes, not saying anything. Elizabeth finally leaned back wiped at her eyes and put both hands on his shoulders. Squeezing them, she stood. "You want something? Maybe something to drink? We might have some coffee? Or a glass of water?"

He shook his head.

"Coffee'd just keep me awake. I think maybe I'll try to sleep a little, and then I'll get up and head over to the Marshal's office real early. Try to be there when he comes in."

"Do you think those men saw you drive away? Would they follow you?"

"I don't think so. I kept my lights off until I was already on the main road. I was on the road before the train finished going by, and as far as I could tell, no one followed me out of the parking lot. I didn't see another car until I was at least 10 miles down the road and then it was coming toward me, not following."

"Okay, well that's good at least." Elizabeth paced over to her apartment window and looked across toward Fall River. The hot water river—part of why Hot Springs was called Hot Springs—was steaming in the cold night air. An extra cloud was rising where a small "Falls" gushed into it, giving a surreal look to the downtown and the streetlights that ran along North River Street.

"Good grief Frank, what WAS Gene doing up there?" She turned and walked over to the counter where she picked up the carved wooden box. "And what IS this thing? That's all he said, 'Give it to Twocrow'?"

"And the money," Frank said. "He said 'Tell Elizabeth I love her, and there's some money that needs to go to Twocrow. It's in a bag by the rock pile,' like that was something you would know. What the hell's the rock pile?"

Gene's sister sank down onto the couch and stared at the window. "I don't know. There are piles of rocks and rock formations all over the place around here. I don't think he'd just put some money down next to one of them, do you?"

Frank shrugged.

"Maybe he meant out at the old quarry?" she asked. 'Didn't you guys used to go out there a lot?"

"Drinking. Hanging out." Frank stopped as he saw the disappointed look on Elizabeth's face. "Hey, we would go drink a couple beers sometimes. Okay? Besides, that's closer to down here, not on the road to and from Rapid." He sat back on the couch.

"He might've been talking about the agate fields out by Fairburn," he continued. "He loved going out there, you know. Said it was one of his 'sacred' places." Elizabeth gave him a quizzical look. "Well, you know Gene. He was learning more about the old ways, and he said he could talk to the spirits there, hear them in the wind, the grass, the rocks and the trees. Maybe he went to the agate fields to hide whatever it was he took from those men?"

She gave him a skeptical look in return. "Look," he added, deciding to change the subject. "I don't have any idea why he was up there tonight. I haven't seen him for over a month. He said he was doing that driving job you talked about, hoping to make good money so we could get a place together soon. But he didn't say what he had lined up. I know it's not a very 'friend' thing to say, but I thought he might be making all that up. Bragging, you know?"

"Frank! Gene never made up anything in his life. You were close enough to him to know that." She paused and coughed violently, holding her hand to her forehead. "Look, I'm sorry. I shouldn't yell at you, especially after you drove all this way in the middle of a freezing night to tell me what happened."

"It's all right. You've got a right to yell. Your brother just got killed."

She interrupted him with a much more violent cough. Frank stood up and moved behind her, placing his hands on her shoulders this time. "What's wrong with you, anyway? You sound like you're getting pneumonia or something."

"No, it's just . . . a really bad cough. I think. I don't know? Probably comes from living in this rat trap." She stood and waved her arms at the walls for emphasis. "Or dealing with that nothing job I have cleaning offices at the State Home. Gene wanted me to go see a doctor up in Rapid, but I didn't think we could afford it. She broke into a series of hacking coughs. Frank moved around to her side to try to offer help, but she waved him away.

"I know he's been worried. Maybe that's why he went up to Rapid on a moment's notice like that. Maybe he's been trying to earn some extra money or something . . . to help me." She stared at her hands. "Oh my God, Frank. Do you think that's why he was up there? Maybe this is my fault!"

"Nothing's anyone's fault," he replied. "You can't think that, okay?"

Frank made his way to the couch and sank down at the corner, leaning his head back. "I should sleep."

"Yeah," she agreed. "Me, too."

He slipped off his shoes and propped his feet up. Elizabeth walked into one of the small adjoining rooms and returned with a pillow and a blanket.

"Thanks." He gave her a grateful look. "Have you ever thought about going back home?"

"You mean out to the Reservation?" she asked.

"Yeah."

Elizabeth shook her head.

"Why not? You got family out there yet. You could stay with your Uncle; or even my family. I know my Mom would love to have you for a while. Be good for her to have some company now that she and dad are split up."

"No!" She paused, embarrassed by the force of her answer. After another series of coughs, she continued. "I'll stay here and fight my own battles. Especially now. If I go back now it'll be against everything me and Gene were trying to do. It'll mean we failed. It's going to get better. I have to believe. YOU need to believe!"

"Well, there's no question you and Gene are brother and sister," he answered. "Both stubborn as hell, that's for sure."

She laughed wryly at that, coughed again, and walked over and kissed him on the top of the head. "I'm sorry I was so hard on you Frank. You've been a good friend—to both of us."

"Yeah," he said, suddenly totally exhausted. "You too."

Chapter Eight

Al Tollefson finished typing out his statement, reeled it from the top of the typewriter and handed it across to Batch Hillman.

"What do you think?"

Hillman started to read it to himself, moving his lips as he read, a habit that Tollefson found disgusting.

"Just read the damn thing out loud!"

"Sure . . . okay," Hillman apologized. "Sorry." He held the sheet of paper out under the nearby lamp. A small clock sitting on the side of his desk ticked loudly and made a little dinging sound as it signaled 3 a.m.

"The body found among the Sandman Elevator Complex's grain bins has been tentatively identified as 18-year-old Gene Darveaux, a resident of the Southern Black Hills community of Hot Springs. Investigating Officer Al Tollefson from the Prairie City Police Department said Darveaux's body was discovered by his officers after patrons at the nearby Railway Café said they thought they heard shots and saw some-one running from the scene . . ."

Hillman looked up. "Really? I didn't know . . ."

"No, you idiot! Not REALLY!" Tollefson slapped the top of his desk in disgust. "Who the hell cares? I couldn't very well say my officers just 'happened' to be cruising around through a grain elevator complex miles and miles away from where they were supposed to be in the middle of the night now, could I? Even if we might be the closest local law whenever something happens out that direction."

"Uh, no," Hillman said, a sheepish expression on his face. "Sorry."

"Just finish reading the damn statement, then we can talk."

Hillman dropped his head slightly and snapped the paper a bit to move more of it under the lamp's light. He moved his finger over to where he had been reading before.

". . . running from the scene shortly before the Burlington's 10:40 freighter came through. The officers found Darveaux's body and determined he had been shot. Darveaux's empty wallet that included his driver's ID card was found in a nearby snowdrift. It is not known how or why he was in the Sandman Complex, but they found a badly damaged car assumed to be his nearby. Tollefson said authorities are looking for family members in Hot Springs. Alcohol is suspected as a contributing factor, and an empty liquor bottle was found near the body. The investigation is continuing, and anyone who might have knowledge of the incident or who might know the victim is urged to contact Chief Al Tollefson at the Prairie City Police Department."

He stopped reading since the announcement concluded with just a listing of the Prairie City Police Department phone number as a contact.

Hillman looked up. "Sounds good. You think anyone will come forward?'

"Who knows? I'm actually thinking of offering a reward. If someone comes in after that, they might know more about places where the kid hung out. That might lead us to a place where he could've stashed the money."

"Yeah, that's a good idea," Hillman agreed. "Maybe you could say something like, 'Chief Tollefson said he did not know whether a reward was being offered.' Make it sound like a reward is possible, or something like that?"

Tollefson nodded. "Okay, add that and then get it down to the *News*." He held out a hand, took the paper and folded it, then stuffed it into an envelope on top of his desk. Pulling a ballpoint pen out of his desk drawer, he began writing a name on the envelope.

"I know the editor who comes in on the 5 a.m. shift down there." He pointed at the name to indicate that's the name he was writing. "When I know he's up and ready to go to work I'll give him a quick call to let him know you brought something by. He's always glad to get a piece like this that can maybe get on the front page and scoop the Rapid City paper. Easy work for him and a little glory, too."

The Chief walked over to a coffee urn and filled up his cup as Delaney came trudging in from the next room. Right now, they were the only ones in the station's main office. "Any luck?" Tollefson asked.

Delaney grunted. "Maybe? Hard to say. Kid is supposed to be living with his sister . . ." he paused and glanced back at the paper . . . "named Elizabeth, somewhere in Hot Springs. He and a buddy—another teenager named Frank Silver Shore—got pinched a couple years back swiping some candy bars from a store over at Buffalo Gap."

He held up some papers. "These were reports I found filed by the Custer County Sheriff's office. They got called in on it 'cause there's no local cop in Buffalo Gap. They say his sister got the two of them out of the County jail after they got picked up. Had to pay a fine and the Sheriff said he sent them on their way with a slap on the wrist. First offense for both. Other than that, nothing else on Darveaux or his sister, or the friend as far as that goes.

"You think he might've been the one we saw running? The café's counter guy said it was a teenaged Indian kid."

"Maybe." Tollefson took the papers from Delaney, looked them over and handed them off to Hillman. "Take these with you. Get yourself a couple hours sleep, drop off this statement at the *News*, and then you and Pete drive on down to Hot Springs and see if you can find either the sister or the friend. Just see where this Silver Shore kid might've been last night and what the sister's been up to; a few things like that. And, maybe they know if he had any 'special' spots he liked to go to whenever he came up this way. A place he might feel comfortable stashing some personal items."

"Okay with you if I just head on home and have Batch pick me up there in the morning?" Delaney asked. "Fairburn's right on the way, just a couple miles off 79."

"You know where Pete's place is?" he spoke to Hillman as he stood looking back at some of the other papers on his desk.

"Sure." Hillman glanced over at Delaney. "That is if you still got your rig parked alongside that old general store building in the middle of town?"

"Yep, still the same, because I bought that old building too. It'll be a great place to store the drugs whenever they come in. Easy in, easy out," the bulkier man replied. "Now and in the future."

He walked over to Hillman's side as he continued. "Fairburn's north entry turnoff is only a few miles south of Hermosa, then just a couple more on into the town. Or you can take the southside entry and that takes you almost right up to my front door after about a mile. My store and rig are both across the street from the old hotel. Just wait 'til you see my sweet new trailer. It's the fucking nicest thing in town."

Tollefson ignored their exchange, walked over to a window and stared out without speaking. Then he tapped the window and pointed toward nothing in particular, picking up his earlier conversation. "And find out if Darveaux has a girlfriend or anyone else he might've been involved with. Especially if she might be living around here."

"Do you think we need to get the Hot Springs law involved?" Hillman asked. "Might seem kind of weird us just coming into town and talking to Darveaux's sister and other people without checking in with them."

Tollefson stroked his chin and nodded. "Yeah, probably." He walked back to his desk and pulled out a law enforcement book and thumbed through it until he reached a page that said Fall River County. "Looks like they've got a consolidated office down there—police, sheriff, Deputy Marshal—all hanging together at the Courthouse building." He picked up the pen again and wrote down the address. "It's up on North River Street," he said as he handed the slip of paper to Hillman. "I think that's not too far from that big indoor pool—the Evans Plunge, I think it's called. You know it?"

"I do, Sarge," Delaney interjected. "I like to go over there swimming some times on the weekends." He smiled to himself as he thought about those excursions. He enjoyed both the natural hot water pool and the pretty girls that frequented the place to show off their new swimsuits.

"Okay, so just swing by their offices when you get into town," Tollefson continued. "Like you say, it'll be sort-of a professional courtesy thing. Besides, they might know where the kid's sister lives. Save you a lot of time and hassle."

He sat back down at his desk and gave his companions a dismissive wave. The two men started for the door.

"And Batch; Pete." They stopped and turned back. "Don't leave Hot Springs until you've tried everything you can to talk to either the sister . . . or this Silver Shore character. If he's a good enough friend to get arrested with, he might be a good enough friend to call for help when you get yourself shot."

They turned together and started toward the door. "Or, like I said, see if you can at least track down some sort of picture," he added loudly, causing them to halt again and nervously look back in his direction. "That might mean making a 'stop' at the sister's place even if she's not around.

"Just watch yourselves and be careful what you say. I don't want to be waylaid by any more damn Indians."

Chapter Nine

Tuesday, Feb. 1, 1955
Morning of the second day

It was 7:30 a.m. when Deputy Marshal Al Twocrow, semi-retired, walked stiffly into the Fall River County Courthouse in Hot Springs. He shuffled down a long narrow hallway and turned the handle on the doorway marked "Law Enforcement Center." The words were embossed on a pane of glass that covered the top half of the doorway. Since it was the only door in the stately old stone building that wasn't solid wood, Twocrow had a good time telling people that he went to work every day in a "half-glassed" location.

"Hey Bill, how's it going?"

The police officer who called out the greeting chortled at his own remark and Twocrow grimaced in response, his deeply wrinkled face crinkled even more by his reaction. Recently he had made the mistake of telling the other police officers and deputies who shared his office space that when he was a young man just out of school—and working at nearby Wind Cave—he had toyed with the idea of changing his name from Alvin to Bill. Ah, the foibles of youth, he thought.

He removed his grey-green Stetson cowboy hat, slapped it against his right leg to rid it of the snow that had fallen on it as he came in from his car, and then placed it firmly back on top of his closely cropped steel-gray hair.

"Yeah, yeah, that's so clever," he replied as he now removed his rimless glasses and waved them around in the warmer air to get rid of the instant fog that covered them after coming in from the cold. "YOU can still call me *Marshal* Twocrow if you know what's good for you!"

The officer, a 10-year veteran named Paul Ramsay, guffawed in response, then pointed toward a bench near the break room where a teenaged Indian boy sat slumped against the wall, nervously rubbing his bronze hands together as he looked around the room. "You got a visitor. Kid's been here since a little after 7."

Twocrow looked in the direction Ramsay was pointing and smiled. "Hey, Frank Silver Shore!" he called across the room. "What brings you here so bright and early on such a cold morning?" He tossed a paper sack with his lunch onto his desk and headed over to the young man, who stood and ran one hand through his longer jet-black hair as Twocrow approached him. The boy's chiseled nose, sharp eyes and high cheekbones gave him an almost hawk like appearance. As Twocrow approached, the boy's worried look changed into a shy smile.

"Hello Marshal," Frank said, jumping up and taking Twocrow's extended hand. "Do you, uh . . ." he paused and looked around again to see if the others in the room were watching them. Since they seemed absorbed in their own duties, he licked his full lips and continued. "Do you have some time to . . .? Uh . . . can we go somewhere more private to talk?"

Twocrow's smile grew deeper and he placed a reassuring hand on the boy's shoulder and gestured in the direction of the nearby break room. "How about in there? That work?"

Silver Shore nodded and made his way toward the room as the old man pulled the door open and led the way inside. "What's going on?" he asked as the door closed behind them and he sank down onto the first available chair alongside a big oak conference style table. The teenager grasped the back of another chair and remained standing.

"Gene's dead," Frank said abruptly.

"What?" Twocrow sat up straighter and pointed to the chair next to him. "Holy Crap! Sit down and tell me what happened?"

Frank pulled out the chair and eased into it. He leaned onto the edge of the heavy wood table and looked as if he might start crying. Seeing the reaction, Twocrow reached out a hand and rested it on the boy's shoulder. "Do you know how it happened?" he asked in a softer, more reassuring voice.

"Shot," Frank responded. "He pulled a hand up to his face to compose himself. "I don't know who, but I found him after it happened. He was out by the Railway Café up north of Hermosa. Called me to meet him and when I got there I found his car in the parking lot. Window was broken out and there was blood everywhere. I went inside, but the guy back of the counter, he said he didn't see anything. When I went back outside I saw some blood in the snow and more going across the tracks."

He stopped and took a deep breath to compose himself. "Some cars came driving up and stopped by Gene's car. So I-I ducked further back in by the grain bins and that's when I found him. But all he could tell me was that three men were chasing him. Then I saw them—the three men—looking around. They saw me, too. Even shot at ME. Oh God!"

"Easy, easy," Twocrow interjected, sliding his chair closer to the teenager and between him and the door, just in case someone walked in. He leaned in closer, his wrinkled brow now furrowed even deeper in concern. "Look, just tell me everything that happened. Maybe Gene isn't dead."

"No, he's dead. I was holding him when he died, trying to find out how he got shot. Then those men came looking and I . . ." his voice trailed off and he stifled another sob.

"Son, do you need something? Water, tea, coffee or something? Why don't I get you something and then you can tell me the whole story, start to finish." He got up and walked over to where a pitcher of water sat next to a small stove. A teakettle sat on one of the gas burners, and Gene checked to see if it had any water. He started a flame beneath it.

"Tea?" He held out a box full of bags. Frank started to shake his head, but nodded instead. The kettle quickly began steaming and Twocrow took it off the flame, dropped a bag into a mug, and poured the hot water over it.

"I love tea," Twocrow said as he cradled the cup and brought it over to Frank, putting it on the table in front of him. "Let the bag sit in there for a minute or two and be careful, it's hot." He walked back to the stove and poured a second cup for himself, draining the kettle in the process. He gave the mug a disappointed look when it didn't fill all the way to the top, but brought it with him anyway.

"All right," he continued, sitting back in the chair. "Now you tell me everything that happened, and don't leave anything out." He nodded at Frank's mug. "Drink a bit of that first. It'll help settle your nerves." The boy nodded his agreement, blew softly across the top of the mug as the steam rose from the edges, took a sip, and began his narrative.

It was a full ten minutes before he finished and the old deputy sat stock still the whole time, not even sipping from his mug. When the boy finished, Twocrow gave a low whistle and finally sipped from the mug and made a sour face. "Forgot to take out the bag," he said, nodding at the offending teabag and sliding the cup back on the table. "Pretty strong . . . and the water's cooled off too." Silver Shore sipped again from his own mug waiting for Twocrow to give him a response to his story.

"So Gene's sister knows?" the Marshal finally said. "It's Elizabeth, right?"

Frank nodded. "I came here middle of the night and told her. Tried to get a little sleep, but I couldn't really. Do you think those men might've followed me? Who do you think they were?" He put the mug down and started to stand. The pocket on his coat caught on the underside of the arm of the chair and he looked down at it. "Oh!" He reached into the pocket and pulled out the brightly painted wooden box. "Here." He handed it to Twocrow. "This was the little box he said to give to you."

The Marshal studied it, turned it over a couple of times and studied it some more. It was carved and painted with tiny scenes from nature—birds, animals, trees and brightly colored flowers. "Mean anything to you?" he finally asked.

Frank shook his head. "No." He reached out for it and the Marshal handed it back. Frank gave it another once over, looking for anything that might help identify it, but the box seemed to be solid with no discernable openings; just tiny carvings all painted in bright colors. "Elizabeth said she's never seen it before either. Really weird." He handed it back. "Anyway, he wanted you to have it, so there must be something he figured you'd know."

Twocrow tapped it idly on the edge of the table then set it down. "Well, for now, it's a mystery to me too, but I'll keep studying it. Maybe it relates to something he told me one of those times we got together." He shook his head, picked it up and slipped it into his own pocket. "You sure Gene never mentioned who he'd been driving for? Or how long? I thought you guys were best friends?"

"We are!" Frank reddened at his sharp response and sank further back in his chair and continued speaking more quietly. "I just haven't seen him for the last month or so. Mom needed help moving back to the Rez 'cause she and my dad were splitting, and . . . well . . . I don't know? Then I moved up to my Dad's place in Rapid. We just hadn't had any time to talk. On top of that, Elizabeth wasn't too happy about our getting together again either." He let the last of it trail off as Twocrow gave him a quizzical look.

"Why not?"

Frank cleared his throat. “Well, since I dropped out of school to get a job, and then I wasn’t working regular, she thought I was a bad influence.”

Twocrow nodded. “Yeah, I can see that, I guess. So, you have some sort of plan? You got a job figured out yet?”

“No, guess not. Just workin’ at odd jobs for now. Frank looked so forlorn; Twocrow stood up and patted him on the shoulder. The younger man glanced up at the craggy old face looking down at him. “I don’t know? I just wasn’t doin’ that good in school, but maybe I should’a stuck it out. Lot of places won’t hire without a diploma.” He sat back in his chair as Twocrow walked to the stove, took the teakettle over to the water cooler and re-filled it. Returning it to the burner, he once again started the fire.

“Gene, he was the smart one,” Frank continued. “I was excited for him to come up to Rapid so we could get a place together and see what might happen. He said this driving job he had was paying real good, and he was going to see if he could get more hours and maybe get me into it too.

“I thought first he was just making it up. But he said it was pretty easy cash and he was hoping to do a lot more. I think especially since his sister had been getting sick a lot, he was thinking she might move up to Rapid, too. Maybe see a new doctor. When Elizabeth and me were talking last night, she had this really bad cough, and she said Gene was worried about her. I think maybe he was trying to make some extra money to help her. You know? But I don’t think the money he told me about—by that rock pile, whatever that is—was part of it. I think that was something else; maybe for the people he was driving for?”

Twocrow nodded. “That sounds like a good possibility. Maybe he ran off with something he shouldn’t have and that’s what got him shot. Does SHE know who he was driving for?”

"I don't think so. In fact, she seemed a little surprised. I mean, I think she knew he'd been doing some driving for someone, but like I said, she didn't even know he was gone last night. He took off after she went in to work."

Twocrow turned the fire off beneath the burner, unwrapped another teabag and dropped it into his cup. After pouring boiling water over it, he walked back and sat down next to Frank. He dunked the bag up and down a few times, took a sip and nodded with satisfaction, taking out the bag and tossing it into a nearby wastebasket.

"All right. I'm going to see if anything has been reported to the Rapid police about Gene's death, and then I want to talk with Elizabeth . . . and you . . . again. Meanwhile, you keep this to yourselves and if anyone asks you about it, you need to act like this is the first time you heard anything. Until you get 'officially' notified, you've got to keep quiet. And tell Elizabeth that, too. You're not supposed to know anything, and if you act like you do that can put suspicion on you . . ."

Frank started to protest and Twocrow held up his hands.

". . . I know you didn't do anything, but no sense letting anyone know that you might've found out about Gene before we did. Okay? Let's keep it to ourselves for now."

Frank stood up. He slipped on his coat. "I'll go back to their apartment and wait for you there. What time do you want to try to get together?"

Twocrow glanced at the wall clock. "You think she'll be up and around by 9:30?" Frank nodded. "Okay. I'll come by the apartment then. They still living up in that second floor flat across from the falls?"

"Yeah. That's their place."

"Okay. I'll see you both then. Now keep your head up and go out of here like nothing's the matter. I'll walk you out." He opened the conference room door and escorted the younger man out to the Courthouse's main entrance. "We're going to find out who did this, but you're going to have to be careful. And you're going to have to help Elizabeth now, too. It's going to be really hard for her." He clasped the younger man's shoulder, gave him a reassuring squeeze, then held open the door and watched as Frank walked back up the street.

"Shit." Twocrow blew out an exasperated sigh and took the small carved box out of his pocket and studied it again. "What about you?" he asked, slowly revolving it in his hands. "What are you all about?"

He put the box back into his pocket as he reached the front door and started to pull the door open. He paused as a glint of light reflected from a window panel running vertically alongside the heavy exterior door. He slowly let the spring-loaded door slide back shut as he turned around to see what had caused the glint of light.

"Mmmm," he muttered, taking two steps toward the top of the stairs. He stood there, unmoving, then folded his arms across his chest and waited as a Prairie City Police Department cruiser pulled into one of the diagonal parking spaces directly in front of the building.

Chapter Ten

The phone rang at the main desk of the *Hot Springs Star* and Maria Tager walked over from her own little desk in the corner to pick it up, glancing at the clock. It was 7:55 and she knew Janeen Wilder, the Star's "do-everything" front desk person, would be in at 8 sharp just like she always was. Maria debated whether to respond or let whoever was on the phone call back. She stood eyeing the phone as it kept on ringing, persistent and annoying. "Oh well, what the hell," she grumbled as she picked up the receiver.

"*Star*. Tager speaking." She held the phone in her left hand, stretched out her right arm and heard the bones popping in the joints of both her shoulder and elbow. Sitting too long writing at her drafty little desk, she thought, as she re-cradled the phone up against her right ear and absently rubbed at her right elbow with her left hand.

"Oh, uh, hi," the questioning voice on the other end was a tired-sounding older man's. "This is Paul Brown. I'm a reporter up at the *Black Hills News*. You the receptionist down there?"

"No," Maria replied, struggling to keep the indignation out of her voice. "Reporter." She waited a beat for the information to be processed by the caller. "Name's Maria Tager. What's going on Mister Brown?"

"Well, it's Paul," he said after another slight hesitation. "Anyhow, we got a dead body report from the P C P D this morning. A shooting. And apparently it's a kid from Hot Springs who got shot—out by the Sandman Elevator complex."

"No Kidding! A Hot Springs kid? Shot? Really? You have a name?" She shifted the phone back to her left hand, grabbed a pencil from her blouse pocket and reached for a notepad from a pile of them on Janeen's desk.

"Darveaux. Eugene or Gene, something like that. My editor got a statement sent to him from the head honcho out there and he handed it off to me for follow up." Maria could hear the shuffling of paper as if the reporter was checking his notes. "Yeah, Gene Darveaux. That's the name. Indian kid, it says here."

Maria wrote down the name. "And he was shot?" She stopped writing. "Did you say P C P D?"

"Yeah. Well, it's the Prairie City Police Department—officially. But they just go by P C P D most of the time."

"Sure. Guess I already knew about that," Maria said in response, even though she wasn't at all sure that she knew anything about that except where Prairie City was located. "Just thought it sounded weird they'd be doing the investigation, that's all."

"Maybe. But the crime scene is right out on the county line between Pennington and Custer Counties, so lots of strange jurisdictions down that way. Anyway, I guess they got a call about suspicious activity over by the Sandman—that's the big grain elevator complex between their place and Hermosa. Sandman Elevator Company. I think it actually might be closer to them than Hermosa, you know? At least I'm guessing that's the case."

Maria jotted Sandman and Hermosa down, picturing the grain elevators in her mind and drawing a quick sketch of one. She nodded and then realized she was nodding at the phone receiver, which wasn't responding. "Oh, yeah, but it's not THAT close to Prairie City. I know where the Sandman is located," she said aloud. "Geez, Hermosa is south and east of Rapid, and seems like that would be way west of the Prairie City police jurisdiction—maybe by quite a few miles, wouldn't it?"

"Well, I suppose. I agree, it's a maybe. I haven't been down that way much myself. Anyway, all we've got for now is this police statement, so thought I'd check to see if you folks might have anything more you could share about the kid? It would help flesh out my story a little, and my editor is hot to get a scoop on the Rapid City *Journal.* Says nobody else has this info. yet and he wants to really run early with it if we can. That is, if you don't mind helping us out?"

"Sure. But, sorry, I haven't heard of him. Why don't you give me your number and I can check it out with an Indian source I've got over at the police station down here." She flipped over another page in the notepad, scribbled Brown's name and wrote down his number as the *Black Hills News* reporter dictated it. "Got it," she said and then repeated the number back just to be safe. "What's your deadline?"

"Couple more hours. Ten, ten-thirty. Our first run is around noon."

"First run. Hah!" She snorted out the words. "We've got ONE run here. It's on Fridays." She tossed the pencil onto the desk and ran her right hand through her long wavy dark-brown hair as she spoke, frowning as the popping sound in her elbow repeated yet again.

"You're a weekly? I thought your paper came out twice a week?" Brown said.

"Twice . . ." she half laughed the response. "No, that's crazy talk. We're lucky to fill up one edition. Besides," the young reporter blew out a big sigh, "It's just me; the editor; and two part-timers—plus our front desk person . . . and our stringers, of course. You know? 'Who had coffee with Who out in the small towns, the clubs,' that sort of *news*." She put special emphasis on the last word and gave another little snort. "But I guess I shouldn't make fun," she added quickly. "The editor says that's what gets us readers and pays the bills around here. So I suppose I should be thankful."

"Well, sometimes I wouldn't mind trading places with you," Brown made a sort-of huffing noise and exhaled loudly. "Nothing but deadline after deadline up here. Never time to catch your breath. Although I guess if you're doing EVERYTHING like you are, that gets pretty hectic too?"

"Yeah, don't I know it," Maria agreed. "We even have to take the photos and develop our own film. I didn't even know how to do that when I got here, and now I'm an expert. I think." She gave a little laugh at that and looked up as the bell over the front door clanged and Janeen shuffled in. Maria gave her a quick wave as the older woman walked past the front counter, dropped a couple of bags next to her desk and started hanging up her coat.

"Well, look, I'll see what I can find out and it'll either be me or our front desk person Janeen Wilder calling you back—an hour, or couple hours at most." She grinned at Janeen as their "do-all person" gave her an inquisitive look, then hung up and said hello.

"Who was that?" Janeen asked, shooing Maria away from her chair and taking command of it herself as she moved over into the space between the desk and front counter.

Maria gave her a quick rundown, jotting down the *Black Hills News* reporter's name and number on another sheet of paper and handing it over to her. Janeen brushed at her short blonde hair and leaned back in her chair, a strange look on her face. "You know, I know a young Indian woman named Darveaux," she said. "Might be a relative. Pretty girl. She works up at the State Home on my dad's wing. I talked with her a couple times—just being friendly and such." She paused and tapped herself above her heart. "Plus we kind of 'connected' 'cause I got some Native blood myself."

"You do?" The younger woman looked a bit incredulous as she eyed her blonde-haired, green-eyed colleague, then shrugged and nodded.

"Well, that's good. You think you might be able to get her address? Or maybe a phone number? I probably should try to get in touch with her."

"Sure. I'll give it a try."

"Okay, yeah, give it a shot. If she agrees, tell her I'd like to talk. But don't say anything about the kid getting shot. You know, in case she hasn't heard anything about it yet. We don't want to be the ones breaking that kind of news to her." The reporter grabbed her coat, circled Brown's phone number on her notepad and slid the notepad into her coat pocket. Re-inserting the pencil back into the pocket on her blouse, she pushed the bottoms of her quilted long pants down over the tops of her Wellington-style boots, buttoned up the coat, and started for the door.

"Where can I find you?" Janeen asked. "In case I need to give you that information right away? Or if any other calls come in?" She was already flipping through a Rolodex on her desk checking for a phone number up at the State Veterans Home.

"I'm going on up to the Courthouse. Cop Shop."

"Going to try to see Twocrow, right?"

She nodded. "If anyone might know Darveaux it probably would be him." Maria paused in the half-open doorway. "And not just because he might know ALL the Indians in town," she said as Janeen made a face. "It's because I think he might know EVERYONE in town plus the entire three-county region."

Janeen's frown turned into a smile and she half-nodded, waving Maria out the door as she pulled a card from the Rolodex, picked up the receiver on her desk and began to dial.

*****

Maria pulled her knit cap down over her ears, took out her car keys and hopped into her pale yellow, 2-door 1948 Dodge Custom Coupe parked in front of the *Star*'s office building. She'd splurged on a loan to borrow $400 and buy the car as a college graduation gift to herself a year-and-a-half earlier and now she was getting ready to make the last payment. It was definitely her pride and joy and she kept it buffed to a bright shine even in the middle of winter.

She glanced at her watch. Twocrow and the other deputies ought to be at work at the cop shop by now. She'd contacted them often around this time of day to get information on stories she was pursuing and it hadn't taken long for her to go from being the "newbie" cute girl, out-of-towner to "that pain in the ass girl reporter always causing us trouble."

She grinned. Even though her face was not the most welcome sight at the police and sheriff's office, she thought she had an ally in the old Marshal since he had been close friends with both her Grandmother Laura and Great Aunt Minnie Thompson. And while she and the Marshal hadn't struck up a firm friendship, as such, she felt like they could become good friends the longer she stayed.

But, since that "staying in Hot Springs time limit" was still up in the air, she was unsure if she should try to grow her somewhat tenuous friendship with Twocrow or just keep up the status quo?

Maria was in the middle of her second year working at the *Star* since coming to Hot Springs right out of journalism school at New York University. While she had earned top grades in the prestigious NYU program, getting a job on any of the big newspapers out East had been a tough option for a young woman. So when the Hot Springs *Star* publisher—a friend of her Great Aunt's—had offered her a chance to hone her reporting skills at the Southern Black Hills newspaper, she had jumped at the chance.

At the *Star*, she'd quickly earned kudos for her writing from many in her adopted community, especially those who fondly remembered the stories done by Minnie and Laura. But she also had rubbed other people the wrong way—especially when she was writing about things that went against longtime local customs or that might offend local bigwigs. And, despite her 5-foot-4 slight build, a disarming tangle of wavy dark brown hair, and her usually quiet demeanor, her "dive right in" reporting style had earned her the reputation as a "take no prisoners" type of writer.

She opened her leather-bound trapper keeper that she kept on the seat of her car. A 9-by-12 notepad was clipped onto the right side, and facing it on the left was a copy of a permanently affixed old photo of her Grandmother Laura and Great Aunt Minnie standing arm-in-arm with Alvin Twocrow next to a big-top tent in Hot Springs' Chautauqua Park. It was dated September 1894 and all three of them looked impossibly earnest and very young. Her mother had given her the photo to take with her to Hot Springs as a way of introduction to Twocrow and while he had been cordial, he had not given her an overwhelmingly warm response. Still, he had been "sort of" friendly and usually willing to talk.

"Oh well," she said aloud, tapping the photo and pointing at Twocrow. "I don't know if we're EVER going to hit it off Marshal, but . . ." She looked at the face of her Grandmother and then at her Great Aunt's and shrugged. "Guess it's either going to happen or not, isn't it? If you're willing to send any support from the hereafter, feel free." She glanced skyward as she said it, hoping their spirits might be listening. Both women had died within 6 months of each other late in 1953 and early in 1954 and Maria missed them terribly.

She reached up to make sure the rearview mirror was in the right position and double-checked her appearance at the same time. She hadn't taken time to put on any makeup this morning, but she still felt good about how she looked. She hadn't had any zits since coming to the Black Hills and felt like the dry climate and thinner air here was good for her fair complexion. People here had often complimented her as being pretty, but she felt like they might just be trying to be nice.

Personally, she thought her face was a little too "craggy," but her Mom had told her once that it was "defined," whatever the hell that meant.

"Oh well," she said aloud, waving her arm in the air and exclaiming with a loud "Ow!" as both her elbow and shoulder again made loud cracking noises at her action. She rubbed both joints with her left hand and pointed back at the mirror.

"You get what you get and THIS is what you get. Take it or leave it," she said to the mirror. So far, most of the men her age were definitely "leaving it." She giggled at her own reaction and shook her head in disgust. "Who needs 'em," she said loudly. Maybe she was just being too sensitive about her looks.

She shifted the car into gear and started north along River Street headed toward the Fall River Courthouse. Driving past the waterfall that cascaded down the hillside along the far side of the river, she gave two young secretaries who worked up the street from her at the Farrell Law Office a friendly wave. The women stopped on the sidewalk to wave back and admire her car. If she ever got a date, it would probably be because she had a cool car, she thought ruefully. Passing between the riverside Gazebo and the Evans Hotel she continued alongside the Sisters Hospital and Union Depot. Braking for the usual congested traffic area out in front of the Vesta Café—the first in a string of sandstone sided buildings just past the hotel on her right—she glanced at her watch again and shifted into second gear.

Just as she was starting to pick up speed again, a good-looking young Indian man darted across the street directly in front of her. Seeing her approaching car, the man, who she thought must either be in his late teens or early twenties, tried to pick up his pace but only succeeded in getting even more in a direct line ahead of her. He half-leaped to one side and slapped down on the hood with his open palm as Maria hit the brakes to avoid a collision. She tapped on her horn in frustration.

He gave her a shell-shocked stare, followed by a flash of anger as he held his hands wide in response.

"What the fuck?" she yelled, not even sure he could hear her through the windshield. She reached across and rolled down the passenger side window. "You see anything here that says 'Crosswalk' you idiot? Holy shit man. I could'a killed you! And you better not've dented my car!"

"Yeah, yeah. So sorry if I might'a dented your precious little car. But don't worry about me, I'll be okay." He held his arms wide again as if challenging her to respond.

"It's not just a precious little car. It's my precious Sweet BABY!" She yelled. "But next time I won't stop, dent or no dent."

The young man raised his hand as if to apologize and stepped off toward the sidewalk. At the curb he suddenly turned his hand around and gave her the finger. His handsome face now clouded with anger, he glared accusingly at her as he started to walk on past her car. Maria narrowed her eyes and glared back, hoping her evil eye response would instill some fear into the young man and prevent any future transgressions.

He just gave her a dismissive wave and hurried away and out of Maria's direct line of sight as she resumed driving. She glanced in the rearview mirror to watch as he strode on past the Vesta and the Evans Hotel before disappearing around the corner in the direction from where she had just been driving.

"You might be good looking, Asshole, but you're still a dumb, dumb, dumb ass!" she grumbled into the mirror. She patted the dash of her precious car as she spoke as if to reassure her baby that she wasn't going to let any stupid idiot cause it to get dented or have an accident.

Increasing her speed, the reporter passed a distinctive rock-walled building known as The Flatiron and then did a quick check to her right for any cars that might be coming downhill from the VA Medical

Center. One close call was one too many, she thought. Entering into a triangular intersection there, she double checked traffic and finding it all clear, drove on, now passing the ornate exterior of the Braun Hotel on her left.

"Okay," she said aloud before adding a satisfied "Yes!" as the Courthouse and the adjacent cavernous wooden Mammoth Bathhouse—stretching out from the edge of the parking lot on the Courthouse's north side—both came into view.

She pulled up to the diagonal parking area directly in front and was surprised to see Marshal Twocrow perched at the top of the Courthouse steps. He was talking to two men standing down below in front of a Black and White Chevrolet Bel Air police car. The car's doors were painted solid white as was its top, which was accented with a large red bulb located almost directly between the driver's and passenger's seats on the roof of the car. The vehicle's passenger side door was marked with a huge gold star encasing the words "Prairie City Police Department."

Chapter Eleven

Maria quickly angled her "sweet baby" two spaces away from the P C P D cruiser and jumped out, extracting a narrow reporter's notepad from her coat pocket and flipping it open as she hurried toward them. She reached in between the top buttons on her coat, removed the pencil from her blouse pocket and patted the coat back into place.

"You guys down here about that shooting up by the Sandman Grain Elevator Complex?" she asked loudly as she approached them. One of the men, wearing a crisp brown uniform, spun halfway around at the sound of the young woman's voice, his hand instinctively dropping to the top of his sidearm as he turned. He exchanged a flustered glance with the other man before looking back up toward Twocrow as if expecting him to respond on their behalf.

"What do YOU know about that?" the Marshal growled, taking the officer's cue. He pointed in Maria's general direction. "This here's Maria Tager, reporter over at the Hot Springs *Star*. That's our local newspaper." He waved toward the two men. "These two boys are down from the Prairie City Police Department . . ." he paused as if debating what to say next, then nodded more to himself than to any of the others. "And, yes, they're here about a shooting they had up that way last night. Found a man's body and an I.D. that said he was from Hot Springs. So they drove down to see if we might be able to give them a bit more information." He paused again and cleared his throat. "About the victim, of course, not the shooting."

Maria was scribbling rapidly on her reporter's pad. She stopped and held out a hand toward the man who had turned in her direction and looked like he might be right out of central casting with his movie star good looks. "Pleased to meet you both. What can you tell me," she eyed the handsome officer's nametag, "Officer Hillman?"

"Not much," Hillman answered, glaring back at his questioner with a look that conveyed nothing but contempt for a reporter who looked like she might be a college-aged co-ed at best. Ignoring the outstretched hand, he added, "Like the Marshal said, we're just trying to find out more information."

Maria pulled back her hand, transferred her pencil over to it, and continued taking notes. "You got a first name, Officer Hillman?" She looked over at the other man. "And, you too, Officer . . .?" The other man did not have a name badge, and his "uniform" looked more like the work clothing Maria recently saw her friend Paul Poundstone wearing down at the Black Hills Power & Light Company.

"Pete Delaney," the heavyset man responded. He was at least 8 to 10 inches taller than the 5-foot-4 Maria and his right hand reminded her of a small ham as he gave her a little grin and reached out to shake hers. His partner frowned as he watched Delaney's reaction. "And I ain't no 'formal' cop like my buddy Batch here. Used to be, back in my Army days when I was an MP. Now I'm just a 'You name it, I do it' sorta guy working for Prairie City and out at the town's airport."

He glanced up at Twocrow and back to Maria. "But I definitely help out the P C P D from time-to-time, since—like I said—I come out of that MP background in the Army," he added proudly, noting Twocrow's questioning look. "And still carrying my military sidearm, too. You know? Just in case." He pulled back the open flap of his coat and patted a wide flat handle of a gun in its holster that he had strapped to his side. "Been carrying this gun for years. One I picked up during the war. Back in '45." He started to unsnap the holster strap to pull it out and saw a look of alarm cross the Marshal's face.

"Don't worry Marshal," he hurried to assure Twocrow. "I got my official permit, 'cause like I said I do a lot of fill-in work for the Prairie City police force." He resnapped the holster and shut his coat before nodding back toward his partner. "Actually," he added, slightly puffing out his chest, "I came along today because **I** was the one who first spotted the kid's body."

"Is that right?" Maria responded, taking more notes as Hillman stepped a couple feet in Delaney's direction, an exasperated expression now replacing his frown as he tried to signal his companion to keep quiet.

"How'd that happen, Pete—okay if I call you Pete?" the reporter continued, noticing Hillman's reaction and moving her slight frame to partially block the officer's advance. Not waiting for his okay, she went on questioning. "I was told the body was found over at the Sandman Elevator Complex. But you're saying YOU found the body? Isn't Prairie City quite a ways east of there?"

"Oh, uh, no . . . not really. I mean, Prairie City's a ways off from there, but like you say, I found the body over at the Sandman." The big man seemed flustered by the young woman's rapid fire questions. "See," he continued, "I saw the body at the Sandman on my way home. I live down at Fairburn and, you know, there's this café—the Railway—out alongside the elevators. It's about halfway home for me. So on Mondays when I work late, after my shift ends around 9, I like to stop by there for a coffee on my way home. Usually catch 'em just before they shut things up around 10."

He looked back to Twocrow as if thinking he ought to explain it to him, too. "So anyway, when I got to the parking lot by the café I saw this suspicious abandoned car with a window broken out and blood all over it, so I called it in to Batch here and . . ." Delaney paused, finally seeing Hillman's warning look that signaled he should stop talking.

"And?" Maria held her pencil poised expectantly above her notepad.

"And maybe we all really should wait to tell you anything more," Twocrow interrupted, also seeing the expression on Hillman's face. "We haven't even notified the possible victim's family yet." He gave Maria a suspicious look. "Which brings up my earlier question: How'd YOU find out about it so quick?"

"Me? Oh. I got a call from a reporter up at the *Black Hills News* . . . who, by the way, already had a name for the victim from the Prairie City Police Department." She gestured in the Prairie City police car's direction. "Said the victim was a kid from Hot Springs named Gene Darveaux. If it's such a big secret, how'd he get THAT info. from your department, Officer?" She swung around and pointed her pencil accusingly toward Hillman. "Did your friend say your first name was Batch, Officer Hillman?" She resumed scribbling as she finished the question.

"Yeah . . . I mean no, it's Gl—Glen," Hillman stammered, turning red-faced as Delaney smirked at his partner's obvious discomfort. As he started walking around toward the driver's side, Hillman waved toward the passenger side door, also covered by a logo that designated it as a Prairie City Police Department car. "Get in Delaney. No reason to keep hanging around here. We ought'a be asking around, see if anyone can give us any more information about our victim."

He looked up at Twocrow. "Will you notify the victim's family, or do you want us to do it? If so, we'll just need an address."

"No worries. I'll let the Hot Springs police know what's happening and they can take care of it. One of us will call your offices when we get it done."

"You said you live out at Fairburn?" Maria turned her attention back to Pete, picking up her earlier questioning before either Twocrow or Hillman could speak again. "Do they even have electricity out there? I thought it was a ghost town?"

Delaney guffawed in response. "Naw . . . well, actually, it IS sort-of a ghost town. Some of my neighbors call it a 'Semi'-ghost town,' " he laughed again and gave her a lopsided grin, accompanied by a shrug. "Some of the houses are falling down and empty, but there's a few of us living in some of the old homes and what used to be businesses and some, like me, got our own trailers. It's a nice quiet outa the way location and the rents go for real cheap. When I first moved there, I got me one of them old downtown stores—the whole thing—for just around 40 bucks a month," he said proudly. "And we got a new main power line coming in there too. Supposed to get it strung and up and running by this Fall. Hell, we're growing!"

"No kidding, sounds amazing," she said, hoping she didn't sound too sarcastic in her response. "How long have you been living there?"

"Couple years now. Moved myself into my new trailer early November and I'm living in that now. Hooked it up to the water and lights from my other place so I have the trailer to live in and my old rental place to store my extra things. It's a great setup. You looking for a place?"

"Delaney!" Hillman spoke sharply to his partner. "Save the socializing and get your butt in the car. We got work to do." The bulky man's smile disappeared and he turned toward the car. Maria moved a couple steps forward and focused her gaze across the car on the police officer before Hillman could get in on the driver's side.

"You spell that with one N or two, Officer Hillman?" Maria asked. Hillman gave her a blank stare in return. "For the correct spelling of your first name?" the reporter added, putting her best "sweet sounding" tone into her voice as she waited with her pencil poised over the notepad.

Hillman just glared across the top of the car as Delaney took his seat on the passenger side and grinned at her again. The officer ignored

Maria but gave a little half salute to Twocrow. Getting into the car he fired up the engine and backed up with a sharp screech of tires before heading down the street.

"Guess I'll go with just the one," she said, turning toward the Marshal and making an exaggerated exclamation mark on her notepad. "Do you know the kid that 'allegedly' was killed? Was it Darveaux?" She walked up a couple of the front steps to get closer to the lawman as she asked.

Twocrow nodded. "Yes, I know him. Darveaux. IF that's who it was got killed," he added. "We're still waiting to hear more on that."

"You know what happened to him?" She finished her climb and stopped next to the Marshal, flipping the notepad over to another blank page.

"Maybe. But, listen, Mar, um . . . Miss Tager, I'm not putting anything 'On The Record' until we find out a few more details about the shooting ourselves and notify next of kin. So until then it's just going to have to be an unidentified young male, tentatively identified as a Hot Springs man and found shot to death outside the Sandman Grain Elevator Complex on the outskirts of Rapid City. Okay?" He turned back toward the courthouse door as Maria lowered the notepad and waved her pencil in Twocrow's direction.

"Sure. But isn't it kind of curious that the *Black Hills News* not only got info. on the shooting, but also had the kid's name included in a press brief they received from the Prairie City cop shop? If everyone's waiting to notify relatives and all, then why put the victim's name into an official press brief? Any comment?" She pulled the notepad back up and waited.

"Okay, look, Miss Tager . . ." Twocrow paused and blew out a heavy sigh. "If we go off the record I'll tell you a few things. So put that damn notepad away and just listen."

Maria lowered her pad and pencil again. "Okay. And please DO call me Maria. I said before that I preferred that, especially coming from you."

He looked away as if embarrassed, then looked back at her expectant face. "All right then . . . Maria. Like I said, it's probably likely that the body belongs to Gene Darveaux. They were pretty certain about that, so they must've found some sort of ID. Probably had his driver's card, or something. But they still need to run his prints to be sure. Darveaux's a Hot Springs High graduate who's been working off-and-on in the community, and a damn good kid, too. I knew him pretty well, and it's a real shame someone like that had to get killed. On top of that he has a sister living and working here, too, up at the State Home. Her name is Elizabeth. Real nice girl, but she's been fighting some sort of illness."

"You already talk to her?"

Twocrow shook his head. "I just heard from a friend of hers that she'd been sick."

"What about those two? They going to talk to her?"

"Beats me? Maybe. But, I might've forgotten to mention to them that I knew her—or Darveaux's friend Frank Silver Shore who they were also asking about."

"Silver Shore?" She shook her head in disgust. "He related to that mean bastard—pardon my French—who used to work down at the Standard station? I had more than one run-in with him after I got here last year."

Twocrow nodded. "One and the same. Hell of a mechanic, but mean as a one-eyed rattler that one. I was glad when he decided to move up to Rapid, but sorry to see his kid go. Frank and his friend Gene are both good kids and I talked with them off-and-on the last couple years they were in high school. Kind of thought Darveaux might be interested in getting into police work." He said the last sentence more to himself than to Maria, then gave another little sigh. "Guess we'll never know now for sure."

"How come those two wanted Silver Shore? They think he might have something to do with Darveaux's death?"

"Yeah, maybe. I asked them the same question and they were pretty evasive about it. Just that he was a person of interest, but they didn't tell me why. I told them the last I knew, his old man had moved to Rapid and they'd have to look for the kid up there. Either that or out on the Rez. Heard his mom moved back out there several months ago. The parents had been having . . ." He paused as if trying to select the right word, and then added, "Issues."

"And Darveaux's sister is a wonderful girl and she shouldn't have to deal with a couple of out-of-town cops at a time when she has to think about her brother's death."

"You going up to the Sandman to check on the crime scene and have a look at his body? Maybe see if you can figure out some things for yourself? I'd sure like to tag along if you are. A picture or two to go along with my story would give us a really great front page feature for this week's paper."

"What makes you think I'm okay with you 'tagging along'?" Two-crow emphasized the last two words and gave Maria an incredulous look as he spoke.

"Hey, I'm great company Marshal. Besides, didn't you promise me an interview one of these days? A 'tell all' about all these years you've put in down here 'policing' out of your 'half-glassed' location?" She chuckled at that and Twocrow joined in, despite his obvious irritation with the young reporter. "We could both kill two birds with one stone. You get some company; I get an interview; and we both get a look at the scene of the crime."

The old Marshal started to shake his head, but she quickly cut back in.

"Look, I promise to keep anything OFF the record that is truly OFF and write only what you say is okay. Okay? I mean, we're going to do a story anyway. Wouldn't you want it to be as accurate as possible? On top of that, you can put in some good words to share with the public—a 'Help us solve this crime' kind of thing. Come on Marshal. Give a struggling young reporter a break. You know what it was like for my Grandma Laura and Aunt Minnie when they were first starting out. I KNOW you do."

She shifted back-and-forth in anticipation then waved toward a sleek new 4-door dark blue Ford Fairlane emblazoned on the door with a white Marshal's Star inside a blue and white circle and the words "U.S. Marshal" in wide white block letters below it. The car was still so new that Twocrow had taped temporary "U.S. Marshal" license plates in both the front and back window corners until the car's new official "U.S. Marshal" plates arrived.

"And, you've got the coolest—and probably fastest—new car around. I'd love to get a high-speed ride in that baby too!" She gazed intently in Twocrow's direction like a kid waiting for the okay to get an ice cream cone.

Twocrow rocked back on his heels and eyed her with a bemused smile. Just for a moment he could clearly see his old friends' Laura and Minnie Thompsons' eyes replacing their young relative's pleading eyes—back when they were the ones staring so intently at a source and he was the one "tagging along" as their honorary adopted brother. He rolled his own eyes and exhaled another sigh, this one longer and deeper.

"Ah, what the hell. I can already feel the spirit of your Aunt Minnie tugging at my sleeve. So, all right, you can ride along. Come on back here about 10:30 and if I'm not here yet, I'll be back as soon as I can around that time." He turned toward the door, then turned back as Maria half-skipped down the steps toward her car. "And you better block off the rest of the day. No telling what we'll end up with once we get up there."

Chapter Twelve

"Well, now what?" Delaney asked as they bumped across several icy potholes on their way down North River Street. They reached a point where the road turned west toward a bridge going across the river or went east on Jennings Avenue toward the North Chicago Avenue turnoff that would head back out of town through Fall River Canyon.

"For one thing you could stop flappin' your gums so much!" Hillman grouched. "Especially when you're talking to a reporter!"

Chastised by his partner's outburst, Delaney slouched back in his seat and looked out at the steam rising off of Fall River as it meandered through the town and on out through Fall River Canyon on its way out to emptying into the Cheyenne. "Sorry," he mumbled. "Didn't think it was such a big deal."

Hillman just grunted before pointing at a flag being raised out front of a large granite building along the right-hand side of the Jennings-North Chicago intersection. "Let's start here." He pointed up over the door where the words "United States Post Office" were carved above a high-arching doorway and just beneath a tile roof overhang. "You'd think they'd know the Darveauxs' address, wouldn't you?"

He pulled the car into a diagonal space in front of the concrete entry walk and jumped out, calling to the flag-raiser before he could get back inside. The man stopped and half-turned in his direction. Noticing their patrol car, he nodded and stood shivering as Hillman walked toward him.

"Something I can do for you officer?" the postal worker asked. He jerked his head toward the door. "Maybe inside? Wind's picking up and chilling me to the bone. Probably should'a put on a jacket before puttin' up the flag." Batch nodded and signaled to Pete to stay put while he followed the man inside.

They moved into the open lobby and the man turned and snapped the door lock to open. Their voices and the sound of the lock clicking echoed through the open space of the lobby area. "George Jenkins," the man said as he turned back to face Hillman and extended his hand, which Hillman shook. "I'm not the postmaster, so if you need to be seein' him, then you're going to have to wait. He's out on vacation down to Florida for a couple weeks and I'm here on TDY to make sure everything stays on track. I'm the 'Fill-In' for all the small post offices in the Southern Hills. Used to be on here full time, but this is a pretty good retirement job." He smiled as he spoke.

"Well, I'm sure you can help me, Jenkins." He turned a thumb up toward his nametag just above his badge. "Hillman's my name. Working for the Prairie City Police Department and we're investigating a murder that took place up in our neck of the woods last night. Couple of the names that came up as being Southern Hills related are Darveaux and Silver Shore. You know where I might find addresses for either of those names if they're here in Hot Springs?"

"Well, sure. Guess you came to the right spot for addresses." The postman chuckled as he extended his arms to encompass their surroundings. Then he frowned. "Murder, you say?"

Hillman nodded.

"Suppose you already stopped down to talk to our law enforcement folks?"

Hillman nodded again. "Yep, we just left a meeting with Marshal Twocrow. He said they'd do some checking around, too, but my partner and I want to see what else we can find out while we're down here." He pointed out the window toward his car to indicate where his "partner" was located. "Long drive down in winter, you know, and on top of that we were up half the night dealing with the body."

Jenkins looked sympathetic. "Sure, I can see where you don't want to head back to Prairie City with just a meeting under your belts. Come on over to the window, and I'll take a quick look at the register." He waved toward the countertop backed by a metal rolltop-covered window and made his way through a heavy wooden door while Hillman walked across the lobby. The sound of a key in another lock clacked into the open space and then a loud raspy noise filled the air as he rolled up the metal covering and pulled out two large books from a row of several stacked onto another counter behind him. He flipped open the first one, found a page and ran his finger down along one side.

"Here's one. Might be anyway? Elizabeth and Eugene Darveaux." Hillman responded with a quick thumbs up. "But they pick up their mail here in a p.o. box. Got some sort of apartment down on River Street, but not exactly sure which building." He pointed toward a bank of Post Office Boxes along one wall. It's 27D. We usually assign boxes with letters associated with last names."

"You know either of them?"

"Naw. Postmaster probably does, but like I said, I'm only a part-timer these days. I'd guess their place is probably down near the Evans Hotel—one of those second or third floor spots they've been renting out down there. You know, some of the people might know them over at the Vesta Café. It's kind-of the main eatery and coffee spot down along North River."

"Okay," Hillman rubbed his chin. "How about the Silver Shores?"

Jenkins shut the first book and replaced it with the second, again flipping over pages. "Pretty sure that they moved out of town a while back," he said as he turned to a page and started moving his hand down along the side once again. "Oh, yeah, him," he said, stopping his finger on a name. "Roy Silver Shore. Mean son-of-a-bitch . . . excuse my language. He used to work over at the Standard station but I heard he had a hell of a run-in with the owner and got tossed out on his ass. Moved on up to Rapid City so we've been forwarding his mail up to the Rapid Post Office. Just sent a few things yesterday, as a matter of fact. You'll have to check in with Rapid for a street address if that's how he gets it delivered."

Hillman took out a small notepad and wrote down the name. "He the only one named Silver Shore?"

"Well, I see here that up to a couple months ago there was also the name Annie Silver Shore, his wife, it says here. But there's a line through that. I remember now that when her husband was still here there was some sort of big altercation and she ended up in the hospital and then moved out on him. Had her own place for a while, but I heard she moved back out to one of the Reservations." He looked back at the lined out name and ran a finger over a penciled line after it. "Okay, here. I list a forwarding P.O. Box for her out at Kyle if you want it?"

"Kyle? You mean way out in the middle of the Pine Ridge Reservation?" Jenkins nodded. "Maybe not." Hillman eyed the names he'd written. "So that was it for them? Just Roy and Annie?"

The postal worker glanced back at the book. "Well, they had a kid who got some mail off-and-on. But looks like he was never officially logged in because he wasn't the primary resident. Probably meant that things usually came in 'Care Of' one or another of the parents. I remember him because he was a hell of a track athlete up at the high school. But I heard he dropped out of school last year after his parents had their big falling out. Not sure where he ended up because we never did get a forwarding for him. Probably living with one of the parents; most likely the Mom, but I can't tell you for sure."

"Well, okay, thanks anyway. I appreciate getting this info. Don't know if it'll be any help, but you never know." Hillman took off his hat, wiped his arm across his brow, and then slipped the hat back on. "You have a good day now." He reached the door and started to pull it open.

"Frank!"

Batch paused, already halfway through the door. "Uh, no; name's Glen . . ."

"No, the Silver Shore kid's name," Jenkins interrupted. "You might want to double-check, but I think his first name might'a been Frank."

Chapter Thirteen

Frank leaned back on Elizabeth Darveaux's couch and stared out the window toward the roaring waterfall cascading down the hillside across the street. As it dropped into the hot water of Fall River—created by the naturally heated water starting from the Hot Brook that flowed out of the springs for which the city had gotten its name—an amazing sight greeted all viewers. There, at the river's intersection with the falls, the cold water from the hillside crashed into the hot water below, and the falls and the river collaborated to form a series of icy artworks on the rocks, trees and grasses.

Half-a-dozen ice sculptures had grown out of the water's action alongside the base of the falls, dramatically fanning out from a point where the water splashed up onto nearby rocks and onto spots that couldn't be warmed by the river. He folded his arms and sat forward as he heard Elizabeth moving around. He should check for coffee or at least heat some water.

As he stood to go out to the kitchen there was a loud knock on the door.

"Hey Elizabeth, you dressed?" he called toward her door, even though he was pretty certain that she was. The door opened a crack and she peeked out, her hair still disheveled from sleep. She started to say something but coughed instead, opened the door and waved a hand holding a hairbrush in the direction of the knocking to indicate he should go and answer it.

"I think it might be Marshal Twocrow," Frank said as he started over toward the front door. "He said he would come over around this time 'cause I told him you'd probably be up. Hope that's okay?"

"Okay, sure" she said softly struggling to suppress another cough. "If it's him, let him in. Otherwise, I'm not home." She swiped at her hair and stepped back into her bedroom.

Frank walked over and opened the front door where the old Marshal stood waiting, his Stetson hat cradled in both hands and a grim expression on his face. "Hello Frank" He nodded. "Hope I'm not too early? I know it's not quite 9:30 yet." The Marshal shifted the hat to his left hand and held out his right to grasp Frank's.

"No, no, it's okay. Come in." Frank swung the door wide and gestured toward the living room. "She's up. Just combing her hair or something." He shut the door behind the Marshall as the old man moved into the room. "I'd offer you some coffee . . . or tea . . . but I don't know for sure if she has any." Twocrow smiled and waved a dismissive hand just as Elizabeth re-opened her bedroom door and came in to join them. She walked over to Twocrow's side and extended her own hand, which he took before giving her a light hug.

"Hello Marshal." She gave a little sob. "I'm glad to see you."

"I'm sorry about your brother," he said with a warm, sympathetic smile. "He was a great young man and it's a terrible loss."

Elizabeth gave him a half-hearted smile in return as tears welled in her eyes. She looked around, spotted a box of tissues and took a couple, sinking down onto the couch and dabbing at the tears as they started running down her cheeks. "Yes," she finally gulped, then coughed. The raspy noise it made caused Twocrow to look at her with alarm.

"Have you seen a doctor about that cough?"

She shook her head. "We don't have the money. I'm sure it'll be okay soon."

The Deputy Marshal slipped off his jacket, hung it on a coat tree next to the door, and then sat down on an old rocking chair across from her. He took out a small notepad, jotted down a phone number and a name and ripped it from the spiral ring that held it across the top. He leaned forward to hand it to her.

"What's this?" she asked, staring at the number and name.

"Doctor friend of mine up at the VA," he answered. "You call him and tell him I told you to." She started to protest but he held up a hand to stop her. "Do it today, okay? And if there's any costs, you have him send them on over to me." She settled back further on the old couch and shook her head slightly as if trying to formulate the right negative reply.

"Elizabeth, you might be getting pneumonia if you don't have it already. Your brother's dead and I don't want you joining him." Twocrow nodded over at Frank. "Besides, Frank and I are going to need your help if we're going to figure out who did this to Gene."

"You think you can?" She coughed hard, stopping her own sentence and shaking her head in pain as she put a hand onto the center of her chest. "God, that really hurt!"

"Liz, do you have any coffee, or tea?" Frank pointed at the small kitchen area of the apartment as he moved across the room behind her.

"No. I'm sorry." She nodded at the window and gestured. "Why don't you go over to the Vesta and get us some? I think I'd like to rest a bit more anyway." She waved her arm toward the kitchen. "There are a couple of small thermos jugs in there. You can take one for coffee; one for tea." Then she handed him the small notepad paper that Twocrow had given her. "I hate to do it, but I think the Marshal may be right. I need to see someone about this cough." As if to accentuate her words, she started coughing again and this time brought up several drops of blood along with phlegm. "Maybe . . . can you call this number first and see if I can get in?"

Frank stared at the blood and hurried over to the phone and dialed. "Um, hello," he said at the sound of a voice answering. "Is this Doctor

Flaten?" He pronounced it FLAY-ton, and Twocrow quickly whispered "FLAH-ton."

"Here, give me the phone," the Marshall added, reaching out and taking it from the younger man. "Paul?" he asked after taking the receiver. Hearing a positive response, he smiled at the receiver. "Yeah, hi. Say, this is Al Twocrow. Hi! Yeah, I know. We need to meet for coffee or lunch again one of these days. Say, listen, I'm calling on behalf of a young Indian friend of mine and wondered if I might get you to take a quick look at her yet today. Might be dealing with the start of pneumonia." He nodded reassuringly at Elizabeth and Frank and stood up, taking the phone off the small table on which it was sitting and carrying it and its springy long cord with him as he continued to talk.

Frank moved over and slipped a reassuring arm around Elizabeth's shoulders, then reached back and grabbed the blanket he had used the night before and wrapped it around her. They sat quietly together listening to the Marshal as he spoke to his friend for a few minutes more. Finally, he turned back toward them, still conversing and put the phone back down on its table. "Thanks Paul. I'll owe you one." He laughed lightly. "Okay, yeah, yeah, I know. Okay, I'll owe you ANOTHER one." He chuckled again. "I'll make sure she gets up there by one. Thanks again!" He cradled the receiver, picked up the piece of notepad paper that Frank had put down next to the phone and jotted something else down next to the name and phone number.

Elizabeth leaned back further and shivered, clasping her arms together to both fight off another cough and try to get warmer. Twocrow nodded toward the door. "Frank, why don't you grab those thermos jugs and run on over to the Vesta to get those hot drinks." He glanced at his watch. "And just get them for you and Elizabeth. I'm going to have to get on the road soon." He pulled out his wallet and handed him a five-dollar bill. As both Elizabeth and Frank started to object, he pushed the bill into the younger man's hands. "You just do that, and get her a hot sandwich or something too. Okay?" Frank nodded. He went into the kitchen, grabbed the two thermoses and moved over to the coat tree next to the door, where he put on his jacket.

Twocrow walked across the room and gave him the notepad paper with the doctor's name and number. "And make sure she gets up to see Doc Flaten by one o'clock. I wrote the building number and his office number beneath his name and phone. He'll be expecting you." Frank moved over to the coat tree and put his jacket back on. "I'm counting on you," Twocrow said. He smiled at Elizabeth. "She probably is too."

Twocrow turned toward Elizabeth, saw the pillow Frank had used the night before and fluffed it up. "You just rest here, let Frank help take care of you, and I'll come back later today when I get back into town. I'm going to drive on up to where they found Gene last night and see if I can find out anything more about what might have happened to him. Can you stay with her?" He asked the question of Silver Shore as he patted the pillow and signaled for Elizabeth to lie back down.

"Sure," Frank said as he half-opened the door. "My old man ain't gonna care if I come back home or not, that's for sure. And I'd rather help Liz anyway."

"All right, good." He walked back to the phone, took his notepad back out of his pocket and wrote down the number off the face of the dial. "I should be back here by five or six, but if it's getting longer for some reason, I'll give you a call. One way or another we'll get back together by evening and try to figure this whole thing out. Meanwhile neither one of you talks to anyone but the doctor or me. Keep your door closed when you're in here and don't answer it for anyone else. You know my voice, so you'll know it's me when I get back. If anyone else you don't recognize tries to call, you just say wrong number and hang up. Okay?"

Elizabeth leaned back against the pillow, then sat halfway back up and shook her head. "But I'm supposed to go up to the State Home to my job. I need to be there by 5."

"Not today," Twocrow insisted. He took the pad from his pocket again and handed it and the pencil over to her. "Write your supervisor's name and phone number down and I'll call to let them know you can't make it in today; maybe even a couple days." He pointed at Frank. "You get on over to the Vesta and pick up some food and coffee . . . or hot tea," he paused and grinned knowingly at Frank. Now skedaddle! I don't want her sitting around here alone for too long." Frank nodded and left, pulling the door closed behind him.

Twocrow reached out for the notepad as Elizabeth finished writing, eyed the name and phone number and nodded. "Okay, I gotta go. I promised someone I'd get on the road by 10:30 so I'm going to head on out." He stopped. "Do you have a photo of Gene I can take with me?"

She nodded and started to get off the couch.

"Just point me in the right direction and I'll get it," he said, signaling for her to sit back. She pointed up at a bookshelf near the window where two large photo albums jutted out on the second row.

"The red one. It's mostly pictures of Gene and me. Some with our Mom and Dad."

He took it down, walked back to the couch and sat down with it on his lap. Elizabeth flipped it open. "Here," she said. "Haven't taken any pictures lately, but the ones on this page are from about three years ago, right after we moved to Hot Springs. That was about a year or so before Mom and Dad were killed in the crash down by Oelrichs. I was a junior and he was a sophomore." She pointed to a series of pictures of the two of them together with a large rock formation jutting out behind them. "He didn't change his appearance that much from then until now."

Twocrow nodded and made a humming sound in his throat. "These are great pictures! Where were you at when they were taken?"

"Up by Spring Creek, on the road east of Hermosa going out toward the Reservation," she said. "I think it was the first time I was ever out there, but Gene used to go fishing there with Dad all the time. It was such a pretty place and they loved . . ." she stopped, choking up and tears filling her eyes.

"It's okay," Twocrow said, taking one of the photos of Elizabeth and Gene out of its sleeve and slipping it into his shirt pocket. "I know it's hard to talk about him being gone. But it's good to have these photos. Good memories." He patted his chest. "I'll take good care of it and get it back to you soon. I promise."

"Okay," she stifled another sob. "It's so hard. My parents had such high hopes when we came here. They wanted us to get our diplomas, make something of ourselves. Then they got killed in that crash, and now look. I'm cleaning rooms. Gene's dead. I just don't know what to do. It's just so hard."

Elizabeth sat back, coughed again, and pulled the blanket tighter as Twocrow stood, placed the open album down on the end table next to the couch and opened the door. "You have to be strong and don't worry," the Marshal said. He put on his hat and touched the brim in her direction. "We're going to find some answers," He exited, pulling the door shut behind him, then turned back and placed his right hand flat against it. "That's a promise."

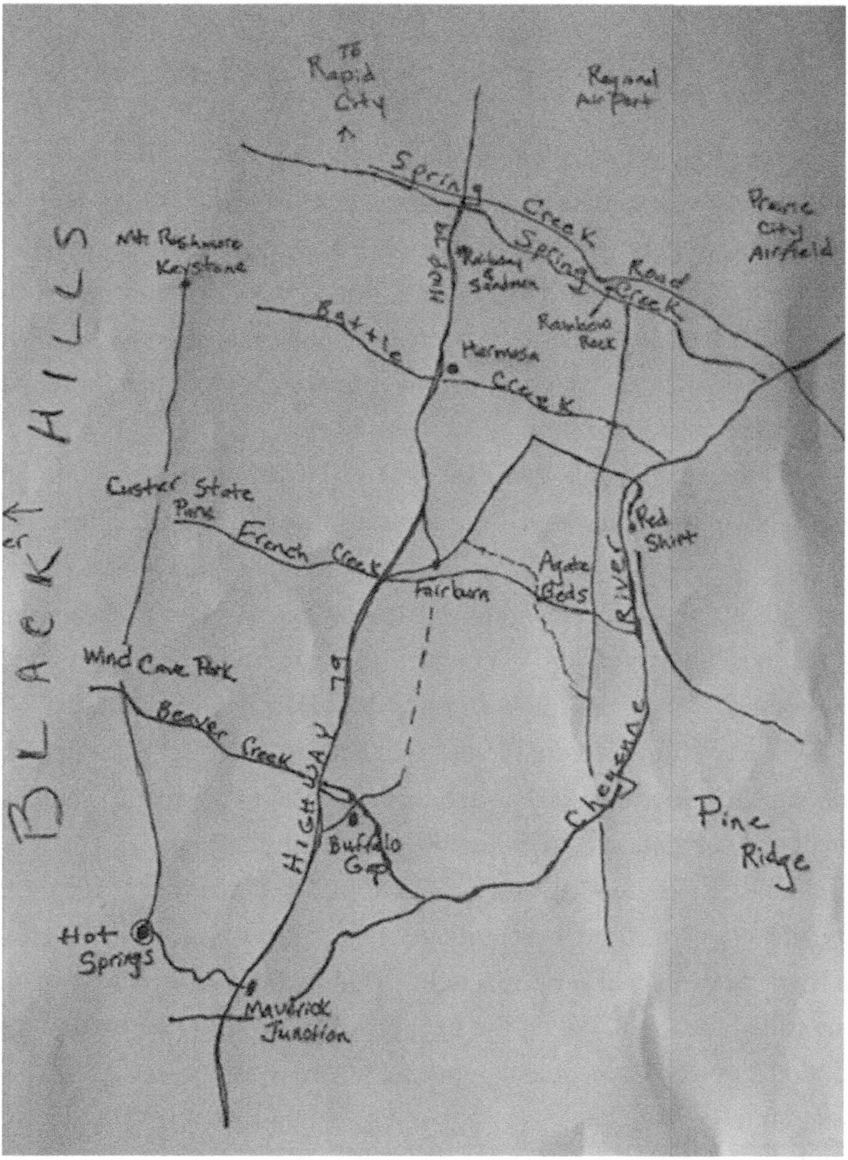
To Rapid City
Spring Creek
Spring Creek
Road
Rainbow Rock
Hermosa
Battle Creek
Mt. Rushmore Keystone
BLACK HILLS
Custer State Park
French Creek
Fairburn
Agate Beds
Red Shirt
Cheyenne River
Wind Cave Park
Beaver Creek
HIGHWAY 79
Buffalo Gap
Pine Ridge
Hot Springs
Maverick Junction

Chapter Fourteen

Frank stood nervously at the counter of the Vesta Café waiting for his two drink containers and a hot roast beef sandwich to go. He had paid the tab and now shifted from foot-to-foot, certain that everyone in the place must be wondering about him and where he had gotten the money. A cheery middle-aged waitress with dark permed hair done up in one of the newest styles moved over to the countertop and plopped down a bag in front of him.

"Sandwich is double-wrapped in waxed paper down along one side and the two thermoses are sitting in next to it. One's coffee, the other tea, just like you asked." She opened the top and pointed inside. "And I went ahead and put in a few French fries for you, too, Hon." She grinned at his shocked expression. "You're that Silver Shore boy, ain't you?" He nodded. "You ran track with my boy Harry last year. That 440 relay. He got himself a conference title because of you." She slipped a few paper napkins into the bag and leaned across to whisper. "There's a small slice of apple pie in there, too. Don't tell the boss."

Frank's eyes grew big and he looked over her shoulder as if expecting "the boss" to come barreling out of the kitchen with a meat cleaver in hand. She laughed at his reaction. "Don't worry, he ain't here now." She rolled the top down on the bag, picked it up from the bottom and handed it over. "Carry it real gentle and there won't be any spills. You have far to go?"

"Naw, just over to the Darveauxs. They live . . ."

"Oh I know the Darveauxs. Are they still in that apartment down by the Falls?" He nodded. "Sweet kids, especially that Elizabeth. She's always been so nice to my Dad up at the State Home. So this food is for her, too?"

He nodded again. She put a hand over the top of the bag, reached back behind her and plucked a couple donuts from a tin sitting on the counter. Plopping them into the bag, she rolled the bag's top shut again and patted him on the hand. "Tell her hello for me, too." She smiled. "You have a good day Hon."

Frank took it from her, gave her a shy, grateful smile and turned to the door just as it swung open, setting off the array of bells hanging at the top. The first man, wearing a police uniform, stepped inside, but seeing Frank, the other one—a big, dumpy looking man with his hat in hand—pushed the door further open and stood holding it for the teenager. Frank stared up at him, sucked in sharply, stopped and then started again, looking down at the bag as he carefully edged his way through the doorway.

"Thanks," he mumbled, stepping outside and turning down the street.

He had taken just a couple steps when a booming "Hey kid, wait up!" came from the doorway. Frank paused, trembling slightly as the big man moved toward him, pulling his hat back on as he extended his other hand in Frank's direction. "You dropped this at the doorway," he said, placing a glove on top of the bag. "Gonna need it in this weather." He half-grinned and gestured toward the steam rising from the river. He started to turn back, stopped and glanced again at Frank. "You look familiar. We met somewhere?"

Frank shook his head, still keeping his eyes down and head half-bowed while holding the bag even more tightly. He was ready to drop it and run if necessary. The man eyed him for a few more seconds and shook his head. "Nah. Don't pay no attention to me." He gave a sort-of snort as he waved a dismissive hand and turned back toward the door. Grasping it firmly he took his hat off again as he stepped inside, the right side of his head, covered by a large thatch of snow-white hair, shining in the cold, noonday sun.

*****

"It's him, I'm positive!" Frank exclaimed. He had raced back to Elizabeth's apartment, risking dropping the hot drinks and everything else but arriving with all the bag's contents firmly intact. "I'm sure he's the guy that was shooting at me last night by the Sandman. I'll never forget that big patch of white hair. We've got to tell the Marshal."

Elizabeth stood and took the bag away from Frank and walked it to the table, risking dropping it as she started coughing again. "I . . . agree," she coughed. "But you heard him. He was headed out and won't be back until later this afternoon. He said to stay calm . . ." she stopped, coughed hard, and sat down in a chair next to the table. The coughing subsided and she continued. "So, we need to stay calm, do what he told us, and then tell him what you saw. Was he with anybody?"

"Well, yeah, that's just it. He was with a cop."

"And . . . you're sure he didn't know you?"

"Yeah . . . I mean, no. I mean, I think he didn't. He kind of gave me a weird look though; asked if we might've met." Frank shook his head. "Geez, Liz. I don't know. I don't think he knew me."

"Just stay . . . cool," she fought off another urge to cough. "Let's just get my . . . visit to the doctor . . . done and . . ." she sat still for a few seconds, wheezing slightly before continuing. "Then we come back here; shut the door . . . and . . . wait!"

Frank nodded and sat down on the couch as Elizabeth reached into the bag and took out the pair of thermos bottles followed by the waxed-paper wrapped sandwich and a piece of waxed paper taped around some fries. She looked back into the bag. "Is that pie?" She reached back in. "And donuts!"

"Waitress was being nice. She said she knows you 'cause you know her Dad up at the State Home." Frank gave her a sheepish grin. "And her son Harry ran track with me last year. Good guy." He pulled the tape off the fries and popped one into his mouth. "Now I know where he gets it."

Elizabeth cut the sandwich in half and handed part of it to Frank. "I'll take the tea if you want the coffee?" He nodded his agreement, opened the coffee and poured some into the thermos cup.

"You have any thoughts yet on where that rock pile might be located?" His mouth was now half-full of sandwich as he spoke and he quickly swallowed and sipped at the hot liquid before speaking again. "I mean, you and me, we might be the only ones who can figure that out."

She sipped at her thermos mug of tea before answering and finding it still really hot, blew lightly across the top before taking a second sip. "When you mentioned the agate fields, I was thinking it might be out there, or maybe in the town of Fairburn itself. Lots of old abandoned houses and stores out there and Gene used to say it would be a great spot to hide something. Could be by an old rock wall or something." She took another sip and pointed toward him. "And doesn't that one creek run alongside the town, too. Could it be a rock formation next to the creek, or something like that?"

"It's French Creek," he answered. "And now that I think about it, there are some cool rock formations along there when it gets closer to the agate field. Might've been one of those he was talking about—although I don't ever remember him saying anything in particular. I can't really figure out anything or any formation that's right in the town itself, though."

"Well, it's easy in, easy out to Fairburn, so we should definitely check it," she said after swallowing the last of her sandwich. "Probably better walk the agate field too. Early morning's the best time out there.

Gene and I went out there walking early a couple times and it's beautiful. Plus, the sun coming up gives you the shadows if there's something that stands out. Like a rock pile. A place for shadows in the morning, rainbows in the afternoon."

She took another soothing sip of tea, found it cooler and took a longer drink. Drinking the tea had taken away her constant urge to cough, especially when she was speaking. "Can you think of anything or any place that's up closer by either the Sandman elevators or the Railway Café?"

He started to shake his head, then stopped. "Well, there is that old gravel pit out west of Hermosa."

"What gravel pit?"

"Maybe that's not the right term. You know, it's that dig spot out along Battle Creek, west of Hermosa where they were digging out sand and gravel for re-building the road. You remember? When they re-did Highway 79 and they dumped a bunch of the bad stuff, I think it's called slag, into in a big pile right alongside the pit? It's kind of on the east side of that little dugout lake where kids sometimes go swimming and diving. But it's not really a rock pile—more of a slag pile. Still, I've heard some kids call it the rock pile when they go there. You know, 'We're going out diving off the rock pile'."

Elizabeth looked unconvinced, but Frank persisted.

"We should at least check it. Okay?" He nodded and held up his hand, bending down three fingers as he spoke. "See, we've got three possibilities already and maybe when we go to those we'll get ideas for more. I mean, what have we got to lose besides time?"

She shrugged and moved back to the couch. "We can make a better plan once we get back from seeing the doctor." She sat down just as the phone began to ring.

Chapter Fifteen

"So that's how you got started in law enforcement? Helping Bat Masterson, Seth Bullock and Teddy Roosevelt apprehend an outlaw gang? And my Great Aunt and Grandmother were involved, too. That's unreal!" Maria shifted around in the spacious passenger side bucket seat of the Marshal's new Sedan. The blue and white temporary license plate reading "Deputy United States Marshal" was taped in the front window corner just to her right and partially obstructing her view. She scribbled a couple more lines on her notepad, emitting a low whistle of appreciation as she did so. "And how old did you say you were?"

"Nineteen. Barely. Your Grandma was 18 and a half and your Great Aunt Minnie was just 17," Twocrow answered, keeping his eyes on the highway but also seeming to be looking back in time. "Over sixty years ago now." He cleared his throat as gruffness permeated his words. "I was working out at Wind Cave at the time. First Indian Ranger, you know?" He pushed the brim of his Stetson back on his head as he reminisced and some of his steel-grey hair spilled out, forming bangs just over his eyes.

"Well, Ranger might be a bit of a stretch," he seemed to be admonishing himself as much as clarifying for Maria. "I was more of a glorified Indian 'host,' giving guided tours, talking about the Great Spirit living there. Things like that. It was before the feds took it over, and the owner back then wanted some 'authenticity' from his guides. He thought 'Real Indians' would do the trick, especially with the story of how the wind from the cave was believed to be the Great Spirit going in and out of the cave to look over his creation every day."

"Wow, this is great." She reached into her coat pocket and gripped a small Leica camera she had brought with her. "We'll have to go out there one of these days and I'll get a photo of you at the Visitor's Center."

She removed her hand and brushed at a stray strand of hair falling down across her eyes. "Or maybe I could get a shot at the entrance. Hey! What the hell . . ." She gave a little scream and careened toward the window, banging her head sharply on the top half of the windshield as Twocrow slammed on the brakes. The car skidded sideways before sliding to a stop in the middle of the road. Three medium-sized mule deer bounded across in front of them, heading out from the hills on a line toward the prairieland stretching out from the highway toward the east.

"You okay?" Twocrow sat gripping the steering wheel, his knuckles popping out white from his bronze skin. "Last thing I expected this time of year were deer on the move. They don't usually trek out to the prairie in the winter." He looked around to make sure there weren't any more of them before easing the car over to the side of the highway.

Maria rubbed the right front side of her forehead and felt for a wound where a small bump was forming. Not finding any blood, she reached down and picked up her notepad and pencil off the floormat in front of her. "Yeah, I'll be okay. Nice driving Marshal. We could've been sitting in the ditch now with a set of antlers poking through the windshield in between us. I've seen that sort of thing before; but never out on this road." She glanced up and down Highway 79 as she said it, looking to see if there were any other cars—or deer—coming their way. A sign alongside the road about a hundred yards in front of them indicated this was the crossing point for French Creek.

"They must've been followin' the creek bed on their way out east," Twocrow said as he pointed to the sign. "Most of the time they can run down through the drainage cut and on up to that underpass about half-mile ahead. Or they'll follow Battle Creek just before you get into Hermosa. But with the snow we got earlier, it's probably plugged up now. Only way across is up and over the highway and right into traffic." He looked out to the east and watched the deer rapidly bounding away from them.

"Three young bucks. Probably weaned out by their mamas and chased out of the herd by the older bucks. They'll be okay now that they're over the main road. No other major roads from here all the way to the Cheyenne."

"Where do you think they're headed?" Maria asked.

"French Creek crosses out this side of Fairburn. Then it runs east all the way past the main town and goes on out toward Red Shirt before it empties into the Cheyenne River. Lots of trees and grass over that way, not to mention hay piles put up by both the ranchers and the tribe. I think it's about 25 or 30 miles out to Red Shirt. I doubt if they'll make it by nightfall, but they should get there easy by end of the day tomorrow if they keep moving."

"I'm still too new to this area to know about all these creeks and rivers and how and where they run," the reporter said, sliding back on the seat again and looking out at a winding frozen stripe of water that was all that remained of French Creek during the winter months. "Isn't there something famous about French Creek? Some famous tree where Indians held gatherings?"

"You're probably thinking of the Council Oak. That's up north and west of here." He crooked a thumb at the window in that direction. "And that's up by Battle Creek, not the French. Like I said, we'll come to that one next."

"Okay. So what's the Council Oak?"

"A giant Bur Oak tree. Been there for centuries. The Tribal groups used to hold Pow-Wows there to talk treaties and how the Hills would be shared by everyone out here together. That was back before your people came here. White Men had different ideas about the word 'sharing.' "

She grimaced and tried to look apologetic, even though she was a little unsure about what "her people" had actually done. She squirmed on the seat and pointed at the frozen stream.

"I keep hearing about Spring Creek, too. Where's that located?"

"Oh, that's even further north of Hermosa. Actually not that far from the Sandman Elevators and the Railway Café where they said they found young Darveaux's body. That creek starts way up in the Hills, out beyond Mount Rushmore. Runs out of Sheridan Lake all the way east to the Cheyenne. There are 5 small rivers running out of the Hills down here—Beaver, French, Battle, Spring and Rapid. Folks call them Creeks, but they're really small rivers.

"They all dump into the Cheyenne and there's a big grassy area between each 'emptying out' point. Makes for great grazing for the deer and antelope, not to mention the cattle herds the local ranchers run out there." He paused. "I went out in that area and lived for a time with Yellow Feather's band—1894-95. It was just after we took care of that outlaw gang actually."

"Why'd you do that?"

"They were my people and I felt a calling. But Yellow Feather was an old chief and after he died, the people with him decided to go back out to the Reservation. Your Great Aunt Minnie spent a lot of time out-and-back visiting me when I was there; making sure I was okay, I guess. Anyway after Yellow Feather died she talked me into coming back to Hot Springs since I didn't have any close family on the Rez. I knew the Sheriff, so I started working at the jail. Then Seth Bullock came down here from Deadwood to run Wind Cave Park in 1903, and I went out to work for him. Rangerin' again. Only that time I really WAS Rangering. I was doing some horse patrolling around the Park, since Seth didn't want anyone taking out any of the Park wildlife, especially the buffalo and elk."

"Keeping people from taking wildlife when they were used to hunting whatever and whenever they wanted. That must've been a dicey situation, huh?"

"Yeah, wasn't easy, that's for sure. But Bullock was a hard-ass and he ran a tight operation. Expected his Rangers to work like lawmen, so when Teddy Roosevelt appointed him U.S. Marshal for this region, he took a lot of the Park Rangers with him as deputies. One of them was me."

"Wow. What year was that?"

"Well, he got appointed at the end of 1905 but it was 1906 when we all got sworn in and started doin' the regular Marshal'n duties. Since I had all those connections in Hot Springs, he chose to keep me down in the Southern Hills. But, of course, we always go where duty calls. So, I've been all around these parts on temporary assignments—down into Nebraska, over to eastern Colorado, Wyoming, Montana. Even up to the Roosevelt Park area in North Dakota from time-to-time."

"Roosevelt Park?"

"It's the National Memorial Park named for Teddy. Mostly on the ranchland he had up near the town of Medora. He was ranching up there before he came down into the Black Hills and made friends with Bullock—before he went back East and started on the path toward becoming President. Your Grandmother was a good friend of his. Your Aunt Minnie too. But I suppose they told you about that."

"Actually, no . . ." Maria's voice trailed off as she thought about all the things she didn't know about either Laura or Minnie Thompson, and especially their relationship with Marshal Twocrow and now the former President.

He reached across and touched the growing knob on her forehead. "You sure you're okay?"

She sucked in sharply and made a little gasping noise at his touch as he stared at her forehead with concern. "Hang on," he said, pulling a handkerchief out of his pocket and getting out of the car. He walked around the front side and down into the ditch, then came back wrapping something in the piece of cloth. As he got back in, he handed it to her.

"Some snow and a couple small pieces of ice," he said as she gave both him and the handkerchief a questioning look. "Hold it on top of that bump and it'll keep it from swelling up any more." She took it and held it to her forehead. The cold on the lump felt good.

He shifted into gear and started driving, gesturing in the direction of a rail line that suddenly appeared near a bend in the road. "The CBQ—that's Chicago, Burlington and Quincy—Railroad runs one of their main lines past here, too. That's another thing that goes back a ways, to the late 1880s and early 1890s, when I was still growing up in Buffalo Gap, living with the Thompsons.

"Line comes from Omaha and then turns north out of Chadron, Nebraska and pretty much follows Highway 79 all the way up to Rapid City where they hook up with the Great Northern. Stops out by Maverick Junction and again at Buffalo Gap, although that's probably soon going to end. They have a small passenger trade there, but all the cattle and grain shipping they used to do closed back in '53. There used to be regular stops in Oelrichs, Fairburn and Hermosa, too.

"Now it only stops outside of Hermosa at the Sandman when there's grain to load. Fairburn got dropped a few years back, right before the war—that'd be W-W-2, that war, not Korea—and I'm sure it's going to completely quit Buffalo Gap one of these days, too. Just not enough folks willing to travel by rail from there anymore. Too easy to just hop in a car and go." He sighed. "Times keep a-changin'."

Maria put the handkerchief onto the floor and picked up her notepad again. Holding her pencil suspended above the pad, she swiveled back toward him. "Okay, two things. First. You lived with the Thompsons? You mean you LIVED WITH my Grandmother and my Great Aunt?"

Twocrow nodded. "For quite a few years. But that's a whole 'nother story."

"No kidding," she said as she slowly exhaled. "No kidding," she added for emphasis. She tapped the pencil on her notebook, and he pointed toward it.

"What's the second thing?"

"Oh," she said, both startled by his quick interruption of her thoughts and the fact that she still hadn't asked the second thing. "You mentioned Fairburn, and I've been meaning to go out to Fairburn and do a story about the agate fields. People keep stopping by the *Star* office all the time asking where to go looking for the Fairburn agates, so guess they must be a big deal, huh? I just don't know that much about agates. Do you?"

"Of course! The rainbow rocks. Iya Wigmuke, we say in Lakota." He pronounced it Ee-yah Weeg-mue-kay. "They're beautiful and striking, that's for sure. You've never seen one?"

She shook her head. "Nope. But I've heard they're really something. Why Iya Wigmuke?" She struggled to say it and he repeated it before explaining.

"Ee-yah Weeg-mue-kay. Rings of bright colors sandwiched together like the colors of the rainbow," Twocrow replied, almost reverently. "Some of them even look like they circle around an eye. And some Lakota spirit leaders believe that's the eye of Wakan Tanka—the Great Spirit. My people have always known about Fairburns. They're said to be the Great Spirit's gift to the Lakota because the only places in the world you can find Fairburn agates are right around here or up in the Teepee Canyon area, west of Custer. In the center of our sacred Black Hills."

He shifted into 5th gear and gestured toward her forehead and then the handkerchief, which she retrieved and put back on the bump. "It is said that the Fairburn agate possesses many mystical powers, including the ability to permit the user to distinguish between honest and false friends. I probably should start carrying one around with me, huh?"

She laughed at that and he pointed past her to the east. "You can sometimes find the Fairburns all the way out to the edge of the Badlands, but more likely than not those out there came from right here—between Fairburn, the town, and the lands stretching on out past Red Shirt. There's a place called Kern's Ranch, not too far from the Cheyenne River. Old Grandma Kern thought she was the first one to find them, but my people knew about them for hundreds of years.

"As a matter of fact," he added firmly, "Lakota think—just like the Black Hills—that Fairburns really should ONLY belong to the People. That's why we have mixed feelings about helping those rock hunters when they come out searching for them. You know what I mean?"

"Yeah, I think so. Like I said, I don't know that much about them. But after hearing this, I'm definitely going to have to learn more." She stopped talking and looked over toward the small cluster of houses and shops on the right as they reached the southwest edge of Hermosa's town limits. "Sandman's coming up in a few more miles, right?"

Twocrow nodded. "And the Railway Café. They're pretty much on top of each other."

A couple miles or so north they dropped down a steep incline and passed a small frozen pond before swinging sharply to the east and then rapidly starting to climb again. After cresting the next hill, Maria could see the entrance to the Railway Café fronting the rail line that suddenly came sweeping in from somewhere out further to the east. Across the tracks stood a small office building and half a dozen rows of large corrugated steel grain bins.

"Where'd that train track go from where we saw it on the south side of Hermosa?" she asked, pointing toward the sweeping curve of the track coming in toward the grain and café complex. "I thought it turned to the east?"

"Well, it does and then kind of wraps around the far east side of Hermosa; almost in a horseshoe shape," Twocrow answered. "Probably not THAT dramatic, but it curves out to where Hermosa used to have its depot and soon curves back around toward where you see it here." He pointed over to their right as they started down the hill. "See over there. Right after it starts coming back in this direction there's a spur line heading almost straight north. That's the line they take when they want to either drop off a bunch of empty cars or pick up others already loaded with grain. That spur runs along the east side of the bins. There's a big loading chute over on that side and they can unhitch the cars alongside it, fill them up over a day or two, and then have them ready to go back the other direction when they're full. They usually haul them on out to Omaha to offload into barges heading down the Missouri River."

Maria craned her neck for a clearer look over the top edge of the temporary license plate, picked the spot where Twocrow was pointing out the spur line, and nodded.

"This time of year they hardly ever move any grain, though, because of the snow and ice," Twocrow said. "They probably hauled a lot of it out of here in early November, and then pretty much shut it down. Usually you see a lot more loads moving again in late February, early March. I'd bet at least half of these big bins are completely full. And that main building," he gestured toward a concrete structure towering over the bins along the east side spur line, "that's probably full-up, too. They'll auger grain into that from the outlying bins, air it out and then load it into the rail cars when the time comes."

He pulled up to a turn-in point that was marked with two signs, one reading “Railway Café” and the other with a large arrow aimed directly at the bins and reading “Sandman Grain & Feed.” Two police cars, one each from Rapid City and Hermosa, sat criss-crossed at the entrance.

Chapter Sixteen

Twocrow rolled down his window. "Howdy," he said, greeting the young Hermosa policeman. The officer was standing alongside his car on the left-hand side "check point" leading toward the shared parking lot for the Sandman complex and the Railway Café. The police had also set up a small sawhorse style barrier so that anyone who needed to get to the café had to make a sharp right turn and check through the Rapid City officer standing on that side.

"Deputy Marshal Al Twocrow. I'm out of Hot Springs." He held out his badge for inspection.

"Hello Marshal," the officer said cordially, eyeing Twocrow's badge and looking in toward his passenger to see if she might have one too. Maria gave the handsome young man a self-conscious smile and automatically straightened her quilted jacket to help eliminate the "bulky" look it was giving to her usually lithe frame. Realizing her reporter's notepad and camera were now visible, she swung her left arm across her body to cover them up while re-adjusting the now wet handkerchief with her other hand.

"Headache?" the young officer asked, pointing at the cloth.

"Got a bad bump and the Marshal wrapped up some snow and ice to keep the swelling down," she replied with another smile. "Thank you for asking."

He blushed, gave her a shy smile in return and then re-focused on Twocrow. "You know about the killing we had here, I suppose?"

Twocrow nodded. "That's why we're here. If it was an Indian boy killed off the Reservation that definitely makes it of interest for the U.S. Marshal's office. You involved in the investigation?"

"Well, sort of, I guess," he answered. "Guess it's kind of up in the air whether it's our jurisdiction or Prairie City's. The elevator and the café are kind of in No Man's Land out here. And Rapid P.D. thinks it might even belong to them, so that's why they have some officers out here, too. Plus they've got a lot more resources, of course, so we're okay with them sending their investigating team over to give us a hand."

"Well, like I said, if it's an Indian it should be part of MY jurisdiction, you know?" Twocrow said firmly. "So I'm going to have to look over the area where the body was found." He pointed toward two more police cars—one with a Rapid City Law Enforcement insignia on the side, and the other with the markings of the Prairie City Police Department. Both cars were pulled up alongside a third car at the far end of the parking lot. "That where they found his body?"

"No, that's just his car. At least we think it's his. All shot up and bloody." He gestured toward the grain bins. "Body was out there among the storage bins. Coroner's office picked the guy up about an hour ago." He pointed at Maria and smiled shyly again in her direction. "Who's that you got with you?"

"I'm Maria Tager," she automatically began to respond. "Hot Springs *St* . . ."

"Tager's out of Hot Springs too," Twocrow interrupted before she could finish. "I'm giving her a closer look at what goes on out in the field on these sorts of things. Too much time working at a desk ain't all that good for a person, if you know what I mean?" He chuckled knowingly and the Hermosa officer gave him a small laugh in response as if he was "in" on what the Marshal meant, even though he had a slightly confused look on his face.

The Marshal glanced at his watch. "Look, if it's okay, we need to get on in there and walk the grounds a bit. I'd still like to get on up to Rapid and see the body too, before it gets too late in the day."

The officer stepped back and gave Twocrow a half-salute. "Sure Marshal. Just stop over by the car first and let them know where you'll be. Don't want any surprises for anyone while they're investigating."

"No problem." Twocrow looked at the officer's name badge. "Thanks Officer Paulsen. You're from Hermosa, huh? Didn't know there was a police station out here. I thought the Custer County Sheriff's Office handled all the police work for the Hermosa area?"

"Well, they're still kind-of in charge. It's just me at the station; I'm the local law here," He puffed up a bit at that and gave Maria another smile as if hoping she might be impressed. "Hired me about six months ago after the town started growing again. We're up to almost a hundred residents now and with all the traffic up and down Highway 79, the town leaders thought it might be a good idea to have someone on board. You know, just in case." He pointed toward the crime scene. "Stuff like this, I guess. Who'd think?"

"Yeah, that's for sure," Twocrow said, half-saluting in return. "Talk to you on the way back out." He rolled up the window and drove into the lot looking over to Maria as they headed toward the parked police cars.

"Thought I should just keep things on the down low with you for now. No sense them getting all stirred up about a reporter being here." He gestured to her face. "How's the head?"

"Better. The ice and snow pack definitely helped."

He nodded and glanced at Maria's notepad, which she had slipped sideways out of her coat pocket. "And I'm going to have to ask you to keep that notepad mostly out of sight while we're on the scene."

"Okay. I understand. And like I told you, I won't write anything that you don't put on the record first."

Twocrow nodded and turned his attention back to the scene in front of them. Now that they were closer, it was apparent that the car under investigation was pretty badly damaged. Maria gave a low whistle. "Lot of holes in that door," she said quietly. "Looks like a lot of blood, too."

They stopped and exited the car. And while the sharp cold air caused Maria to suck in her breath, Twocrow seemed oblivious as he pulled his hat down tighter and started toward the other lawmen, two working inside the vehicle and a third, sporting the insignia of the Prairie City Police Department, standing nearby. He held out his badge as the man eyed it and then tipped his own hat in their direction. "Morning Marshal." He glanced at Maria, seemed a bit puzzled by who she might be, but said nothing further. "Hell of a thing. Kid was shot up pretty bad."

"Yeah. Looks like he left a lot of his blood inside there," Twocrow agreed. "Hard to believe he walked away from this. Where'd you find the body?"

"Well, I didn't," the officer said. "Couple of our other officers found him. One of them was our head man, Al Tollefson." He pointed southeast from where they were standing. "Kid's body was over there between those first two rows of bins. Got it marked off. He was shot up—probably got into a fight over a bottle. I heard there was alcohol involved."

Twocrow followed the outstretched arm with his eyes and pulled up his right hand to further shade against the glare of the bright sun, which hung low in the southern sky.

"We got a little snow about 4 in the morning, so some of the tracks and things were partially covered up, but it's pretty clear to see where he went down. They're still trying to figure out why he went out there, unless whoever shot him was still after him. That's the main mystery, I guess. Like I said, maybe for the whiskey. Empty bottle was laying on the ground beside him." He pointed again. "Anyway, it's right over there."

"Hard to see anything from this angle, especially with that sun." Twocrow looked back at the car. "What's going to happen here?"

"They're about done dusting it and then we've got a tow truck coming to pull it on into the main station in town. I guess it'll go on over to either the Rapid cops or . . ." he stopped and gestured toward Twocrow " . . . or your shop, I suppose?"

"Mmmm," Twocrow half-spoke, half-hummed in response. He waved to Maria to wait where she was. Stepping in closer to the damaged car he looked inside, giving a cursory nod to the other two men, one sitting on the passenger side in front and the other in the back and obviously on site just to process the scene. "You mind?" he asked, signaling that he'd like to pull open the driver's side door.

"Sure, go ahead," the officer in front answered. "Appreciate it if you could keep your gloves on though."

Twocrow gingerly pulled open the door, peered in at the steering wheel and dash, then knelt down to examine the inside of the door. Seeing nothing unusual, he stood. "When you get this all done, can you send a copy of your report over to the Marshal's office? Down in Hot Springs; not up in Rapid." He took off his right-hand glove, pulled out a card and laid it on the dash. The officer grunted an okay, keeping his focus on what he was doing.

"You find any alcohol inside?"

The officer shook his head.

"No. Nothing. Not even a whiff. Why?"

"Just eliminating some things. Thanks." Twocrow stepped away from the car, slipped his glove back on and turned toward the Prairie City officer. "We're going to walk around over there," the Marshal said, nodding at the bins. "Then we'll probably head on into the Coroner's

Office. Thanks again for your help." The officer tipped his hat in response and half-leaned back against his car as Twocrow and Maria walked away.

They had gone only about half-a-dozen steps through the snow when Twocrow stopped suddenly and turned around. Maria was wearing low-heeled leather boots with no protective covering, and the boots' flat bottoms caused her to half-skid to a stop, caught off guard by the Marshal's sudden change in direction.

"Do you know if they took the body into the Pennington County Morgue?" Twocrow called back to the Prairie City cop, taking a couple steps back in his direction.

"Not positive, but I don't think so. Looked like they loaded him up in a hearse from one of those private funeral parlors in downtown Rapid that the Sheriff likes to work with. Guess I'd be surprised if the body's destination was the County Morgue."

"Well, what the hell!" the Marshal exclaimed. "Look, I need you to get on the horn to the Pennington County Sheriff and tell him I need that body moved over to the Morgue for a complete autopsy. First thing! Tell them I'll check in with them soon and that the body can't be touched by any funeral home until the autopsy's complete. You got that?"

The young officer looked frightened by the Marshal's outburst and just nodded respectfully in response.

"All right then. So what are you waiting for? Get on it now!"

The officer turned toward his car, pulled open the door and reached for the mic on his two-way radio as Twocrow spun back toward Maria. He took just one step in her direction before once again stopping and turning back just as the officer pulled the radio mic's cord out of the door to prepare for his call.

"Did you say your head man was one of the officers who found the body," Twocrow asked him, speaking in a much calmer voice as the officer warily eyed the old lawman.

"Yeah, that's right," the young man responded. "It was him and Deputy Hillman. Hillman's kind of our second in command."

"Yeah, I met him earlier today," the Marshal replied. He rubbed his hand up under the front of his hat, pushing the brim back a couple inches, then gestured toward the officer. "Both your top cops working late on a weeknight? That the usual routine for you guys?"

"Well, yeah . . . maybe," the officer hesitated, as if not sure if he should say anything more. "Actually, I don't know for sure. I'm just a member of the team, you know? We only got seven guys on our force. And that's for the airfield, the township and the whole Prairie City community. "So the head honchos have to draw a night shift or two each week, too. Just the way things are out our way."

"Sure. All right. Thanks." Twocrow pointed at the mic in the man's hand. "You go on and get that call in. Get that autopsy going. Sorry I got a little sharp with you, but that's something that can't wait." Twocrow gave a half-wave, pulled his hat brim back in place and walked away, catching up with Maria. He started to walk past her, seemed to think of something more and stopped again. Turning back around, he took a couple steps back, once again causing his young companion to slide awkwardly to one side to avoid him.

"What about Delaney?" he shouted over to the officer, who was now seated halfway into the car while holding the mic in both hands.

Startled by Twocrow's sudden yell back at him, the officer slid back out of the car, stood up behind the open passenger side door and leaned across the top to respond. "What? Who?" He asked.

"Delaney? Big, heavyset guy. Patch of bright white hair on the side of his head. He was with Hillman when they came down to Hot Springs earlier today."

"Oh, Pete!" The cop kind of nodded as if verifying with himself that he had the right name. "Well, he's not really part of our police force. He just works in and around the town. He's kind of a 'general duties' guy, I think." He smiled. "Hangs out with Batch . . . Deputy Hillman, I mean . . . a lot of the time. I think they're good friends from back in their Army days. Heard them talking about that a couple times." He paused. "Why you asking about him?"

"Well, I thought HE was the one who found the body."

The officer looked puzzled. "Um, well . . . again maybe. I mean, sure, I guess he might've been the one. I heard he was out here, too, but he wasn't there when the Chief briefed us, so I assumed it was just the Chief and Batch who . . ." He hesitated as if unsure what to say next, then added, "you know, were the ones who found the body."

Twocrow contemplated the man's response. "All right, thanks. I probably just heard that wrong." He tipped his hat in the officer's direction. "Okay, I'll let you finish up with that call into the Sheriff's office." He turned yet again and resumed walking, this time striding quickly past Maria before the reporter had time to react.

"Something seem wrong to you about that?" Maria asked, hurrying back alongside the Marshal and puffing in the still cold late-morning air. "I thought it was pretty clear that Delaney said he was the one who found the body. You heard that, too, didn't you? He seemed like the kind of guy who'd want to get credit, especially in front of a bunch of city cops who probably don't hold him in the highest esteem."

"Well, what does your 'investigative sense' tell you?" Twocrow asked. "I mean as a reporter and all?"

"Unusual," Maria answered half under her breath. "Seems like they would've told the others that Delaney had been here first and called it in." She rubbed a gloved hand across her chin, her breath visible in the cold air despite the bright sunshine. "That and the fact that both of their top two guys came out here to respond. That seems even more unusual. At least it does to me."

Twocrow didn't say anything, as if waiting for her to continue the thought. "And . . ." the young reporter said, picking up on the cue, ". . . wouldn't it be even more unusual for both of the head guys to be on duty on the late night shift—I mean, at the same time and everything? Besides shouldn't one of them be staying at the office? You know, in case something else came up?"

"Mmmmm," Twocrow nodded his agreement.

They crossed over the railroad tracks and went down the embankment past the first row of bins over to the second row where some red flags were stuck haphazardly into the frozen ground. They circled south to a point where several more flags were leaned up against a couple of the bins in the second row. Footprints surrounded an indentation in the center of the flags and a large patch of dried blood marked the center spot of that indentation. A set of tire tracks that had started over at the entry road that ran from the parking lot up to the Sandman Office Building were clearly imprinted in the new snow. The tracks came to a stop just outside the flagged-off location.

"Probably the funeral home's transport hearse," Twocrow said, pointing at the tracks. "Gonna be hard to pick out anything in particular here. Looks like half the cops from both Pennington and Custer Counties have already traipsed through the place." He moved up near the bloody splotch on the ground and knelt down beside it.

Maria walked around to the north side of the flags and stood staring in the direction where the tire tracks had come and gone. She took the small Leica camera out of her left side coat pocket and held it up. "Okay if I snap a crime scene shot or two from this angle, and then maybe one just over your shoulder?" Twocrow shrugged in response and continued examining the ground while she moved about taking the photos.

The reporter moved back away from the marked perimeter, walked between the two bins across from it in the first row and took a couple more shots from that spot. Turning to look over toward the railroad tracks, she also snapped a photo of that scene too.

Walking back between the two rows of bins toward the tire tracks, she reached a spot where a faint set of footprints, spaced out as if the maker might be on the run, veered off sharply in the direction of the Railway Café. The prints were just barely visible because of the light early morning snowfall. She followed them to a point where a second set of prints with deeper indentations came from out alongside the bins and joined with the first set. Then both sets went on together beyond the first row of bins and leading in the direction of the railroad tracks.

"Hey, Marshal!" At the sound of Maria's voice, Twocrow looked up from where he was still examining the other scene, a look of irritation on his face at being interrupted. "When you get a minute you might want to come and take a look at these footprints."

Chapter Seventeen

Maria snapped two more quick pictures in the direction the prints were pointing and slipped the camera back into her pocket. Walking carefully alongside both sets of prints, she paused when she reached a spot where two other footprints, a bit sharper in their appearance, appeared side by side. Their deeper indentations seemed to indicate that whoever made them had stopped and stood here for a time before moving on.

She moved widely to her right to avoid stepping onto either set of prints and stood waiting for Twocrow to join her.

"Looks like a couple of people came this way just before it snowed!" Maria said loudly. She gestured toward the footprints. "First person might've been running because those footprints are kind of far apart. And then someone else came after that first person and maybe stopped right here before moving on."

As Twocrow came toward her from the flagged-off area, she studied the scene, pulled out her camera again and snapped another shot of the footprints from this new vantage point. At the sound of his feet crunching in the snow, she turned and snapped a photo of the Marshal as Twocrow walked toward her.

"What are you doing? And what's so important to get me away from my investigation of the body's location?"

"Well, I was just thinking a photo of you walking away from the crime scene might be a good illustration, that's all," Maria replied, quickly putting the camera back into her coat pocket before the Marshal might respond by taking it away from her. "Don't worry, I'll run that shot past you if we decide to use it, just to be sure it's okay."

"You be sure you do that," Twocrow said gruffly. "This what you wanted me to see?" He eyed the pair of footprints next to the young woman and knelt down to the right side of them. He exhaled sharply, reached out and plucked something from the snow.

"What's that?" she asked.

"Shell casing." Twocrow gingerly held it up and the sunlight glinted off it. He moved the casing's open end closer to his nose. "Recently fired, so it might've been from last night. Maybe from whoever was standing here. Remind me to ask the Coroner what kind of bullets he's been digging out of the victim's body."

She took the notepad out and jotted down his request.

He looked up in the direction of the café and back again at the crime scene, carefully balancing the spent casing on the edge of his fingers in the process. "Kind of strange," he added as he turned it over in his hand and stared at it more closely.

"What?" Maria asked.

"Last time I saw a shell casing like this was over at the firing range. One of our guys who'd gone off to Europe during the war came back with a PPK he found on the battlefield."

He paused at the look of bewilderment on Maria's face. "I'm pretty sure this bullet casing came from a German military handgun called a Walther P-38. It's usually called a PPK for short. Hell of a gun, but not very common around the U.S. I always thought it would be nice to have one if I ever got the chance. I think a lot of our military cops took them off the Nazis and then kept them for themselves."

He gingerly turned the shell casing over again, moved his free hand to his coat pocket and extracted a handkerchief. "I'm thinking this might've come from a gun like that. But I'm not sure, so I'll have to check into it." He dropped the casing into the folds of the handkerchief and slipped it back into his pocket.

"What kind of gun do you use?" she asked, nodding toward Two-crow's sidearm.

"Smith and Wesson 10," the Marshall responded, unholstering his weapon and turning it on its side to show the reporter. "It's also a .38 but a little heavier, especially for the caliber. Still, it's a great gun. Bullock liked them. So he issued them to all his deputies way back when. I just never got away from it, I guess. First gun I ever took to a firing range."

"Sort of like a first date, huh," she chuckled, quickly swallowing her response and returning to a more stoic look as he appeared slightly irritated at her little joke.

He turned the gun over again and ran a finger along the barrel. Making sure the chamber was empty and the safety was set, he grasped it by the front end of the barrel and held the stock out in the young reporter's direction. "Here, what do you think? Has a real nice weight." He thrust it toward Maria. She flinched but took it and awkwardly held it out in front of her before handing it back. "Heavy," she said.

"Six shot revolver." Twocrow turned it on its side. "It's heavy but I like the weight. Lot of police like a lighter weight .357 magnum, but I'm not sure if it'd be right for an old dog like me." He tapped the top of his gun. "Still, I think I want to get a new one; something with adjustable sights. The sights on this one are fixed. About the only thing I don't like about it."

She nodded as if she understood but the puzzled look on her face finally drew a chuckle out of Twocrow. "Probably not something your average newspaper reporter would be thinking about, I suppose? Especially if she grew up in New York City."

"Oh, I didn't grow up in New York City," she objected. "I just studied there. My home was in Connecticut. That's where Grandma Laura settled after she moved away from here and went out East to make her mark as a reporter. But, I'm sure you already know a lot about that—at least from what Aunt Minnie told me." She stopped as he grimaced at her remark. "Which wasn't really all that much, by the way. And that's why I want to get the whole story from you! You OWE me."

He made a noncommittal throat clearing sound in response and gestured with the weapon in the direction of the faint path that both sets of footprints took away from them. "You're right about having me take a look at these prints though. Thanks." He pointed. "It does look like the first set are from someone running and they continue heading directly away and on up toward the café. So, based on what Frank told me earlier, I'm going to venture a guess that that particular set is his; probably the fainter ones filled with more snow."

He slipped the gun back into his holster and took a few more steps toward the rail line. Kneeling down again, he pointed at the deeper footprints. "I think the second set has to be from whoever it was that was shooting at Frank. Someone who was bigger and heavier; followed him and shot at him as he was running away. This spot with the prints together is probably where he stood when he was shooting. You got any theories?"

"Me?" Maria was startled at his request, but walked up and knelt beside him, wanting to keep involved. "Well, I suppose the second set of prints could've come from one of those Prairie City police officers who found the body," she said. "I mean they might've been looking around at all the footprints, too. Doesn't mean they were the ones who shot at Frank, though. Does it?"

"Possible," Twocrow agreed. He looked back toward the crime scene. "Based on the direction of both sets of prints, they didn't come from the victim, that's for damn sure." He stood up and moved slowly along beside the second, deeper indentations. "There's a couple more up here that are even clearer than those you found."

He reached down to his holster and made sure it was snapped shut across the top of his pistol, then signaled for Maria to follow him. Twocrow walked up to where the footprints reached the edge of the tracks before continuing between the rails and on toward the Railway Café.

"Well whoever made these—both sets—was headed directly toward the front of the café," the reporter said. She walked up beside him and pointed at footprints between the rails and continuing on the other side. "They're clearly headed over toward the Railway Café's front entrance." She pointed at the prints between the rails. "But only one set of prints is between the rails, the deeper ones from the follower. Do you think the first person who was running might've jumped across?"

Not waiting for his response, she motioned in the direction of Darveaux's shot-up car. "You think those cops over there already talked to the folks working up in the café?"

"Ummm-hmmm, you would think so," Twocrow responded, returning once more to his half-humming, half-snorting manner. He stepped up between the rails, the highest point between the café and the grain bins, and stood looking back toward where the body had laid. Glancing quickly over to where the officers were still going over Darveaux's car, he slowly swept his gaze back toward the café.

"Come on, let's just make a little stop in there before we go on up to Rapid City. Even if those cops did talk to the folks inside, it won't hurt to ask one more time. Plus it'll give me a chance to call Hot Springs and check in with my office."

"And give me the chance to go pee," Maria moved her feet anxiously and pulled her legs together as she said it. "I was just going to ask you if we could go in for that purpose if nothing else." She gave him a shy smile. "It's either going to be that or I'm going to have to run back out there among those grain bins." She chuckled as he scrunched up his face at her suggestion. “Sorry, but when a girl’s gotta go, well, a girl’s gotta do what a girl’s gotta do. I’ve got a really weak bladder.”

“You’re definitely related to Minnie and Laura,” he answered, waving her forward as he stepped down across the tracks before reaching back to help her avoid slipping as she came across. “You know, just now, when you were talking, I could hear both Laura’s and Minnie’s voices clear as a bell—and see them standing there too.”

“Oh yeah?” She smiled. “Marshal, you REALLY need to tell me more about those ‘younger’ days that you all shared together.”

This time his humming was more of a pronounced snort as he strode on toward the café door, a lopsided grin on his face that was turned away from Maria’s view.

Chapter Eighteen

A small bell rang merrily above the café entrance as they pushed open the door and walked inside. A middle-aged man putting clean coffee cups onto a shelf behind the counter gave them a curt wave and pointed toward an array of tables and booths alongside a wall covered with large-paned windows. "Sit anywhere you want. No one coming in anyway. Not with all THAT going on." He frowned and waved in the general direction of where the police were working on Darveaux's car. The window second over from the door was partially boarded over.

"Um, I really need to find a bathroom!" The urgency in Maria's voice made the man quickly turn his arm to direct her toward a door at the far end of the room.

As she hurried away, he picked up the coffee pot behind him and pointed at it with his free hand. "Coffee?"

"Sure," Twocrow answered. He nodded in the direction where Maria had disappeared behind the door. "Don't know about my young friend there. You'll have to check with her when she returns."

"Thought she might be your daughter?" He looked at him more closely. "Or Granddaughter?"

"Granddaughter of a good friend," Twocrow answered, ignoring the dig. "She's pretty new to our neck of the woods, so I'm just taking her along on some of my road trips." The door to the bathroom banged open and Maria emerged with her coat over one arm. Embarrassed by the violent reaction of the door, she gave them a pained look, reached out and snagged the door handle and gently re-shut it before walking back in their direction.

"Sorry, but I was getting a little desperate for that potty break," she said as she approached them. "And I didn't mean to bang open the door so hard. Hopefully nothing's broken. My apologies." The counterman just gave her a 'no problem' shrug and held up the coffee pot with a question mark on his face.

Maria looked up at a colorful poster behind him that depicted two high school-aged teens holding bottles of 7-Up beneath the headline "Fresh Up With 7-Up."

"Might go for one of those instead," she said, pointing toward the poster. "Or maybe a Coke?"

The man nodded. "Sure, got 'em both. Choose your poison."

Maria eyed the poster again. "Okay. I'll take the 7-Up," she answered as Twocrow sank down into the nearest booth and slid in, carefully placing his hat down on the bench beside him. Maria took the other side, shoving her coat in ahead of her and undoing a scarf that she still had wrapped around her neck.

The window beside them provided an unblocked view out toward the grain bins and also a clear view of the narrow roadway that led out toward the Sandman Elevator Company's small office building. The raised rail line running parallel to the café filled part of the space in between them and the bins, but there still was a direct line of sight out in the direction to where Darveaux's body had been found.

Twocrow zipped open his own jacket and pulled it back, letting the warmth of the café's heated air wash over him. He shrugged out of the coat, displaying both his badge and sidearm just as the proprietor walked up with a coffee pot and oversize cup in one hand and a green soft drink bottle and a root beer-style mug in the other.

The man gave a low whistle. "U.S. Marshal, huh? Guess this killing's a bigger deal than I thought."

"Maybe," Twocrow responded in a noncommittal voice. "Every killing's a big deal as far as I'm concerned."

He looked back over the counterman's shoulder. "Hey, you got a phone I can use to make a call into the Pennington Sheriff's office? Might take a few minutes if you don't mind?" The man jerked his head back toward a phone mounted on the wall alongside a pair of swinging café style doors that led into the food preparation area. He put the mug and bottle of 7-Up down in front of Maria and started to pour Twocrow's coffee.

"Right over there by the kitchen. Help yourself." He dropped a menu at Twocrow's spot and handed another one to Maria.

"Might be some charges on your line," Twocrow said as he edged out of the booth and walked over to the phone. "I'll leave you a card and you can let us know if there are. My office will pick up the tab." The man gave a little wave and nodded his okay. As Twocrow lifted the phone's receiver and made his call, the man started pointing out menu items to Maria. They both stopped talking as the Marshal raised his voice to make a point.

"Listen," he said. "I need a COMPLETE autopsy on that body, including a tox screen on the blood and an 'official' cause of death. I don't care if it's obvious the kid was shot. I want it from the Coroner, so you retrieve the body and get it the hell over there sooner rather than later! This one's my jurisdiction and I need some answers!"

He paused as he listened and turned his back to the proprietor and Maria as he added. "And then have either the doctor or someone from his office call me with those results later today or first thing tomorrow at the latest, no matter the time. Pretty sure they've got my numbers."

He nodded as if reassuring himself that the urgency of his message had been "received," and hung up. He pointed at the phone again. "Okay for one more call?"

"No problem. Make as many as you need."

Twocrow put the Pennington Sheriff's card away and extracted another before taking the phone receiver off the hook and giving Maria a small smile as he prepared to dial. He pointed toward the boarded-up window. "So what's going on there with your window?"

"Damn Indian ..." the Café owner paused as he gave Twocrow a wary look. "Sorry." Then he shrugged. "Well, no I'm not sorry. It was that damned Indian kid . . . the one they're looking for, not the dead one, of course. My night man told me he rocked it last night before he took off. It was while he was running away from them cops that showed up."

"Rocked it?"

"Yeah, my man said a rock just suddenly hit the window and shattered it. And when he went outside to see who had done it, that kid yelled something at him before he ran over to his car and drove away. Wasn't until the kid was already gone that he learned the cops had found a dead body out by the bins. Otherwise he might've tried to stop him from leaving. You'd think if the kid killed that other kid he wouldn't go throwing rocks at our windows before he left." He gave them a questioning look. "I mean, you wouldn't would you?"

"Yeah, that's what you'd think all right," Twocrow agreed. The dial tone that had been coming from the phone receiver was replaced by a beeping sound, indicating the receiver had been off the hook too long before any numbers had been dialed.

He once again started to dial but stopped and re-cradled the receiver. Taking the photo of Gene and Elizabeth out of his pocket he turned toward the proprietor and held it up. "You ever see either one of these two before?"

The man walked over and took the photo from him, scrutinized it closely and handed it back with a shake of his head. "Not that I can remember. Should I have?"

"Not necessarily, but thought I'd ask, just in case."

"I could check with my night man. But he won't be here for a few more hours. If you want to leave the picture and phone number, I can let you know what he says."

"Not now. Do you know if your night guy gave those Prairie City cops a description of the kid that ran off?"

"Yeah, said he did." The man held out his hand for the photo one more time, took it and examined it even more closely. "Pretty girl. Those two kind of look alike." He gave them a wry smile. "And I DON'T mean just because they're both Indians. Are they related somehow?" Twocrow nodded. "You think the boy might be the one who broke my window?"

"No, most definitely not," the Marshal said as he returned the photo to his pocket and gave Maria a knowing look. "He's just someone else I'm checking into." Twocrow contemplated returning to the phone, decided to wait on his call and walked over to the window instead. "Looks like you got all the glass picked up. You still got that rock?"

"Naw, my guy must've cleaned it up when he swept up the glass. Just pisses me off that somebody'd do something like that. Especially when I go out of my way to serve Indians here in the first place." He stood looking indignantly at Twocrow as if daring him to say something contradictory.

Instead Twocrow turned away from the window, moved over to the unbroken one next to the door and looked out, trying to picture a line that would lead out from the boarded window alongside it.

"Maria, you mind coming over here and telling me what you see?" He signaled to the reporter who took a quick swig from the 7-Up bottle before sliding out of the booth to join him. Maria walked over to Twocrow's side and stared out of the wide glass pane the Marshal was touching with his fingertips.

"I don't know? There's the bins, the railroad tracks, the…" she paused as if a light bulb was coming on. "And past the tracks. Those are OUR footprints. Right?" She turned excitedly toward Twocrow. "It's pretty much on a direct line, isn't it?"

The Marshal nodded, turned back toward where the proprietor was standing, and pointed at the wall behind him. The café owner looked over his shoulder and back at the Marshal. "What?" he asked. "Why you pointing back there?"

"Did you notice anything up on your wall?"

The café owner looked at the wall and shrugged. "Well, sure, there's a little grease and dirt, I guess, but nothin' too serious." He gave them another wry smile. "Nothin' that'd get the place shut down, though. That's for sure."

"You mind if we take a quick look?"

"At the wall?"

Twocrow nodded.

"Okay, what the hell? Knock yourself out." He stepped away and took a seat on one of the revolving stools as the other two walked around behind the counter to replace him. The Marshal leaned back into the counter, held up his hand and slowly extended it on line toward the boarded up window.

"That look like the right line to you?"

Maria nodded and drew an imaginary line in the air swinging her arm up from Twocrow's hand and touching the wall. Twocrow walked back around to the front of the counter and moved over to the window. He stretched out his arm to where it followed the same imaginary line of Maria's outstretched hand. "There," he pointed above and behind the young woman's fingertips. "You see that?"

The reporter leaned back for a better angle and looked up as Twocrow came back to the front side of the counter directly across from her.

He pointed toward a small hole in the wall about three or four feet above Maria's head, splinters of wood radiating away from it. "You got a ladder or step stool we can use?" Twocrow asked the owner as the man stood up from his seat and walked over to see what they were looking at. The man nodded toward his kitchen.

"Sure. In there. I'll go get it." He walked away while Twocrow pulled out a large jackknife, flipped open the blade and stepped back around behind the counter. The owner came back through the swinging kitchen doors dragging a small stepladder and Maria traipsed over to meet him as Twocrow nodded his thanks.

Maria took the ladder out of his hands and pulled it open, propping it against the wall next to the Marshal, who immediately climbed up until he was even with the hole. Shaking slightly, he dug the knife blade into the wood alongside the hole and pried. Within seconds, a metal object popped out and rattled onto the floor and Maria nearly pounced on it as she hurried to retrieve it. She regained her feet and held it up toward Twocrow. The owner sidled in for a closer look as the Marshall stepped back down.

"Is this what I think it is?" Maria asked.

"Yep," Twocrow answered, taking it from his young companion's hand. "That's the working end of a bullet." He looked at the proprietor. "And that's probably what came through your window. Not a rock. A bullet."

He walked over to the booth, picked up his coat and rummaged around in the pocket. Pulling out his handkerchief containing the shell casing that they had found outside in the snow, he unwrapped it, laid the spent bullet alongside and moved both of them over into a brighter light.

"And I'm willing to bet that these two together are going to make up a cartridge that was fired from a Walther P-38 pistol."

Chapter Nineteen

Hillman sat back in his chair and eyed the remains of his lunch with a satisfied sigh. "Don't know if we'll get any information here, but that's a hell of a meal." Delaney's response came in the form a soft belch and he looked around to see if anyone had noticed. The other tables and booths were all filled now and everyone seemed more intent on eating the good food than paying attention to any out-of-towners in their midst.

Their middle-aged waitress walked over with a pot of coffee in one hand and a check in the other and the lawman gave her a dazzling smile and pointed at her wavy hair. "I like your hairstyle," he said. "You're right in with the latest, aren't you?"

Her face turning red, she tried to mask her pleasure at his observance, and then gave him a flirty smile in return as she refilled their cups. "Anything more I can get you boys?" she asked, tentatively holding their check out but not putting it down before getting a response.

"Nope." Hillman took the check and leaned back, rubbing his hand across his belly. "Glad I don't live around here or I'd be gaining twenty pounds in nothing flat. Great service, great food and a pretty waitress." He grinned at her again, his movie star good looks even more enhanced by the action. She gave him yet another flirty smile in return.

"Glad you liked it Hon," she said. "I see you're here out of Prairie City," she added, lightly touching the police department patch on Batch's left shoulder and then letting her hand slide down his arm before straightening back up. "What brings you boys all the way down to Hot Springs on such a cold day?"

"Just out gathering some information on a shooting we had up our direction," Delaney interjected, trying to get some of the waitress's attention for himself after watching the exchange between her and his companion.

"A shooting! Oh my!" She gave a slight gasp and took half step backward. "And it had something to do with someone from here in Hot Springs?"

"Maybe," Hillman said, glaring at Delaney. "We're still looking into that. For now, we're just trying to track down a young man who might've been in the area where they found the body of the person who got shot. Just looking to see if he might be able to provide us with some help. He might not even know what he witnessed, so that's why we'd like to try and track him down." He pulled out his notebook and opened up the pages as if checking on a name.

Looking down at a blank page in front of him, he flipped the book shut, turned his face upward and gave her yet another of his winning smiles. "You wouldn't happen to know a young man by the name of Frank Silver Shore, would you?"

*****

"Shit!" Delaney grumbled as they crossed the street to where they'd parked their car. "I *thought* that kid looked familiar."

"And you didn't see which direction he was headed when he walked away from you?" Hillman held his hands wide as he spoke, waving them in all directions as if trying to draw something out of his partner's subconscious memory.

"Well, it was definitely that way," Delaney answered, pointing away from them and down River Street to the southeast. "I handed him his glove. He said 'thanks.' I asked him if we'd met somewhere. He said 'no.' And then he turned and walked away."

He pointed again. "In that direction. And it's down there, somewhere by the waterfall, that the waitress said Darveaux and his sister were living. So, I'm thinking that's where that Silver Shore kid was headed. But after we talked and I went back inside, I honestly didn't see where he might've gone. He could've gone straight down the street, or could'a turned up one of those side streets. I'm tellin' you that's all I remember." He reached the car, jerked open his door, then slammed it shut again, gave Hillman a helpless look in return, and emphatically added a second "Shit!"

Hillman grasped the hard-plastic bill of his mostly leather hat and slapped it down alongside his leg in frustration. Rubbing his other hand across his face, he blew out an exasperated sigh, then re-settled the military style hat back on his head and pulled the bill down just over the tops of his eyebrows.

"Well, you said he had a bag full of food just like that waitress said, so he had to be taking it somewhere to share with somebody else. And my guess is that's Darveaux's sister. That post office guy said the Darveauxs have a place down around this part of town, and the waitress just agreed. So we gotta try to figure out exactly where. Somebody around here has to know them and where that is."

He drummed his fingers on top of the patrol car, and then pointed across the river toward a large parking lot. The mostly empty lot was fronting a big stone church where a woman was sweeping off the entrance steps. "Do you suppose the good folks at that church might have an idea who their neighbors are … and where they all might live?"

*****

Frank pulled his car up alongside the curb in front of Elizabeth's apartment building and hurried inside to help her down the stairs. Earlier, Marshal Twocrow had told the V.A. doctor they'd be there by 1 p.m. but then the doctor's nurse had called them back to ask if they could come by 12:45 instead. That was just 15 minutes from now, but fortunately they were not that far away from the medical center so he told her he was sure they could make it.

He took the stairs two at a time, doubled back to his left and rapped on her door. "Liz, it's me. You ready?" The door opened in response and she stepped out, dressed in a heavy wool coat and a scarf pulled across the top of her head. "Car's right out front, so you won't have far to walk," he said, offering his arm to help steady her as they made their way back toward the stairs. The doorway across the hall creaked open and an older woman looked out toward them. Frank gave her a little nod and she quickly pulled her head back and shut the door.

"Don't worry, that's just Gertie," Elizabeth said. "She's ALWAYS interested in what Gene and I might be doing." She rolled her eyes, then added, "But don't get me wrong. I like her. At least she cares."

"Wait here and I'll get the car door open," he said as they reached the bottom of the staircase and moved toward the narrow passageway leading out to the street. She leaned up against the wall for support as he stepped outside and hurried across the sidewalk to his vehicle. He cleared off the passenger side seat and propped the door open. Starting to stand back up alongside the car, he suddenly stopped and leaned back down inside the passenger door instead as a police car marked with the words Prairie City Police Department cruised slowly past. He ducked down even lower as he saw the driver gesture in his direction and then make a sweeping movement with his arm as if outlining an area or group of buildings to his companion.

"Oh no, damn it," Frank muttered. He glanced back toward Liz's building and saw that she was starting to push open the door. "Liz!" He half-called and half-hissed her name and she stopped partway out. He pushed his hands in her direction as if trying to signal that he wanted her to go back inside. She gave him a quizzical look before finally seeming to understand. She stepped back and let the outside door go shut again.

Frank eased himself up between the partly open door and the roof of the car and looked down the street. The police car had reached an intersection and was turning right across an old iron bridge that led into the parking lot of the beautiful new stone church known simply as United Churches—housing the congregations of the Baptists, Presbyterians and Methodists who had chosen to all worship there together. He waited until the car swung into their gravel parking lot, slowly drove up and stopped by the Parish House next door to the church entrance where a woman was wielding a broom.

A police officer exited the car and walked up to her. After a couple of minutes they moved together to the door and she rang the bell while talking further to him. The door opened and a man in clerical garb smiled out at them, listened for a few seconds and then extended his hand and invited the officer inside.

Frank jumped to his feet and hurried back to the entry door.

"Come on!" he urged, almost pulling Elizabeth through the doorway while looking back over his shoulder toward the police car. Already the pastor and the officer had re-emerged from the doorway and the officer was pointing past the patrol car and making a sweeping motion with his hand toward the buildings over on their side of the river.

Frank urged Elizabeth to crouch down and pointed past his car in the direction of the church. "Those cops I told you about are right over there in the church parking lot, talking to the Pastor," he explained. "We should get moving before they come back in this direction."

She coughed hard in response and ducked lower as she made her way on his arm over to the open car door and slid down inside. Frank shut the door behind her before crab walking in between his car and one parked behind him. He eased ahead, pulled the driver's side door open and jumped in behind the wheel. He glanced back at the police car. The

Pastor was gone and the car was still sitting there running as if its occupants were planning their next move.

"You sure that's them?" Elizabeth asked, looking miserable as she scrunched down on the passenger side seat.

"Positive. They must be trying to figure out where you and Gene live and thought they'd check in at the church. Do you think the Pastor over there knows that you live over here?"

"I don't know? Maybe. We've been in our apartment for over a year, so I'm sure a lot of the neighbors know about us by now. I mean, we're those Indians! The outsiders. Lots of folks are probably concerned about us being here. I'm sure they can find out from anyone in the building which apartment is ours as soon as they walk in. What do you think we should do?"

He sat very still for several seconds and then turned toward her. "I need to go over to the Marshal's office and see if we can get ahold of him and let him know what's going on. But first I'll take you up to the doctor's office and leave you there. Then I can head over to the Courthouse and have someone there get him a message, or maybe even try to give him a call. That sound okay to you? I don't think I can come into the doctor's office with you anyway."

She half murmured her response, already sounding exhausted just from the short walk out to the car. "Yes. Sounds good. I'd go with you to the Marshal's but the way I'm feeling I probably should get on in to see that doctor first. Sorry, but I really am feeling terrible."

He nodded a vigorous approval, started the engine and checked his rear view mirror before pulling into traffic. He gasped, and then clamped his jaws shut and pulled out onto the street. Behind him and only about a block and a half away he could see that the Prairie City police car had now re-crossed the bridge and was signaling to turn back up the street in their direction.

Chapter Twenty

"What time is it?" Twocrow increased his car's speed as he spoke.

"Almost 1:30." Maria answered after glancing at her watch. "You sure you want to go all the way back to Hot Springs before going into Rapid. We weren't that far away, you know?"

"Yeah, I'm sure. Sorry you're not going to see what happens with the body, but I want to give the Coroner time to get the autopsy done anyway. Plus, I'm worried about Elizabeth and Frank. I don't know why I have this feeling, but I just got a really bad vibe about those Prairie City cops. Like they could be a real danger to the kids. Call it Cop Sixth Sense, I guess."

"Cop Sixth … There's no such thing." Maria was firmly grasping the passenger side armrest with her right hand, her knuckles slightly white from the pressure. She stretched her neck in his direction trying to see the speedometer. "You sure you know the proper way to drive this thing? How fast are we going, anyway?"

Twocrow glanced down at the gauge and made his dismissive half grunting, half humming noise. "About One-ten." He barely turned his head in her direction as he answered.

"A hundred and ten! Miles per hour!"

"Yes." He shrugged. "Look, I just took a special training course for these new cars. Learned every little thing about how to handle them." He stopped talking as the car reached a small bridge and went slightly airborne as they crossed it. As the vehicle settled back onto the highway, he pushed the accelerator even higher, causing Maria to gasp both in surprise and pain. Her head was still sore from their earlier mishap and while the bump had diminished a headache had replaced it.

"And that included driving it at super high speed?" she blanched, her stomach churning as she asked the question. "It almost feels like we're flying instead of driving."

"It was a very comprehensive course. And yes, don't worry, we had special training and testing on how to drive at high speeds, just in case we got caught up in a car chase, or had to respond as fast as possible to an emergency situation. Things like that. We drove on a practice course, but it was very realistic. A lot like this road as a matter of fact." They came to a second small bridge and repeated what had happened at the first, the car roaring as it elevated, thumped down and re-accelerated. "More or less," he added softly.

"Did you pass?"

He cocked his head slightly her way, his facial muscles tightening as he glared and once more made his non-committal half-hum, half-snorting noise he'd used with her earlier.

"We'll be fine as long as we don't meet up with another group of deer trying to cross the road. Then you might hope we really can fly instead of just going fast."

"Yeah, thanks. I'll keep that in mind." She looked uneasily out toward her right, seeing if she could spot any sort of animal movement. The grassy upslopes leading from the prairie west toward the foothills—a prelude to the actual Black Hills that lay behind them—seemed devoid of wildlife but she was still nervous. "You know when I was saying earlier I thought it would be cool to ride in your really fast car? I didn't actually think we'd be driving '*really* fast.' That was just a figure of speech on my part."

He smiled to himself, replaced it with a grimmer expression and glanced in her direction. "When we get back to town I'm going to need your help."

The off-hand statement caught her by surprise and Maria half-turned toward him in anticipation, releasing her grip and taking out her notepad once again. It really was the last thing she had been expecting him to say.

"Okay. Sure. I'd be glad to. But how?"

"Just to be safe, I want to get Elizabeth Darveaux and Frank Silver Shore out of the Darveaux apartment and put them somewhere a little more secure—and obscure as far as that goes. It would just be for a couple days until I have a better understanding about this Prairie City cop and his buddy. And, once I know Elizabeth and Frank are safe, I'll feel a lot more comfortable heading back up to the Pennington Coroner's office for a look at Gene's body. That's something I really need to do yet tonight or first thing in the morning latest. You okay with helping me out on that?"

"You mean, getting his sister and their friend into a 'Safe House'?" She laid the pad back down on her lap and slid the yellow graphite pencil back inside her coat pocket. "Are you're thinking they could stay at my house?"

He eased back on the accelerator as they approached the Maverick Junction intersection and turned on the car's flashing red light. As the Marshal's car wheels squealed in protest at the sudden right turn, a car approaching the Fall River Canyon turnoff from the south pulled over to clear the way. Twocrow completed the Fairlane's turn around the corner and headed down into the canyon toward Hot Springs. Now on the two-lane Fall River Road—also known as U.S. 385—he had backed off to only 65 miles per hour in the winding 45 mph zone. Twocrow kept his overhead red light flashing and it filled the interior of the car with a whirring, clicking sound.

Maria resumed her grip on the armrest, indicating she was not all that reassured that her 79-year-old driver had actually passed that driver's training he'd been bragging about.

"I guess I AM thinking your place," he said, picking up the conversation where they'd left off a mile or so before. "I doubt those two from Prairie City, if they're on the wrong side of things, would even think that you'd be involved. So it should be safe for all of you there."

She sat quietly, thinking about his request and after a few seconds he added, "Listen, you don't have to do it. It's just a re . . ."

"No, no I'll do it," she interrupted. "No worries." She pulled herself up straighter in her seat as they reached the Hot Springs city limits and proceeded down South River Street, the city's name for the south end of the highway as it snaked its way through town. The street name switched to South 6th, then changed again into Chicago Street before hitting the T-shaped crossing at Jennings Avenue. Twocrow did a quick check of traffic to his right, then turned left down the hill for a block to where the road once again became River Street, this time North River Street running parallel to the warm, steamy Fall River.

He drove about a block and a half and pulled up to parallel park alongside one of the stone buildings almost directly across the street from the waterfall. He turned off the engine and glanced at his watch. "One-forty-five. They're probably still up at the VA seeing Doc Flaten, but I'd like to be here when they come back so they can pack up and go right over to your place. If you want me to drop you over at the newspaper office, we can come back and pick you up there after they return?"

"Hey it's not a problem. I can wait with you. Why are they at the doctor's? You never said anything about that, did you?"

"Elizabeth is sick," Twocrow said. "I thought I told you."

Maria started to shake her head no and paused. "Well, you said she wasn't feeling so good, but I don't remember anything about them going to see a doctor. At least not that I recall." She shrugged. "No big deal, just clarifying? What's wrong with her anyway?"

"Well, that's what she's seeing the doctor about, to try to figure that out. Personally, I think she might have pneumonia. Or, at the very least, she's on the verge of it. I don't think it's anything you'd have to worry about catching if you've got any concerns about that." He opened the door as he spoke and started to slide out.

"Oh, no, that's okay," she said as she pushed open her own door and popped up and out onto the sidewalk. "I'm just surprised that's all." She started toward the front end of the car and the Marshal joined her while pointing toward one of the doorways. "It's that one," he said. "They live up on the second floor."

She studied the chiseled stone sided building, just one of the numerous pink sandstone structures that faced out onto River Street and made up one of the signature trademarks of this Southern Hills community. Washed by the mid-afternoon sun the stones almost seemed to glint a golden brown instead of their normal pinkish to red cast.

"Looks like they live in a pretty nice place," she said as they approached the doorway. "Compared to my place, I mean. I'm in an old fake log cabin up on College Hill. Kind of a dump, but it's cheap."

"Well this place is nice on the outside, but not so much on the inside. Pretty run-down and drafty, actually," he answered. He reached out and pulled open the outside door and they walked into a dingy passageway that opened further into a dark, slightly musty smelling wooden hall. A rather rickety wooden staircase, it's steps worn down to significant grooves in their centers from years and years of use, occupied the middle of the hall with doorways on either side designating first floor apartments.

Twocrow pointed at the stairs and up. "They live up there. On the left and back forward toward the street side." She started up ahead of him, the steps complaining with groans and creaks as they made their way up. Two-thirds of the way, Maria pulled to a stop as an older woman moved into view at the top of the staircase. She stared down, a look of concern on her face. She took a step or two closer, leaned hard with her right hand on a cane and rested her left hand on the bannister.

A glint of recognition filled her face. "Marshal Twocrow, that you? Thought I saw you coming toward the front door when I looked out," she called past Maria and down to where Twocrow stood three steps behind Maria. "I was just about to ring up the police department, but now that you're here I won't bother."

"Hello Gertie," the Marshal responded. "What's the problem?"

The woman appeared to be in her mid-to-late 70s, or maybe the same age as the Marshal. She was wearing a heavy wool sweater and a scarf draped around her neck, and while she was still partly leaning on the cane, she didn't seem totally dependent on having it. She stepped back a couple paces as Maria continued on, reached the top and stood waiting for the Marshal to finish his climb. Despite his advanced age, Twocrow didn't even seem winded as he extended a hand to greet Gertie. Maria, on the other hand, was puffing after the 20-stairstep climb.

"Have you met Maria Tager before?" he asked the older woman. "This here's Gertie Gentry," Twocrow added, pointing toward her and not waiting for the woman's answer. "She lives across the hall from the Darveauxs. And she's a longtime friend of mine."

"Ain't you that reporter girl?" Gertie responded. She lifted her cane and pointed it at Maria. "You're the one that works over at the Hot Springs *Star*? You're Laura Thompson's girl, ain't you?"

"Grand-girl . . . daughter . . . granddaughter," Maria was flustered as she tried for the proper response with the accusing cane aimed at her face. "I'm Laura's granddaughter. My mom's her daughter. And, yes, I'm a reporter for the *Star*."

She held out a hand to the older woman, and after first eyeing it suspiciously, Gertie lowered her cane and held out her own hand for a tentative shake. "I like some of your stories," she said. "Sort of reminds me of your Aunt Minnie's writing. Used to read her when we all lived out by Buffalo Gap. That was way back before she moved over to live and work in Hot Springs, back when her dad, Colonel Jack Thompson, still ran the Gap newspaper, *The News*. Then when me and my husband retired and moved over here, I guess I started reading some of her stuff in the *Star* too, you know?"

"Great Aunt," Maria corrected, moving seamlessly back to the beginning of Gertie's rambling explanation. "Minnie was my Great Aunt. Laura was a reporter here too, you know? Before she moved out East and did some work on newspapers back there." She smiled. "Both of them are gone now, but I inherited their investigative reporting genes. You might say newspaper writing is in my blood."

"Well, that's got to be true," the older woman answered. "Never seen anyone dog a story like your Aunt Minnie." She leaned back on her cane, which she had now planted firmly on the floor between her feet. "I swear, you look like you could be your Aunt Minnie's twin sister—when she was your age, a'course. You got that same sweet face and bounce to your hair. That dark brown hair's just like hers, too. I mean 'til it got so white during those years when she was sick and all." She patted the young woman on the arm. "Sorry about her loss; and your Grandmother's death, too."

Twocrow gave her a wan smile at the mention of Maria's now-deceased relatives before turning to look down to his left toward the doorway leading into the Darveaux apartment. "Elizabeth at home, you think?" he asked, inclining his head in that direction.

"Well, that's what I was going to call about," the old woman answered. "I saw her go out with a young man—Indian *boy* actually.

They maybe left here about 12:30 or so. But then about 30 or 40 minutes ago I heard a lot of banging and crashing sounds over at their place, and I was pretty sure she hadn't come back home yet. I wasn't sure if I should go over and check things or not, so I just kind of laid low. But now I haven't heard any noises, or ANYTHING so far as that goes, for going on 15 or 20 minutes. Maybe more, but I doubt it. Anyway, I got a bit worried that maybe somebody did something to her place—or maybe to her if she came back and I didn't see her when she come in. Haven't seen hide nor hair of that brother of hers, so figured he wasn't involved."

She half-hobbled, half-strode down the hallway, thumping her cane from time to time as she moved toward the apartment with Twocrow and Maria trailing behind.

"See." She pointed at the door with the cane, which Laura thought was beginning to look more and more like a part of her arm and not necessarily a support piece. "Looks to me like somebody might of broke the lock. So maybe that's the noises I was hearing? You don't think that boy did something to her, do you? I'm almost positive it weren't her brother I saw her with. But I don't see as well as I used to. Still, I'm pretty sure I'd know him. And like I was saying, I ain't seen him all day and usually I do."

"No, no, I think that she probably left with a friend of theirs. Friend of mine too. Boy by the name of Frank Silver Shore. You must remember him, don't you? He's that high school friend of Gene's. I asked him to come and drive her in to see the doctor." He put a hand on Gertie's shoulder to stop her from going any closer and eased past her to look at the door. It was clear that the lock had been broken as there were tiny splinters of broken and exposed wood radiating out from the latch. "You've probably heard her coughing the last few days, haven't you? She's been getting pretty sick."

"Well, sure," she said. "Guess I have now that you mention it. Don't hear as well as I used to either, you know? But some of her coughing did get pretty loud." She gestured toward the hallway window on the street side. "So that boy was takin' Elizabeth in to the doctor's office then?" Twocrow nodded. "Well, that makes sense. Sure it does." She pointed her cane back toward the Darveaux apartment door. "So who do you suppose was in there making all that racket?"

Twocrow put an arm on hers and directed her toward her own doorway. "Maybe you and Maria should wait over there by your apartment while I just check on that. Okay? You say you haven't heard anything inside there for a while now?"

"No. No noises for at least 15 or maybe 20 minutes, I'd say."

"Well, then I'm sure it's okay, but you just let me check on that. And don't be alarmed. I'm going to take out my pistol now. Best to be prepared for anything, don't you think?"

"Sure," she said, eyeing the Smith & Wesson as he removed it from his holster and chambered a round. He motioned for Maria to step back and stand with Gertie across the hall. "You want me to get my .22 rifle and back you up?" she queried, a determined look on her face. "I keep it loaded right inside the door." She tapped on her own door with her cane. "Bet I could still pop a rattler or two if needed—either the snake or the human kind."

"Well, thanks. That's a real nice offer Gertie, but I'm sure it'll be fine." He gave Maria a little nod as if to insure that she wouldn't let Gertie do anything of the kind, and then he stepped over to the side of the door, away from the center. Rapping lightly, he waited expectantly for several seconds. Hearing nothing, he gestured for Maria and Gertie to slide further back alongside the stairway railing and then knocked again, this time much louder and harder. The force of his knock caused the door to disengage from its broken latch and swing part way open.

"U.S. Marshal!" He called, holding the gun upright in the ready position. "Anybody in there?" He pushed the door again and it swung further open displaying more splinters of wood on the floor. Twocrow carefully swung the door all the way open and gave a low whistle. He held a hand up toward the women, signaling them to stay put before he slipped inside. After about a minute, he re-emerged, setting the safety as he slid the gun back into its holster.

"Well," he said, gesturing for the others to join him. "Nothing to worry about from anyone inside. But based on the looks of things, I'd say it was lucky Elizabeth went to the doctor to take care of that cough."

He stepped back and flipped on the light switch as the women moved up beside him. The living room was in a shambles with books, papers and anything else that wasn't a large piece of furniture scattered indiscriminately about on the floor.

"What in the world were they looking for?" Maria's voice was almost a whisper as she found that her throat had constricted from the fear she was feeling over seeing what had happened to the apartment.

The Marshal advanced back into the room and picked up a photo album lying on the floor at the corner of the couch. He quickly flipped through the pages and stopped as he reached a page that had a photo similar to the one he'd been carrying around of Gene and Elizabeth—this one had them pictured with both of their parents. Also on the page were a pair of impressions where two other photos had been mounted but now were missing.

"They took photos of the Darveauxs," Maria's voice was returning to full strength as she stepped forward and touched the page. "Now they know what Gene's sister looks like if they can find her."

Chapter Twenty-One

Tuesday, Feb. 1, 1955
Mid-afternoon to 10 p.m.
on the second day

"Okay, I see. So just be patient is what you're trying to tell me?" Twocrow cradled the phone receiver on his shoulder as he took out a notepad and wrote something down. "Listen, it's really crucial that I get some sort of report from you as soon as possible. And Doc I'll be more'n glad to come up to Rapid and wait if need be."

He listened intently to the reply and nodded. "Okay. I understand. I'm going to give you my home phone number and you have someone give me a call as soon as you have anything more to share. And if I don't answer, just call me back every 30 or 40 minutes after that. I'll be at that number from 5 o'clock on. And like I said, I'll be glad to head up to Rapid yet tonight if you have something for me to see in person. Okay? Good. Thanks Doc. Much appreciated."

He hung up and glanced over at Maria, who was sitting alongside his desk. "That was the Pennington Coroner. Said it's too soon, but he should have something for me by end of the day." He immediately lifted the receiver and dialed again. "Now I'll call Doc Flaten up at the V.A. and see if he has anything new to report on Elizabeth," he said as Maria gave him a questioning look at his action. She could hear the phone ringing and then a muffled woman's voice as he started the conversation.

"Look, I'm sorry," he said after several minutes of back-and-forth, "but do you mind if I talk directly to the Doctor? It's very important. No, it doesn't matter how long it takes. I'll hold." Twocrow leaned back from his desk and pointed toward the phone receiver as Maria gave him another questioning look. He held his hand across the mouthpiece as he spoke to her, keeping the receiver to his ear.

"Doc Flaten's nurse says Elizabeth is still there at the doctor's office, and he has her making arrangements to keep Liz overnight at the clinic while he treats her further. He's already started her on two IVs and an inhaler. She said it's lucky Elizabeth came in when she did or she'd be dealing with full-blown pneumonia. The nurse said Doc Flaten thinks they caught it just in time."

He picked up some papers from his desk and studied them while continuing to wait for the doctor to come to the phone. "Something seems really off about this Prairie City report," he waved the papers toward her. "They say alcohol was probably a factor, but I can't ever remember that kid drinking anything besides a beer. And even that was pretty rare. I've gotta check into that further, that's for sure."

Maria was sitting in a metal folding chair alongside his desk and once again holding his wet handkerchief to her forehead, which had started aching again where the small lump had formed.

Jim Dolan, a young Sheriff's deputy who had been flirting with Maria on her recent stops at their offices, walked across from the break room area carrying a glass of water and a wet washcloth. He handed her the glass and pointed at the handkerchief. "You need to use this clean washcloth and give me that ugly thing," he said. "Sorry Marshal, but that thing looks really gross." He reached out to take the handkerchief and handed her the washcloth and two white tablets in exchange. "Brought you a couple of aspirin too."

She nodded gratefully as she swallowed the aspirin with some of the water and held the clean cold washcloth up to her brow. "That feels great! Thank you." She gave him a warm smile as he held the dirty handkerchief at arm's length, swinging it dramatically in front of Twocrow before turning to take it away.

"Just toss it in the wastebasket," the Marshal grumbled as Dolan grinned toward Maria before giving Twocrow a thumbs up in acknowledgement.

Maria smiled back and swiped the cool new cloth across her forehead, wetting the top of her brow before laying it down on the corner of the desk. Standing, she removed her coat and placed it neatly on her metal chair's seat to provide a little padding. Patting it lightly and shifting it a few inches further forward so it wouldn't fall through the chair's open back side and onto the dusty wood floor, she sat back down and gave a little sigh.

"That's much better. Okay, so what about Frank?" She asked after she was settled. She reached over past the wet cloth and tapped on a note from Frank that they had found on Twocrow's desk when they had arrived back at his office. Dolan said the teen had brought it in to the office about 20 minutes earlier, just around the same time she and Twocrow had been exploring the Darveauxs' trashed apartment. "Is Frank still waiting there with her? Did he say anything about going back up to join her at the doctor's office? I mean, after he dropped off this note?"

"Well, I'm not sure if he is or . . ."

He held up a hand and spoke into the phone receiver. "Yes, I'm still here. No problem. I'm glad to wait, thanks." Twocrow cradled the phone on his shoulder and shook his head with a sigh. Tossing the police report back down he took up Frank's note from under her fingers and spread it open flat on his desktop with his free hand, pushing it back into the center of his desk.

"He just wrote that he recognized one of those Prairie City police officers as one of the men he thought was out at the location where Gene died. He says he needs to talk with me as soon as possible. I just assumed he would go back to be with Elizabeth after he left here because that's the sort of thing he would do." He picked up the note once again and gave it an intensive stare, his brow wrinkled in thought.

"After what the nurse said, I think it's pretty definite that she'll be spending the night up there at the Clinic," he said. "So, I think that takes you off the hook for putting her up at your place."

"Yeah, I guess." Maria was disappointed to be losing the opportunity to help out. "But what about Frank?" She asked. "He can't stay overnight with her up at the VA, can he?"

"Well no, I doubt it," Twocrow replied. "We'll still have to find a safe spot for him, unless he sleeps on the floor over at my place."

Maria brightened. "Well, then HE should still come and stay with me. He can sleep on my couch."

"What? No! I can't expect you to take him in without her being there too."

She held her arms wide and gave him an incredulous look. "He's not an axe murderer or anything like that, is he? Isn't he just a scared teenager who needs someplace safe to crash for the night? I can handle having him stay over at my place overnight. I'm a big girl Marshal."

"Sure you can and yes you are. But how would it look? What'll your neighbors think? What are people going to say?" He gave her a semi-frightened look. "Even more important what would your Great Aunt Minnie and Grandma Laura say if they were still alive and I allowed this sort-of arrangement? They might be gone in body, but their spirit definitely still affects my thinking and what I look to as being right or wrong. I couldn't live with myself or their ghosts if something bad happened to you."

"Nothing BAD's going to happen to me! And I know exactly what my Grandmother and Great Aunt would say!" she responded, a heated tone creeping into her voice and her face reddening as she spoke. "They'd say 'Do what's right to help this poor kid!' And 'Do what's right to help solve his friend's murder!' I still have a lot to learn about the relationship you had with Grandma Laura and Aunt Minnie, but if they were the same strong women then that I grew up knowing, loving and learning from, then you and I both know that I'm right!"

She accented her final sentence by pointing her index finger straight at his face before dropping her hand back to the wet washcloth; retrieving it and holding it back to her forehead. "Ow," she added for emphasis.

"Well . . ." he paused. "Um . . ." The sound of a questioning voice came over the phone and looking relieved by the interruption, he held up one finger for her to wait as he took his hand off the mouthpiece. "Oh . . . uh, yeah, hi Doc. Al Twocrow here. Yeah, I know you know that already. Sorry. Just talking to someone in the office while I was waiting. So, what's the story with our girl?" It was obvious he was flustered by Maria's dramatic reaction and grateful to switch the conversation to something new.

He wrinkled his forehead again as he listened to Doctor Flaten's explanation of what was going on with Elizabeth, nodding at several points and uttering a few "Uh-huh's" and "I see's" in response. Finally, it was his turn to talk.

"So, you'll keep her up there for a couple more days. And if this new medication you have does its job, she could get back home by Friday or maybe Saturday at the latest, right?" He listened again and now smiled toward Maria, who took several deep breaths to calm herself down.

"Well, that's great—both that you can keep her there for the treatment and that this should do the trick," he continued after listening for a few more seconds. "Well, thanks again. Listen, can I talk to Frank before he gets out the door?" He waited a few more seconds and then shook his head. "Oh hell. Yeah, I see. Well . . . okay. I'll head over and try to catch up with him there. Thanks again Doc for seeing her like this. I owe you big time. Hey, I'll check back in with you tomorrow."

He hung up and nervously tapped the top of the phone while avoiding looking in Maria's direction.

"So it sounds like she'll be taken care of," Maria said in a much calmer voice and not waiting for him to explain. Carefully refolding the washcloth, she smoothed it out and placed it back on his desk. "So, where's Frank?"

"That's a damn good question, but I think I know the answer. He's a pretty smart kid so I think I know that his message for me might be trying to tell me he's getting to someplace safe and waiting there for me to come to him." He stood and pulled his coat off from the back of his chair where he'd draped it upon their arrival.

As he pulled it toward him a small, brightly painted box fell from one of the pockets and clattered onto the floor next to Maria's feet.

Looking embarrassed, the Marshal started to reach for it but Maria beat him to it, sweeping it up and placing it on the corner of his desk next to the washcloth. "Pretty," she remarked. Then she picked it back up to look at it more closely.

"Wow, my grandmother used to have a little box just like this. My mom said Grandma got it from her mother when her family lived at the trading post out near the reservation. She called it her treasure keeper."

She placed it back on the desk and now Twocrow retrieved it and studied it carefully. "That's right," he agreed. "I remember that now. Wow, that was a long, long time ago. We were just kids." He eyed the box. "Do you know why she called it that? Did she or anyone else ever say anything more about it?"

Maria laughed. "Oh sure, but I thought it was just a story. Mom said that Grandma claimed there was a secret compartment inside, to keep her very best treasures hidden. Like I said, she thought her grandma—my Great Grandma—got it from an old medicine man when they were living at that trading post next to the reservation. That would've been WAY BACK in the day, wouldn't it?"

The Marshal nodded thoughtfully while slowly rotating the box in his hands. He held it up to the lamp on his desktop and studied it even closer.

"You think this box might be that kind of treasure keeper?" Maria asked. She leaned in closer to join in his examination. "Where'd you get this one? Why'd you have it in your coat pocket?"

"Well, it came from Gene Darveaux who gave it to Frank just before he died. I stuck it in my pocket this morning and flat out forgot about it until now." He set the box down, drummed his fingers on it a couple times, and then opened his center desk drawer and put it inside. Picking up his coat again, he shrugged into it as he walked around the desk. He stopped and reached across to the corner of his desk to snag his hat and started to walk on. Maria gave him a questioning look.

"We'll have to get back to the mystery of the box later," he said half over his shoulder. "That is, IF there even IS a mystery to consider. Right now, I think I'd like to get out of here and go meet Frank."

Maria nodded in agreement. "Yeah, I haven't even met him yet, but I feel like I have and I want him to be safe too." She leaned back in her chair. "Listening in on your phone conversation, it sounded like Doctor Flaten told you someplace Frank might be headed. You said you were going to 'catch up with him there,' to use your own words," she said, cocking her head to one side. "Come on Marshal, you figured out where he might be going didn't you?"

"He told the Doc he was going over to the Indian Cultural Center and hoped to meet me there later after I got back into town. He probably still figures we're over at the crime scene or up in Rapid at the Coroner's

Office and won't be back until late afternoon. So he obviously didn't want to risk being seen before then."

"Well, that makes sense," Maria said. "So why are you questioning where he's at? Shouldn't you just head over there and meet him."

"Have you ever run across anyplace called the Indian Cultural Center here in Hot Springs? Or, for that matter, ANYWHERE around this community?"

She thought about that for a few seconds and finally shook her head. "I guess I never have now that you mention it, but you know I'm still relatively new to town."

"No. You haven't heard of it because there ain't such a place," he said as he buttoned up his coat. He plopped his hat down on the back half of his head before pulling it forward into the position she almost always saw him wearing it, the front brim just above his grey, bushy eyebrows. "But I'm pretty sure I know what he was talking about."

He started toward the door. Halfway there, he turned back and waved his right hand toward her. "How's the head?"

"Not too bad. I'll be okay."

"Good." He nodded to the door. "So, are you up to coming along, or not?"

"Oh! Sure. Of course." Expecting to be left behind and startled by his invitation, she jerked to her feet, nearly knocking over her chair in the process. Her sudden movement caused her previously neatly arranged coat to slide backward through the chair's gap and drop into a heap on the dusty floor. "Oh damn it!" she grouched, blushing with embarrassment at her own slapdash reaction.

She made a quick move toward the floor to pick it up and suddenly felt a small wave of dizziness washing over her. She grabbed at the top of her chair to keep from falling and sat back down.

Seeing her reaction, Dolan sprang up and hurried over to help her as Maria grimaced and held her hand to her forehead and took a deep breath.

"Hang on Maria," he interrupted as he reached her side and knelt down to grab her coat off the floor. "Let me help you with this, okay?"

"Ummm," she said, putting her hand back to her forehead. "Just give me a few seconds. I'll be okay." She blushed, shook her head to clear the cobwebs and stood back up.

"You sure you're okay?" He took her elbow and draped one arm around her shoulders to support her.

"Yeah, thanks," she said gratefully, slightly leaning into him as he helped her put her coat on.

Seeing the now dusty backside of the garment, Dolan reached out and swiped rapidly at it as Maria continued to pull it on tighter and button it up. "Oh," she exclaimed as his hand brushed across her backside.

Dolan turned bright red and backed off a couple steps. "Oh, shit. I mean, uh, sorry, I was just . . ." he stopped talking and held both hands out in apology. "So sorry."

She smiled shyly in his direction. "Hey. It's okay. I know you weren't trying to do anything bad. Is there still a lot of dust and dirt back there?" She tried to look over her shoulder as she also looked back at him. He nodded. She grabbed the bottom edge of the coat and twisted it toward him. "Can you just brush it a couple more times before I go? I don't want to look bad when I go along with the old grouch over there."

Dolan smiled back, took hold of the coat's bottom edge and pulled it out toward him before brushing back-and-forth on it a couple of times. "There, looks like new again."

Maria reached out and squeezed his arm. "Thank you!"

"You coming along or going out for coffee with Dolan?" Twocrow growled from his place at the doorway where he was still waiting and glaring at the young people's exchange.

She gave the Marshal a glare of her own in response as she started toward where Twocrow was impatiently holding the glass-topped door half open. Maria reached his side and turned back to give the deputy a little wave and even bigger smile. "Thanks for helping me Jim, and I'll see you again soon, okay?"

Not waiting for his answer, she turned back toward the Marshal and was startled to see he already had left the doorway and was rapidly moving down the hallway. "So you think you know where Frank might be going?" Maria puffed as she adjusted the last of her coat buttons while hurrying to catch up to him as they headed down the hallway toward the main outside door.

"Yeah, I have a pretty good idea anyway," he said gruffly over his shoulder. "I think what he said to the Doc was a coded message for me, just in case someone else found out about Elizabeth and him being there and pressed the Doc to help locate him. With Elizabeth safe and out of reach for a while he could plan to get back together with me without being out in the open." He stepped out onto the front landing leading to the steps where Maria had found him talking to the Prairie City officers earlier in the day.

"You see anybody watching us?" he asked her, looking up the street in the direction of the big wooden structure housing the Evans Plunge warm water pool as he spoke. She took that as an invitation to check in the other direction and quickly did so.

"No, no one—at least not who you mean," she answered. "But I'll keep watching as we drive, just to be sure we're not being followed."

Twocrow nodded his approval and went down the steps toward his car with Maria once again pushing herself to keep up. She was amazed at how quickly he moved around for a man his age. And while her upper body was still aching from their late morning mishap, he didn't seem to be affected at all. "Do you work out or run? You know, things like that?" she puffed.

He shook his head as he reached the car and unlocked the driver's side door. "Just got a good metabolism, I guess." He chuckled.

"What's so funny?"

"Just the way you said that. It was exactly the same words your Aunt Minnie used to use when we were out and about together. She said I was the damndest person to keep up with that she ever had to follow—both 'planned and unplanned,' if you know what I mean?"

Maria eyed him across the top of the car and gave him a knowing smile. "Why Marshal, you mean you sometimes purposely tried to evade my Great Aunt Minnie?" She reached down and pulled open the passenger side door, then slid in before he could answer.

"Don't get me wrong, I loved Minnie dearly, but there were times when she could be so damned exasperating and relentless," he said, responding to her question as he got in behind the wheel and started the engine. "Your Grandma Laura too, back in the day when we were all growing up together out by the Gap. Not that I was glad that your Grandma moved away and never really came back, but there was more than one time that I was glad I only had one Thompson gal at a time to try to deal with."

Maria settled back and smiled to herself. "It's funny you should say that," she said. "Because a couple of times—after Aunt Minnie came out to visit Grandma and we'd all be together for a few weeks before she came back here—my mother used THOSE exact same words. Although," she looked out of the corner of her eye in his direction, "sometimes her words were even a little stronger."

For the first time all day, he responded with a genuine laugh.

"And guess what?" she added, shifting around to check and be sure they weren't being followed. "I think I might've inherited that persistence from both of them."

This time, the old Marshal responded with the same half-snorting, half-humming reaction that he had been using with her earlier in the day.

Chapter Twenty-Two

Delaney stood watch over the gas station attendant as he finished filling up the Prairie City police car with gas. Hillman was inside the station—visible through the window—completing a telephone call to Sarge. The attendant topped off the tank and walked around with a partially frozen wet rag in his hand.

"Don't know if it'll do much good to wipe off the windows in this cold." He pointed skyward. "Even with the sun shining I think it's just gonna smear it more than wash it."

"Yeah, don't worry, it'll be okay," the big man said, pulling a ten dollar bill out of his wallet and handing it over for the gas. He glanced at the dial on the gas pump and noted the amount. "You can give the change to my partner in there. I'm getting back in the car to stay warm."

The attendant gave him a tip of the cap in response and hurried inside. After just a couple more minutes, Hillman walked out counting the change as he walked while folding up a handwritten receipt from the station. He walked around to the driver's side and got in, handing the money and receipt over to Delaney before starting the car.

"Get that receipt to Sarge and he can probably reimburse you out of petty cash as soon as we get back."

The big man nodded. "What'd the Sarge have to say? Why'd he want you to call instead of just talking on the two-way?" He pointed toward the police car's intercom as he asked.

"What he wanted to tell me he didn't want going over the police radio. Never know who might be listening in?" He blew out an exasperated sigh. "Sarge is pissed, of course, but what the hell are we supposed to do? I thought we made a lot of progress even though we didn't find the girl or anything in their apartment. But hell, even if we were able to track her down, she probably wouldn't know shit anyway."

Delaney grunted his agreement and settled back in his seat as they pulled out onto the street and started back out of town toward the Fall River Canyon Road. "So, what's the plan? Did Sarge make contact with the pilot?"

"Yeah, and just like we figured he's going to have him drop down onto the Cheyenne River bottom landing strip out at Fitz's place, just after sun-up. So, you'll need to get your ass out to the agate fields by 6:30 or 6:45, latest, and be ready. Pilot knows to look for you and your truck and that you'll signal him with a red flag, aimed in the right direction.

"We'll be going with long-range radio silence until he sees you, unless we've got some kind of emergency. If there's a problem on our end or he's got trouble we'll just call each other direct at that point. Better safe than sorry. So you having the flag is doubly important. If he doesn't see you waving that flag to point him in the direction he's supposed to go, he'll abort the flight and this time he ain't gonna wait around for a third try.

"So you and me can stay in touch by walkie-talkie and after the pilot passes your checkpoint, you can let me know he's on his way," Hillman waved at the car radio as he spoke. "That's when he'll switch his radio over to our Prairie City police channel and he and I can talk direct without having any interference—either static on the radio or from someone listening in who shouldn't be. I'll just talk him down from there and we'll be ready to make the handoff as soon as he's on the airstrip."

"Okay."

"And I'll stay in contact with you on the walkie-talkie, too, and let you know as soon as the pilot's getting ready to set down at the airstrip.

Up 'til then if you think anything—anything at all—seems wrong or we need to stop things, we can still do it right away. The last thing we want is for him to land and then have something else get screwed up. No more screw-ups!"

"You got it."

"Sarge said the pilot's still planning to have somebody riding shotgun, just like the other night," Hillman continued. "So he's got some firepower along if something does go wrong. But hopefully everything's going to go smooth as silk—just a quick in-and-out for all of us. Drugs delivered; payment made; nothing but big profits ahead."

"What about the cash? How you supposed to pay him?"

"Sarge took it from the private account. He said he drove down and dropped an envelope with your name on it at the Fairburn Post Office. Guess your telling him about that paid off, huh?" Delaney smiled at the praise.

"Anyway, he asked the postmaster to hang onto it for you, which he said he was more than happy to do since the request was coming from an officer of the law." He snorted as he said it. "Anyway, as soon as we get back to your place, we'll swing over and pick it up before I leave town.

"I'll take the cash back to my place tonight and then have it with me when I drive out to Fitz's place tomorrow. As soon as I get the pilot paid and the drugs are all offloaded, he can crank it up and get the hell out of there. Like I said, easy in, easy out. After that I'll just wait for you to meet me there."

"Shouldn't be more than a 30-40 minute drive for me to get down to Fitz's from that eastside entry to the agate fields," Delaney said. "We can load the boxes onto my truck and I'll bring them back up and store them at my place until we can get them ready to distribute."

"Yeah, that sounds like a plan," Hillman answered. "You got a good dry place for them?"

"Yeah, like I was saying last night, we can use the back room in that old store next to my camper. That's the side I used to live in, and I just hung onto it for storage after I got the camper. I spent all day Monday cleaning it out. We can stack the boxes in there and then go through them on the weekend."

"Good, good, although I doubt Sarge'll want to wait that long. Don't be surprised if he decides to come down to your place tomorrow afternoon to get started. He's got a lot riding on us getting this done right, you know."

"Yeah." Delaney nodded, "for sure." He sat back, quietly watching the course of the steamy Fall River on his right as they drove. They rode in silence along the next four miles of the winding Fall River Canyon highway, but when it straightened out for a final half-mile stretch leading up to Maverick Junction, the big man broke the silence.

After coughing lightly to get Hillman's attention, he held up one of the photos they had taken from the Darveaux apartment and pointed toward Elizabeth's image. "You think the Darveaux kid's sister will report the break-in at their apartment to the local cops? Sort of been worried about that."

"Maybe. But even if she does, there's nothing to tie us to it." He reached into the inside pocket of his coat and extracted the second photo of the Darveauxs when they reached the intersection with Highway 79.

"Good to have these photos, but I wish we could'a found something … anything … that would have given us a clue as to where that dumb-ass brother of hers might've stashed our cash. I guess the good thing is that nobody but us and him even know that he took a bag of money from us in the first place. You said that other kid running away didn't have anything with him, right?"

"Well, yeah," Delaney said, puzzled by Hillman's comment. "But what's that got to do with anything?"

"Sarge said he's going to spin the kid's shooting around toward those recent burglaries we been hearing about up in Rapid City and Black Hawk. Make it look like this dead kid might'a tried to make off with more than his fair share and whoever he was working for found out and went after him.

"That way, if the break-in in Hot Springs gets reported, the local cops could put two-and-two together and think that whoever was after Darveaux would just naturally come looking for wherever he was living, too. You know, maybe seein' if he had any of their booty locked away at his home. Something like that."

"Geez, that's damn smart," Delaney said, rubbing at his chin as he gave a low whistle of appreciation at his partner's explanation.

Hillman gave a noncommittal grunt in response, signaled to his left and turned out of Fall River Canyon and north onto Highway 79. Even though it was only 3:45 shadows were already stretching out from the foothills toward the two-lane blacktop. It would start getting dark soon.

"You gotta hand it to Sarge, don't you?" Delaney continued. "He's definitely smart as hell about things like that."

"That's true," Hillman said, turning on the headlights and then drumming his fingers along the top of the steering wheel as he drove. "Now, if he could just figure out where that Darveaux kid disappeared to after he drove off, and where he might've stashed a leather bag with 50 thousand dollars."

*****

"What's this place?" Maria asked as Marshal Twocrow wheeled his car into an obscure small driveway, drove down a narrow lane past a little grove of ponderosa pine trees and pulled up to the front of a small single story wood frame house. The house was not much larger than a large storage barn or a lakeside vacation cabin.

"This? It's my house," he replied, pulling up closer to the front and then continuing around toward the far side where a detached single car garage sat at a 45-degree angle, its doorway jutting out toward the tiny house. "Yeah, I know, it's small," Twocrow added, noting Maria's cursory study of the place. "But, it's cozy and suits me just fine. And I got it because it's a one-person hideaway. But no room for 'guests,' which is why I wanted Frank and Elizabeth to stay over with you instead of just putting them up myself. Somebody would end up on the floor and I can guarantee you it wasn't going to be me."

He pulled past the corner of the tiny house and the back end of a beat-up old 1941 Plymouth came into view. He stopped and lightly tapped the horn.

"Who . . .?" Maria stopped before she could really get started with her question as the driver's side door on the car swung open and a slender young Indian emerged. He smiled and gave the Marshal's car a sheepish half-wave.

"Hey! I know that guy!" Maria stared daggers in the boy's direction. "He threatened my baby!"

"He what? Your . . . baby?"

"My car. Okay? Never mind," she muttered. "Now that I know what he's been dealing with I guess I can forgive him."

Twocrow gave her a questioning look in return and she waggled a dismissive hand back-and-forth. "Like I said, never mind."

"Okay." He nodded toward the young man. "Then come on out and meet Frank Silver Shore." Twocrow gave her yet another questioning look as if waiting for her to give him a reason NOT to make the introductions. Frank pushed his car door shut and started walking in their direction.

"Sure." She started to open her door and then swiveled back toward the Marshal. "But how'd you know he was going to be here?"

"Cop Sixth Sense of course," he chuckled, cutting off her question and opening his own door as he spoke. "That and the fact that Frank, Gene and I met here on so many different occasions that they just started calling it the Hot Springs' Indian Cultural Center."

"Hot Springs Ind . . ." she stopped and smiled. "Oh! So when he told that to the doctor . . ."

"Mmmm-hmmm. Our own little 'code.'" Twocrow answered. He clicked open his door and started to get out. "Come on."

They both got out and Frank stopped walking, momentarily confused by the sight of the young woman. His smile was quickly replaced by a look of fear as he obviously recognized her from their early morning encounter.

"Frank Silver Shore meet Maria Tager." The Marshal pointed at Frank and then at Maria. "You can trust her. She's on our team," he added, still noting the flash of fear in the young man's eyes.

"Don't worry. I won't bite," she reassured him. "Despite what I said this morning." She reached out to shake his hand and Twocrow gave her another questioning glance. "No problem about what happened earlier, okay? Bygones?"

He gave her a tentative handshake, then his handsome face brightened with a shy smile. "Okay. Thanks."

He turned to face Twocrow. "I thought I should come here to wait. Hope it was the right thing to do," Frank began explaining. "I've had time to think about any possibilities for Gene's 'rock pile,' and Liz and I talked about it too. But, nothing definite comes to mind. I'll try to write down some possibilities whenever I think of them."

"Good," Twocrow answered. "And it might be something really obvious. You just never know." He gave Frank a reassuring pat on the shoulder.

"I decided to come up here," Frank continued, " 'Cause I saw two men … earlier, over by Elizabeth's place when we were leaving for the doctor's office . . . and I wasn't sure what I ought to do? I was scared to go back there."

"Yeah, I kind of figured," Twocrow answered. "You did right, coming here. And that was smart using our code word for my place. What'd those men look like?"

"Well, I'm pretty sure one of them was that big guy with the bright white hair who shot at me last night. But he was with a cop, so that was kind of weird. I don't know if it's one of the cops I saw with him by the grain bins, but it might'a been. Anyway, after I got Liz up to the doctor and the Doc said he was going to keep her there, I decided I better find another place to go, just in case they knew where she lived. Or in case they were waiting for her. Or waiting for me as far as that goes. You know?"

"Definitely a smart decision because we stopped in there and it looks like whoever you saw has already been inside their place. It was a mess. It was clear they were looking for something, and maybe not just you. It's just a question of whether they found anything or not. Unfortunately, it looks like they might've taken a couple photos out of Elizabeth's photo album that she got the photo out for me. If that's the case, then they know what she looks like. You weren't in any of their photos, were you?"

"No. At least I don't think so." Frank swallowed hard. "So, either way, I can't go back there tonight, that's for sure. You think they know where I live up in Rapid? Can I just stay here with you?"

Twocrow shook his head. "I might be headed back up to Rapid yet tonight and I don't want you here by yourself. I've been talking with Maria here about that and we've got a solution," Twocrow said, moving forward and clasping Frank by the shoulder.

"Now, listen. You might not like what I'm going to say next, but I need to tell you about my plan for where you're going to be spending the night."

Chapter Twenty-Three

Maria pulled her car up in front of the door of the single car garage that fronted her faux log house and jumped out. She rolled open the overhead garage door, straining at the door's weight until it slid past the halfway point on its track and rolled upward. Turning around, she pointed toward a spot directly in front of the small walkway that led up to her house's front door to indicate to Frank that he should park his beat-up old Plymouth in that spot. Then she jumped back into her own car and drove it into the garage.

Exiting and checking to see that Frank had understood her signal, she grabbed the thin rope hanging off the door handle and maneuvered the door shut. As Frank nervously walked up the pathway in her general direction, she hurried across the gravel driveway and gestured toward the front of the house. "Go in there."

He veered left. "Thanks for forgiving me for this morning," he said as he reached her. "I'm sorry I threatened your car. I was just . . ."

"Yeah, I know, okay? Marshal Twocrow has given me all the details and now that I know what you were going through . . . well," she stopped. "Well, hell, I might've threatened to bash somebody's car in too. Usually you can win as long as it's not moving at you at too fast a pace." She grinned. "Listen, stop worrying about that, okay? Like I said earlier, bygones."

He gestured toward her house. "Are you sure about this? I still don't know if this is such a good idea," Frank muttered as he waited for Maria to unlock the front door. He looked nervously at the neighboring houses. "Won't your neighbors get upset?"

"About what? What's to get worried about?"

"Well, you know?" He shuffled his feet and gave her a bashful smile. "You bringing in such a good-looking, hunky guy like myself to spend the night."

She stared at him in surprise and then burst into laughter. "Oh, yeah. That! I love it! Neighbors be damned!" She grabbed him by the shoulders and turned him from side-to-side. "Check it out neighbors!" she called to no one or anyone who might be watching. "I'm bringing home a new Boy Toy for the night!" She leaned her shoulder into the door, pushed it open and half-dragged him inside.

Now both laughing, they moved past the small entryway into the living room where she indicated a couch in the center of the room. "Just toss your coat and stuff over there. You got anything else out in your car? Any change of clothes, for instance?" She brushed at her nose. "No offense, but you're smelling a bit ripe."

He blushed and turned to slip his coat off. "Sorry," he said over his shoulder. "I didn't plan on being down here for even one night, let alone two or three. It all kind of happened at the last minute after I found Gene and then took off to get away from those guys who were shooting at me."

"Geez," she said solemnly. "When you put it that way it makes me feel bad for even mentioning anything about your clothing."

"No, no it's okay. I know I smell bad. I even smell bad to myself." He pointed toward a little hallway leading off toward her bedroom in the back. "You think maybe I could take a quick bath or a shower?"

"Of course," she answered. "Listen. You get in the bathroom and toss out your dirty clothes and I'll get them going in my washing machine."

"But . . ." he stopped, embarrassed. "Won't that take a while? And how you going to get them dry?" He looked around. "Holy moley, you're not rich enough to have your own electric clothes dryer, are you?"

She laughed. "Not hardly. Guess I wasn't thinking." She paced out to the kitchen and stared at her little washing machine standing in the corner near her sink. She glanced up at the wall clock and turned back toward Frank. "Hang on," she said. "I need to make a quick call."

She took the telephone receiver off its hook on the wall and dialed a number. After two rings, Janeen Wilder answered at the office of the Hot Springs *Star*.

"Hey Janeen! It's Maria." Maria said. "Yeah, hi. I'm back in town and I need a favor. We've still got some men's clothes out back by the press area, right? I mean, in case someone needs an emergency change if they get covered with ink, or something like that?"

"Sure," Janeen answered. "Why? And where are you? Been a little worried not hearing anything."

"I'm at home. Don't worry everything's okay? Look, I need whatever men's clothes you can round up—shirts or slacks, blue jeans. Doesn't matter. I'll head down to get them soon, and I can explain then. I don't want to talk about it on the phone."

"All . . . right," Janeen hesitated as she spoke. "Yeah, okay I guess."

"Great!"

"Oh, and I reached my friend up at the State Home and she said that the Darveaux girl called in sick today, so I haven't been able to reach her at all," Janeen added. "I called over to the Hot Springs School, too, and got a couple of things about Gene Darveaux and then called the guy up at the *Black Hills News*. Hope that's all right? I tried to reach you at the Marshal's office, but the other cops there said you and he had already taken off for Rapid."

"Of course it's all right; definitely not a problem. Look. I'll head down there in a few minutes and we can talk in person. Thanks Janeen."

She hung up and turned back toward Frank. "Okay, problem solved—maybe." She gave him a little shrug. "I'm going to head downtown to the newspaper office to meet up with my office manager. I'm pretty sure between us we can round up a few clothes that you can wear tonight—maybe even yet tomorrow. Then we'll take your things from the washer and hang them up in the kitchen to dry as soon as I get back."

"Umm . . ." again he looked embarrassed.

"Listen, we gotta do this. I can't stand having you stink up my place overnight, and I'm definitely not letting you go back down to your friend's place where you might be in danger from those goons, whoever the hell they are." Frank started to protest again and she held up a hand while reaching for her coat. "No ifs, ands, or buts about it. Okay?"

After a few more seconds of hesitation, he finally responded with his halfhearted approval. "I guess. Suppose there's no other options, huh?" he added aloud. She smiled, gave him a little wave and started through the door. "But hey, lady," he called after her. She stopped and came back in. "What do I wear until you get back with something? You don't want me sitting here just wrapped in a towel, do you?"

Maria blanched at that image, stepped back inside and shut the door. "Hang on," she said, walking quickly past him and down toward her bedroom. A few seconds later, she emerged, holding a fluffy blue bathrobe.

"No way," Frank exclaimed, stepping back as if shocked that she would even suggest it.

Maria shoved the robe hard into his chest and said. "Yes, way! And don't even think about not getting cleaned up before I return." She pointed toward the kitchen. "You know how to start a washing machine, right?"

He gulped at the intense expression and sound in her voice. “Well, sure,” he mumbled.

“Then strip off those stinky clothes, and get them into the machine as soon as I’m out of here! The sooner they’re washed, the sooner you can have them back all clean and dry.”

“Okay.” His voice level had dropped so low she could barely hear him.

“And Frank,” she added, stopping again by the door. “My name is Maria, and even if you think I sound like a mean old lady, I’m really not that scary.” She gave him another curt smile and started out, then popped her head back in, startling him all over again. “Get your clothes in the washing machine before I return—IF you know what’s good for you! And that’s NOT a suggestion!”

*****

“So, you’re going with the duck-tail look, huh?” she said, pointing to his wet head and swept-back hair style as Frank walked from the bath-room wearing the mish-mash of clothing Maria had picked up for him at the newspaper office. The oversize pants were rolled up to keep from dragging on the floor. “I saw Gene in a photo with his sister and he had a flat top. Thought you might’ve had one too?”

“Yeah, once, a year or so ago, but not any more,” Frank answered. “We both wanted to be ‘with it,’ you know, once we got re-settled in the big city. Figured we’d probably stand out like sore thumbs if we kept our flattops. Gene was already starting to grow his hair out too.”

“Well, you’re right. That’s smart,” she replied. Then she grinned at him. “Besides, you look kind of cute with that new do, no doubt about it.” She walked into the kitchen smiling to herself as he blushed at the compliment and pretended to drop something onto the floor so he could look down instead of just looking embarrassed. "Just don't let it get too long so you turn into one of those Greasers," she called from the kitchen as she stirred some vegetables cooking in a pan on top of the stove.

She put a lid back on the pan and leaned around the corner of the door and winked at him. "Unless you DO happen to look like James Dean, of course. I mean, what girl wouldn't want to be seen hanging out with a guy who looks like James Dean?"

"I used to tell Gene he could be the Indian version."

"Of James Dean?" she asked, surprised at his response.

Frank nodded. "Yeah. Believe it or not, he kind-a looked like him. Same build; same sort-a Cool Cat look. Only he didn't have the attitude. Just the coolness." He gave her a "You know what I mean?" smile and she nodded and waved for him to join her in the kitchen. As he walked in he swiped at his hair with a pocket comb that he carried with him and the action caused his shirt, still not fully buttoned, to spread open and display a large bruise on his upper right side.

He sat down at the table as she brought over the pan of mixed vegetables and plopped a loaf of bread down beside it.

"How'd you get that big bruise?" She pointed at his chest as he hurried to fasten the last of the buttons.

"From last night, running from those guys who were trying to shoot me. I had to sort-of 'dive' across the railroad tracks to get away. Landing area was a little on the 'hard as a rock' side, if you know what I mean?"

"Geez," she muttered. "You sure you're okay?"

"Yeah. Does hurt a little, but I had the nurse take a quick look at it when I took Elizabeth in and she said nothing seemed to be broken."

Maria gave him a sympathetic look and walked over to the refrigerator. As she pulled out a plate with a brick of butter on it, she said, "Your friend Gene sounds like he was a really great guy." She placed the butter on the table and then sat down across from him. "Sorry I didn't get to meet him."

Frank sighed and slumped back a bit in his chair. "Gene and I used to really have a gas hanging out at the quarry or going diving at the Pit up along 79," Frank said, tears forming at the corner of his eyes. "You know, I can't believe he's gone. I just don't know what I'm going to do without him? You know?" He started to cry and she stood up and walked over and put her hand on his shoulder.

"I lost a close friend like that, too. When I was in my last year in college," she said. "It's really hard, but eventually you figure out a few things and try to get on with your life."

He gulped and brushed at his eyes. "Where'd you go to college?"

"New York," she answered, before quickly adding, "It was close to where I grew up out in Connecticut" as she saw a look of wonder fill his face.

"Man, I'd love to go to New York sometime," he said. "You ever see any Beatniks?"

She laughed at his off-hand remark. "Sure, but that wasn't my crowd. I stayed over by my college more often than not." She sat back down at the table. "You ever think about going to college?"

"Me? Naw, I ain't got the jets for anything like that," he stared sheepishly at the floor. "I still have half-a-year of classes just to finish up my high school stuff." She gave him an inquisitive look at that and he hurried to explain. "I was trying to figure out some things, too, like what to do with my life after my folks split up. My grades got in trouble and I ended up dropping out last spring. Couple of months back I moved up to Rapid to be with my dad. I don't like being around him much, but I'll still probably end up being a grease jockey just like him. Don't know much about doing anything else, I suppose."

He stared at the ceiling then looked back toward Maria. "Only I'm plannin' on being a lot nicer guy than that son-of-a-bitch," he added, a bitter tone to his voice. "You ever meet him?"

"Yeah, sorry," she said. "He definitely could be a piece of work to deal with. I had a couple of *arguments*"—she paused to hold up air quotes and put emphasis on the word—"with him myself. I don't think he thought my opinion was worth much, especially because I was a girl. But when it came to my baby . . . my car . . . I sure as hell knew what I wanted and what was needed, so it pissed me the hell off when he wouldn't listen!"

She stopped and burst into laughter as Frank leaned back in his chair as if trying to stay out of her line of fire. "I guess I get a bit passionate about things like that, especially when I know that I know a hell of a lot more about things than some people are willing to give me credit for.

"Plus my head's been pounding again from the bump I got earlier so I'm sure that's adding to my crankiness." She leaned back in her chair. "Sorry about that and about my 'happy' comments concerning your old man."

"Uh, well, I don't blame you," he said. "Guess I feel the same way whenever he gets on my case. It's like my opinion and what I know don't count for nothin'."

"Anything."

"Huh?"

"Sorry. It's my writing background again. I'm always wanting to correct the wrong use of a word, and instead of saying nothing it should be anything." He looked back with confusion and she waved her hand airily and grinned. "Never mind."

"Okay," he agreed but still seemed confused over what she had just said. He took a bite from a piece of bread he had buttered, placed it back on his plate and gave her an inquisitive look.

"You got a boyfriend, or someone you're dating?"

She hesitated as she thought about her earlier exchanges with Deputy Jim Dolan and then finally responded with a tentative, "No, not really." Now it was her turn to blush.

"No time for that, I suppose," she continued. "I don't think anyone around here would be much interested in me, anyway." She made a sweeping gesture around herself, and added, "You know. I'm kind of a Plain Jane."

Frank shook his head hard in disagreement. "Wow, are you off base on that one," he said, then stammered, "I-I mean, Plain Jane is the last thing I'd call you." He looked away, as if embarrassed by his own boldness, finally reaching out and grabbing his glass of water and gulping at it.

"Well . . ." she gave him a warm smile before continuing. "Thanks. Some people tell me I look a little like my Great Aunt Minnie, whatever that means? I suppose I'm never sure how I come across to folks. My Mom says I have 'defined features.' "

He stared across at her. "Does that mean pretty?"

"Hah! Sure." She chortled and blushed again at the same time. "I'm especially cute when I get bruises and bumps on my forehead and the black eye I'm bound to add to the mix by tomorrow or the next day. That run-in we had with those deer this morning is probably going to leave me worse for wear."

Chapter Twenty-Four

Frank finished eating, swiped at his plate with the last of his bread and moved his chair away from the table. Maria smiled. "Anything more I can get you?" She stood and took her plate then reached across for his.

"No, thanks. I'm fine. I appreciate everything."

She put the dishes into the sink and then walked over to the living room. "Sorry if I sounded a bit too authoritarian before." He looked confused. "You know, when I went off to get the clothes and had you getting your things cleaned up." She gestured toward a small makeshift clothesline where his clothing was drying over top of a wrought-iron heating grate. "I apologize for that."

She moved into the room and went directly to a linen closet at the beginning of the hallway leading down to the bedroom and bathroom. Taking out some sheets and blankets, she pointed at the couch. "We can make up the couch for you to sleep, if that's okay?"

"Yeah, for sure," he responded, moving on into the room and taking the sheets from her to start the process. "It's really great of you to do this."

"I'd want someone to do the same for me if I was ever in need."

They pulled the sheets into position on the couch and then tucked blankets in on one end. She walked down the hall and returned with a pillow in hand, tossing it on the other end.

"It's okay. I can sleep without one if that's a prob . . ."

"Don't be silly," she interrupted, puffing up the pillow as she spoke over her shoulder. "Hey, you want some ice cream and a piece of cake?"

"Ice cream!" He looked incredulous at her offer. "AND cake? Wow, sure. That would be amazing! Are you sure you're not rich?"

She walked out to the refrigerator as he excused himself to go back down to the bathroom. As she returned with the bowls of dessert he shuffled back to the living room. She could clearly see by the hollow look in his eyes that the events of the day were starting to wear on him.

"That rock pile your friend told you about. You told the Marshal you might have some ideas about it. What do you think Gene meant?" she asked as they started in on the dessert. "It had to be someplace you all knew, didn't it? Marshal Twocrow told me earlier that you don't really remember anything Gene called the rock pile?"

"No, but he must have," he responded, holding a spoonful of ice cream suspended above his bowl as he thought about it. "I told Elizabeth it might be up at the Pit—that's a gravel dugout place up between here and Hermosa where we used to go. It's over to the west a couple miles off Highway 79," he added quickly, noticing the confusion on her face. "We'd go out there swimming or just to hang out."

She nodded. "Sure. Makes sense. Nothing else comes to mind?"

Frank shook his head. "No. I don't think so. Liz and I went over all the possibilities but nothing seemed right." He sat absently stirring his spoon in the bowl then took another bite.

"Hadn't thought much about it before, but she wondered about the agate beds." He was half-shoveling part of the cake into his mouth as he spoke and the words came out sounding like "Ugut budz." Embarrassed by the muffled way he had said it, he swallowed before saying again, "Agate beds."

"You mean the agate fields out east of Fairburn?" she asked.

"Well, yeah, I guess. Fields, beds, whatever? And I'd say they're slightly northeast, not straight east. I always thought about them being more in a southeasterly direction from The Railway Café and the Sandman elevators where I found Gene's body."

Maria held out her hands with an "Okay, get on with it" expression and he gave her a sheepish grin in response.

"Anyway, Gene and I used to go out there to relax and kill time. But I think for him, they were kind of a primo hangout spot. I don't know? Maybe?"

He took another bite of cake as he thought further about it. "He'd go out there for a couple hours at a time, and then he'd drive over to meet me at The Railway Café after. Like I said; maybe." he scraped up the final spoonful of ice cream as he thought about it further. "Actually, it's possible he might've headed out there when he was on the run. There probably are several spots out there that would work to stash something you're trying to hide?"

"Like a big bag full of money?"

He smiled. "Sure, like a big bag full of money. What do you know about the agate fields?"

"Not much. I've just heard the stones are pretty cool."

"You've never seen a Fairburn agate?" Frank re-scraped his bowl to make sure he had the last of his dessert and then pointed his spoon toward her. "Hang on." He walked across the room to where he had put down his personal items. Pushing in among them, he pulled out a small smooth stone and walked back over to her.

"This is a Fairburn Agate." He extended a bright multi-colored rock in the palm of his hand for her inspection. "I've had this one since I was little. My mom gave it to me. For protection."

She stared at it with awe. "Wow, beautiful. It is like a rainbow rock, huh?" She took it from his hand and turned it over, then handed it back. "What do you mean she gave it to you for protection?"

"Well, an agate is supposed to protect young people from harm or evil spirits. It keeps them safe from harm. I believe it still keeps me safe."

She looked up at him with a questioning expression on her face. "Still? I thought you said it protects *young* people?"

"Hey, I'm still a kid at heart." Maria laughed and he continued. "Anyway, I just feel better keeping it close to me whenever I can." Then he shrugged. "You never know, do you?"

She grinned. "Sure, you never know."

He tossed the stone up in the air, caught it and then eyed it again. "What did you just call it? A rainbow rock?"

"What?"

"A rainbow rock? You called it a rainbow rock."

"Yes." She pointed at the rock. "That's how Marshal Twocrow described it to me. Because of those bands of colors. Like a little rainbow. Why?"

"I mean, now that you say that it reminds me that Gene said something about a rainbow when I first found him. He was trying to tell me what happened. Before he said rock pile, he said rainbow or rainbow something, I think. But he stopped because he was having trouble talking. After he started again, he called it rock pile and that's what stuck with me."

Frank's face lit up as he eyed the agate in the palm of his hand. "Maybe that's what he started trying to tell me. That it was over at the agate fields where he hid the bag. Maybe there's some sort of rock pile there at the agate fields—the rainbow rock fields. We should go out there and check?"

"Sure," Maria agreed, revved up herself by Frank's excited response.

"You know what?" Frank exclaimed, moving back to his little stack of things and putting the small stone back in among them. "I'm going to do it! I'm going to go check out the agate beds first thing tomorrow morning. Early. At dawn."

Maria gave him an incredulous look. "Tomorrow? At dawn? You gotta be kidding. In this weather? You'll freeze your ass off." He blanched at her harsh reaction, the enthusiasm in his face quickly dampening. "Sorry," she added, "but I really think you might. Especially if you go out there so early. WHY in the world would you want to go out there at dawn in the first week of February? That just seems crazy."

" 'Cause sunrise is the best time; to check something like this, I mean. The way the land is structured . . . by the agate beds especially . . . the morning sun backlights anything that is even close to being a rock formation, or a rock pile. In an area like that it just jumps out at you whenever you see something, especially when the sun's really low to the horizon, like it is right now. Shadows last longer.

"Going out there at dawn is good any time of the year, but especially in the winter. Trust me on that." He grabbed his empty bowl, walked over and picked up hers and carried both of them off toward the kitchen as he continued talking.

"When Gene was getting into all this stuff about connecting with the Great Spirit and learning more about how the Lakota People are linked to nature, he said we needed to go out to places like the agate fields. Or up to Wind Cave. He said that's so we could see how we're—The Lakota People—how we're part of the earth; part of the land," he said, pausing at the kitchen doorway.

"He was really into it. He said a member of his family used to be a medicine man—that's like a spirit leader and healer all rolled into one—and he thought that was really cool. That's why he wanted to learn about the old ways, too. To be like that relative. I think he thought someday he might be a medicine man.

"He swore he could hear the wind, the trees, even the rocks, all of those things, speaking to him. On top of that he was learning how to speak Lakota. He wanted to be part of everything that makes the Lakota people who we are." He leaned into the corner of the archway between the two rooms and stood looking at her as he spoke.

"Gene said it was always kind of cool to see how the light and shadows could make things stand out during different times of the day, whether it was out at the agate fields or up at Wind Cave park. But even the tiniest little places would be highlighted more at sunrise because that's when the Great Spirit emerges to look out on the Lakota People. That's why he said dawn would always be the best time."

"Did you ever go out there at dawn yourself to check it out?"

"One time, just to see if I could see what he was talking about. But, really, I'm not much of a morning person," he answered. "I guess I take after my Mom that way. She used to say that the best sunrise is one that is straight overhead when you wake up. Like at noon."

Maria laughed. "I can TOTALLY identify with your Mom about that."

"But like I said, I did go out there that one time really early. And I went with him at dawn up to the Wind Cave Park a couple times, too. So I could know what it was like when he was there. What he could see. He always had this faraway look in his eyes like it was just him and the land and I wasn't even there. Just him, the Great Spirit, and the land. So I quit going with him."

"Wow," Maria said. "Like I said earlier, he sounds like he was an amazing guy."

"Yeah, he really knew a lot. He was getting . . ." he paused as if trying to think of the right explanation and then shook his head and continued on toward the sink. "Actually, he was getting a little too much off the deep end for me."

Caught off guard by his matter-of-fact change of tone, she stared at him in disbelief before bursting into laughter. He turned back and grinned, joining in. His laugh was deep and melodic and Maria caught her breath at how nice it was to hear him laughing after how morose his voice had sounded earlier.

"But," he said as he made his way back into the living room. "If we're gonna solve this thing we gotta do it like Gene would do it. So, I'm guessing that he would go to someplace exactly like that to hide whatever it was that he found. It would be someplace where he felt it would be safe and secure."

She crossed her arms and hugged herself tightly, nodding as she thought about what he was saying. "And, whatever that place is, it's some place he called a rainbow rock or a rock pile. Or both," she said.

"So, going out there really early in the morning, do you think that sounds too crazy?" he asked, watching her reaction. "I just want to DO something. Otherwise I feel like I'm letting him down."

"No. No. Now that you explained it, it doesn't sound crazy at all. In fact, I think you might be on to something." She stood and walked over to the closet by the front door and looked inside as he went back across the living room and settled onto the couch. "How cold do you think it'll be out there? What do you need to wear to stay warm?"

"I dunno. Boots, scarves, a heavy sweater under my coat." He gave her a curious look as she continued to stare into the closet and then pulled out a pair of ankle high leather boots. "Why?"

"Must be the journalist in me again, but now you've got my curiosity up. So if you're locked into going out there, I think I need to go out there with you."

"You? Why? You sure you wanna do that?"

"Yeah," she said while still digging in the closet. "But you're going to have to drive. No way I'm taking my sweet baby out on those crummy dirt roads."

"Why do you call your car a sweet baby? I mean, isn't it just a car?"

She glared at him. "Good thing I'm over here or I'd slug you for saying something as stupid as that. If a guy can talk all day about his car's 'sweet' engine, why isn't it cool for me to call my entire car a sweet baby?"

He shrugged, started to say something and then thought better of it and just shrugged again.

She turned back to the closet and pulled out a heavy deep red quilted coat. Holding it out in front of her she swung it around toward him. "This ought to work for me, and we'll have to get a couple more things for you, too." As if to emphasize her resolve, she added, "And yes, I'm sure I want to go out there with you in the morning."

"Okay." He smiled. "Thanks!"

"I probably should let Marshal Twocrow know. Don't want him to be worried when we're not here first thing tomorrow."

He nodded. "Yeah, but wait until morning. Otherwise he'll just try talking us out of doing it."

"Yeah, probably. Anyway, it'll be an adventure." She laughed lightly and nodded as if reassuring herself. "So what time do we need to leave?"

"Well," he said gravely. "Before I tell you, maybe you better sit back down, because I don't think you're going to like what I have to say. Not even a little bit."

Chapter Twenty-Five

Wednesday, Feb. 2, 1955
4 a.m. - noon on the third day

Frank's old Plymouth coupe hit an across-the-road rut and bounced hard. Maria grabbed at the binoculars case she had brought along and pulled it tight against her body to prevent it from flying onto the floor.

"Criminy Frank, that's like the fifth time!" she groused. "I thought you said you knew this road?"

"Sorry." Frank grasped the steering wheel tighter and stared intently toward the dirt road on which they'd been driving. "I DO know the road, but I've never driven it in the dark before. It has more potholes and ruts than I remember."

"Really? Hard to believe!" she glared over at him. "How much farther?"

"There's a fence with a gate coming up. That'll be one of the spots where we can walk in. I'll let you out there and then drive down alongside the fence—maybe half-mile or so—and go in from a second gate down there. It's a little over a mile walk across to the middle of the agate fields . . ." he paused as she gave a small groan. "But it's a flat walk." He paused as if re-thinking that. "Well . . . pretty flat. It's really not that hard of a walk, although guess I've never tried it in winter."

She exhaled sharply as she swiveled on the seat and stared at him. "Be honest before we get out and freeze our butts off walking to God knows where. Would this be the way Gene would've driven to get back here? Think hard. Do you EVER remember him talking about a rock pile when the two of you were here?"

Frank started to respond then pointed ahead, "Hey, we're here." He flipped his lights up to bright, illuminating a triple strand barbed-wire fence and grunting in satisfaction. "There. See. That's the fence and gate I told you about," he said. "Knew it would be coming up soon."

He turned off the lights, pulled the gearshift to neutral and set the hand brake. A faint glow from the coming dawn was just fringing the far horizon.

After staring at it for a few more seconds, he turned off the motor and looked over at her. "Honestly? About Gene, I mean. I think there's a fifty-fifty chance that if he came out here that night, he might've driven down along the gravel road that runs over on the far side of the field instead of here," he said. "It's a bigger, wider road that turns south off Highway 44—and that's the main road coming out of the southeast side of Rapid City." He nodded back toward the road that they had just followed. "That would've been a lot easier for him to drive on instead of coming in on this dirt one, especially if he was hurt."

"Really? Then why didn't WE drive in on that road first?" She didn't care if the sarcasm in her voice came through loud and clear, but Frank seemed oblivious.

"Well, first of all, driving my car over to that road would've taken us a lot longer—just to get around to it," he answered. "Even though that east side road is a lot easier to navigate, it would've taken us another hour, at least, to get to where it begins since it doesn't connect up from the south or southwest side.

"With a pickup or truck you can take another dirt trail that's about seven or eight miles north of here to get across. That trail runs straight over from the Fairburn road to the main gravel on the other side. But with a car you first have to drive up north of Hermosa, and then head east on Spring Creek Road for about 20 miles. After that you can turn back south to where that eastside gravel road intersects and comes down off 44. The gravel over there is an easy road to get to when you're coming down from either the north or east, but it's hard as hell driving to it from the south or the west."

"Which is where we're at," she nodded. "So, since he was up in Rapid to start with, it probably would've been easier for him to reach than it is for us coming from down here. That's what you're thinking? But we might be on the wrong side, right?"

"Well . . . yeah, if he even came here. But I don't know for sure. I think he'd drive on whatever road was the most direct route for him at the time. But I'm sure he'd try to get to someplace he felt comfortable about or knew well. Like I told you last night, he loved coming out to this agate field. We came out here together quite a few times, and I know he would come out on his own. Plus he drove out a couple times with his sister, too. He just loved walking around out here."

He pointed out the window toward the three-strand wire gate. "Anyway, this would be our main spot to walk in from, because we always drove over from Hot Springs or came in from the north side access road into Fairburn if we were driving down from Rapid. We'd park right here by this barbed-wire gate and go walking around; sometimes for hours at a time."

"But you never heard about a rock pile? Never? I mean, what do you think that means?"

"Who knows?" He threw his hands wide. "I wish I knew for sure, but I don't. Maybe he found a stone formation out here and called it the rock pile. Maybe it's some kind of little cliff or a cave or maybe it's just a hole in the ground with a pile of rocks in front of it." His face was taut and his voice had risen about an octave.

"Geez, lady, I honest to God don't know!" he said with the sound of angry frustration filling his voice. "I'm going into this halfway blind, too, you know? I TOLD you that you didn't have to come out here with me. Coming along was your idea, you know, not mine!"

He turned away, opened the car door and then looked back and spoke again, this time a bit less emphatically. "But I'll tell you this, flat or hilly or whatever, I still think our best chance of spotting ANY kind of rock formation or rock pile out here will be just as the sun is coming up and backlighting it. Like I said before, that's why I wanted to come out here early in the morning and I'm sticking with that theory. Okay?"

Maria's features softened at Frank's exasperated response. Picking up the binoculars case, she slipped its strap over her head and pulled them onto her lap. Then she gave him a wry grin and patted his arm. "Okay. Okay?" She moved her hand to her left hip and side of her butt for emphasis.

"Both my butt and my aching head don't do so well on pot-holed roads at 5 in the morning, especially when I make myself get out of bed at 4 a.m. just to start the trip. Makes me grouchy, but that's on me and I should be the one to apologize." She grimaced. "Seems like I've been doing a lot of that lately."

"All right. Okay." He looked embarrassed. "And I'm sorry, too, for getting so pissed off. It wasn't called for."

"No, I don't blame you. I'd be pissed off at me too." She grinned, opened her door, and slid out, immediately shivering as the cold air hit her full in the face. Frank got out on the driver's side and she leaned toward him across the top of the car. "And please, please, please don't call me 'lady.' Call me Maria," she said. "You're not that much younger than me, and it seems weird when you call me lady. Sorry, but that seems like something you ought to be saying to my mother. I'll call you Frank and you call me Maria. That's gotta be our deal."

She stepped back, not giving him a chance to reply and rested a hand on the top edge of her still-open door. Then she pointed straight ahead toward the glow forming on the horizon. "All right, suppose we better get moving? 'Second star to the right and straight on 'til morning.' Right?"

"Huh?"

"You know, like out of Peter Pan?"

"Peter Pan?"

"The cartoon movie? Remember? When Wendy asks Peter how to get to Neverland."

"Sorry, never saw it," Frank answered. "What's Neverland?"

"You're kidd . . . Never mind," she sighed and shut her door. "Let's start over." He responded with a blank expression as she waved a hand in frustration. "So," she resumed, pointing again at the ever-growing sliver of light on the horizon, "I should just go through that gate and walk straight toward the sunrise. Right?"

"Yes," he agreed. "And like I said, I'll drive down along the fence line a little further to where there's a second little gate just before you reach the bottom edge of the fields. If Gene came out here, he would've gone in either this gate or that one for sure. There aren't any other good options. I can walk across from there. If I start at an angle along that southwest corner and go northeast I should meet up with you when we reach the heart of the main agate beds. From there we can walk back together on a path that's in-between and check out that route, too."

He started toward the gate and she trudged along behind, swaddled in her heavily padded red winter parka draped down over quilted pants to keep her legs warm. She pulled her wool scarf tighter around her neck and shivered again. "How's your forehead?" he asked.

"Still sore, but better. Lump's gone down," she replied. "And the cold actually seems to be helping it, too."

"Well, just sit down and rest if it starts to bother you. I'll find you if you do." He eyed her coat. "No way I can miss you wearing that thing."

"Hah! You're just wishing you had something this warm yourself. I think you're just jealous that I thought of it first." She headed over to where he had reached the fence.

"So, listen," he said as she moved up alongside him. "You're going to walk about a hundred yards or so across this open area in front of you before you reach a harder bare ground and then followed by a rocky area that leads into the edge of the agate beds." He pointed out ahead of them, but it was too dark yet for her to make out much of the landscape. "Just a bit further on from there, where the ground changes from flat to more rolling hills, that's the start of where you might see some special rock formations or rock outcroppings. Those are the things that Gene might've called a rock pile. So you'll have to look sharp."

"Don't worry, I always look sharp," this time she responded with a slightly wicked grin.

He eyed her array of heavy clothing again. "Yeah, sure, I guess. Actually you sort of look like a big fluffy red bird if you ask me."

"Well, at least I'll be keeping warm while you're definitely going to be freezing your butt off with that skimpy stuff you have on. You should've dressed warmer."

Ignoring her comment, he stopped short of the gate and turned back. "Like I said, it shouldn't be a hard walk, especially since we haven't had much snow. It'll just be cold."

"You really think we might find something?" Her voice was now partially muffled by the scarf that she'd pulled up to the middle of her face.

He cocked his head toward her as if trying to decipher what she was saying, then shrugged. "That's a definite 'Maybe.' It is kind of a long shot, I suppose. At least when we get done looking around here we'll know for sure that this ISN'T Gene's hiding spot, right?"

"Or that it IS," she responded, trying to lighten the tone of her voice and further cut into the tension that had developed between them. "Who knows, maybe we'll be able to start and stop our search right out here? We'll find Gene's so-called rock pile. Find a big bag of money. Case closed."

She looked back at the horizon where the glow of light was now turning an orangey red color. "Red Sky at morning, shepherds take warning," she chanted, pointing toward the reddish line along the horizon.

"Another Peter Pan thing?" he asked, looking toward the spot.

"What? No. Haven't you heard that old line: 'Red Sky at Morning, Shepherd Take Warning; Red Sky at Night, Shepherd's Delight'? Some people say 'Sailor' though, instead of Shepherd."

"Well, I guess I have now. Is that a silly cartoon saying like the other one or something real?"

"Ummm?" She paused to think about it. "I think it's something real because it has something to do with weather patterns and stuff like that.

"I think that If the morning sunrise is red or orange, it means there's a storm coming later in the day, and if it's a red or orangey sky at night—like when the sun is going down—that means it's going to clear off and be nice weather ahead. I'm not positive, but that's the old saying. Like I said, sailors use it too, but since they're out at sea they say sailors instead of shepherds. Helps them plan for what weather to expect."

She stepped past him, moved up to the fence and grabbed the gate-post. Pushing it toward the fence's anchor post, she grasped at the wire loop holding the two posts together and began wrestling the loop upward, trying to get it loose.

"O-kay . . . Sure. Shepherds take warning! Sailors too!" Frank called out as he joined her, reaching around and across the top of the fence and grasping the gatepost just under where Maria was holding it. He exhaled a little grunt as he pulled it toward himself while she pushed.

The wire holder gapped open and Maria pushed at it, sliding it upward and away from the fence post. The barbed-wire gate went slack in her hands and she let it drop onto the ground. "Tough to do," she said. "You think it's okay if we leave the gate open for now?" He contemplated her question and looked around. Seeing no cattle or horses anywhere, he nodded his okay.

"But if you do see any cattle or horses moving this direction, come right back and shut it. We don't need to deal with livestock getting in here and chewing up the sacred ground with their hooves."

Maria turned in a complete circle, studying the landscape as if expecting herds of cattle and horses to suddenly appear despite the bitter cold. Frank anxiously watched her reaction and reached back down to grab the gate post.

"Maybe we should just shut it," he said. "Better safe than sorry."

He stepped to one side and waited for her to go through before pulling it up tight and straining to re-hook it. She reached across the top wire and grasped his arm, helping him with the job.

Succeeding in getting it latched, he glanced at her hand on his arm and smiled. "Great teamwork, huh?"

"For sure," she responded. She rubbed her hand up further onto his arm, gave it a little pat and then turned and started walking. Frank leaned against the gate's anchor post watching her go. He started to turn toward his car but turned back instead and called out to her. "Hey . . . Maria? Did you remember to let Marshal Twocrow know we would be coming out here?"

She turned back. "Yeah. I mean, sort of. I thought it was a little too early to call him at his home, so I phoned the Dispatch Center down at the Cop Shop and asked them to leave him a message so he knows. They said they'd have it 'Prominently Displayed' for him when he comes in." Her words came out with a shiver in her voice and she hugged her arms across her chest as she talked, anxious to get moving again to help keep warm.

"Okay, yeah, that should work." Frank nodded. "All right. Good luck. See you in the center of the agate field. And Maria," he sounded solemn as he spoke. "Whatever you do, be careful."

Giving him a little wave and a smile of reassurance, she turned her back to him and resumed walking. He watched for thirty seconds to be sure she was headed in the proper direction, then looked around once more before doing a shiver of his own before hurrying back to start his car. Flashing the lights twice to signal he was heading out, he cranked the steering wheel right and shifted into low. Keeping the lights on low beam to focus on the grassland ahead of him, he drove alongside the fence line heading southeast toward the other gate.

At the sound of the car's movement, Maria turned to watch as it passed over a small hill and dipped down out of sight. She shivered again, flapped her arms back and forth for warmth and resumed walking, suddenly feeling very isolated.

Chapter Twenty-Six

Maria gazed out toward the horizon where the sliver of light was now forming into a bright streak and sucked in sharply as a gust of icy wind hit her exposed face, bringing tears to her eyes. She was grateful that the wind wasn't a steady breeze and that the temperature wasn't any colder. She pulled her scarf up higher to cover both her mouth and nose, leaving only her eyes and the bottom of her forehead exposed.

The thermometer outside her little house had read 15 degrees when she had left to join Frank after he'd gone out to get his car started for their drive out to Fairburn and the agate field. He had warned her that his car heater didn't work very well and once inside she realized that he wasn't just saying that. Aside from providing protection against the wind, the inside of his car wasn't that much warmer than it was in the outside air.

"I didn't know you drove a refrigerator," she chattered, snuggling further down into her heavy quilted coat and then pulling her hat down over her ears to try to keep them warm.

"Ha, ha, ha very funny." He looked embarrassed by her comment. She tried a smile to show she was just joking, but her teeth just chattered more at her action. "Sorry," he added, seeing her shaking. "I'm sure it'll warm up as soon as we get moving along. The heater's always slow to get fired up."

"At this time of day, me too," she said, finally getting a chuckle out of her companion. "Look, don't worry about it. I'll be fine. I just like to complain."

Several times he'd apologized further for the poor performance of his old car's heater, but she waved him off, especially after they had reached these rough backcountry roads. They were the last place she wanted to be driving her own sweet car, especially in the dark.

After rising at 4 a.m., they had gulped a quick breakfast and started out through Fall River Canyon en route to Highway 79. There had been hardly any traffic, which was lucky since Frank's car's engine struggled in the morning cold.

After turning north on the main highway they still hadn't met or passed a single car as they drove the dozen miles, or so, up to the gravel road that was the south Fairburn turnoff. From there, they had followed a fairly smooth graded gravel road to the east that had first led into the mostly abandoned "semi-ghost town" of Fairburn. After passing through the town, the road subsequently turned into the rougher dirt road that went east out of the town and on out to the agate fields.

*****

Earlier when they had reached Fairburn, it still had been almost completely dark. The tiny community had no corner streetlamps to illuminate either its streets or its eclectic mix of buildings that ranged in style from partially falling down old retail stores to a scattering of mostly abandoned clapboard houses and sheds.

Several of those old buildings had loomed from the shadows as they slowly drove into town after passing over a railroad track on the south-west side. Just across the tracks and to the north was a boarded up train depot. And directly in front of that now abandoned building Maria could make out a spur rail line that at one time might've served as a place for trains to pull over from the main line to stop. There, she thought, passengers either must have got on board or disembarked when the town was thriving as part of the rail line's regular route.

Just across the tracks on the east side was a large, warehouse-looking building that was partially falling down from neglect. A narrow dirt road led off toward it.

"Fairburn used to be a big timber shipping center and that was the place where they stored the logs before they were loaded onto flatcars," Frank had explained. "They haven't shipped anything from here for quite a while now. I heard they're trying to sell the building."

As they drove further into the heart of the town a couple of lights had finally greeted them. They were shining from what might've once been a fairly elegant hotel and dining room, probably built back in the days when that depot had still been in operation.

Located above the hotel's wide wooden front porch were two ornate, cast-iron light fixtures, each sheltering a large clear light bulb. Each of the bulbs emitted a glaring whitish light that overlapped with the light coming from the other one. Together they lit up a double entry—one side leading straight ahead into the "lodging" section of the building, the other turning left toward a door labeled "Dining Room."

A single, smaller wattage yellow bulb, this one projecting from above the back door and unprotected by any sort of fixture, was shining out beneath the sloping roof of a rickety back porch. She thought that it seemed to be a last-minute add-on to the two-story building. The bulb struggled to light both the porch below it and a brick pathway that led out toward a pair of outhouses at the far back corner of the hotel's yard.

Above and slightly in from the tiny porch, smoke wafted from a brick chimney, but there were no lights in any of the windows on either of the building's two floors.

"Nice 'accommodations,' huh?" Maria pointed toward the outhouses. "It would scare the crap out of me—no pun intended—to have to go out there to go to the bathroom in the middle of the night." She swung her arm back toward the main building, gesturing at the smoke. "But, somebody must be living in there. Either that or the town's 'ghosts' have taken up residence. Looks like somebody might've remade this old hotel into some kind of apartment building, doesn't it?"

"Not that many people actually live in Fairburn, you know? Maybe 40 or 50, if that," Frank answered. "They're scattered all around the town as far as I can tell, so there's probably SOMEONE living there, too."

A lightly graveled street in front of the hotel appeared to have been the community's Main Street at one time. Directly across from the hotel stood a badly weathered "general" store. Its two side-by-side centrally located doorways seemed to indicate that it had now been sub-divided into two living spaces inside. Like the hotel, this building also had smoke coming from a small brick chimney, this one centered halfway back between the two sides.

"That looks like a building right off the Main Street set from 'High Noon'," she said with a laugh, referencing the hit movie that was finally being shown in the Hot Springs' Theatre, the town's entertainment mecca.

Maria followed her short laugh with an exclamation of surprise, pointing off toward the far side of the ramshackle building to where the front end of a fairly wide mobile home occupied the darkened adjacent lot. "Wow, look at that! The ghosts in that one are living pretty high off the hog." Frank gave a noncommittal shrug in response.

"I mean, *Really* high off the hog," she added with emphasis in her voice, trying to impress her companion with what she was saying. "That trailer is one of those new Pacemaker Tri-Levels. I was reading about how they're all the rage down south for people who drive down there to spend the winter months. You know, the folks they call Snowbirds? Somebody in this old town seems to be doing A-Okay money-wise to live in a ritzy trailer like that."

She pointed to the right side of the trailer where a newer dark-colored pickup truck was parked. The pickup's box was fitted all the way around with a split-rail siding box. "And driving an expensive pickup truck too."

"I guess," Frank answered, glancing past her. He stopped, then pulled through the intersection and took a longer look back across Maria's body through her window. "Sorry," he said as she shifted further back in her seat in order to give him a better view. "That pickup looks familiar, but I'm not sure why."

"So you weren't just using that old, 'Oh, I didn't stop in time so I have to look back across your body' ploy as a way to check out my boobs, huh?" She chuckled.

"What?" His blush was visible even in the semi-darkness and in spite of his dark skin. "No! No, I-I wouldn't . . ."

She punched him lightly on the shoulder. "Geez, relax; I'm just teasing you. I couldn't resist. Lighten up, will ya?" She grinned and tapped him again before pointing back through her window. "So you think you might've seen that pickup truck before?" She glanced his way and he was still looking straight ahead, his hands clamped tightly on the steering wheel. "Frank!" He glanced at her. "Look across my body through the window. Don't be an idiot!"

Still red in the face, Frank nodded, trying to regain his composure as he carefully leaned forward to look past her body. "Yeah, but I probably saw it over in Hot Springs or someplace nearby," he finally said, gesturing with a circular wave of his right hand. "And I don't know who might live in that fancy trailer? Maybe one of the regular residents just wanted an upgrade from trying to live in whatever ones of these old houses and stores are still standing. Can't blame him, right?"

She nodded back at the battered storefront. "Yeah probably. With the smoke coming from the chimney it definitely looks like somebody is either making a home inside that old store or using it for something else. It's not abandoned, that's for sure." She pointed past the Pacemaker along the darkened street out toward where the outlines of a couple more buildings indicated that this Main Street of the community continued further to the south. "Do you know what's down in that direction?"

"Sure. That's the French Creek edge of town," Frank answered. "And there's just a few more old houses down there if I remember right. But I don't know if people are living in any of them or not. That's the main reason why it's called a 'semi' ghost town, 'cause it's mostly empty of people. At least those who are still alive." Now it was his turn to chuckle as she grimaced at the thought.

He reached another intersection and turned north. "I've heard that Fairburn was a booming place back 50 or 60 years ago—1890s, early 1900s. I think they thought there might be gold or silver around in these mesas or over in the southern hills. Or maybe even in French Creek itself. That's where they 'officially' discovered gold in the Black Hills, you know?" Not waiting for an affirmation, he added, "There's an old abandoned mine just out to the west of here too. We drove right past it when we came into town. It's on the back side of that hill where we passed the depot. I don't know if I'd want to go in there, though. Probably full of snakes hibernating for the winter."

Maria shuddered at the image of a bunch of hibernating snakes and scrunched tighter against the car seat. One thing she truly hated was snakes, especially the poisonous prairie rattlers and big bull snakes that populated this region.

"Even back when the railroad stopped here, 15 or 20 years ago, I heard it was a good place to spend a few days if you wanted to tour around in the southern Black Hills," Frank continued. "If you drive back south on Highway 79 a few miles toward Buffalo Gap, you can take the 7-11 road—you might'a heard it called the 'Gap' road—over toward the Red Canyon. From there you can head on up to the east entrance to Wind Cave Park. Even though it's just a gravel road, people still do take it 'cause it's kind of a cool drive. There's a couple'a big ranches and lots of horses out that way, too, including at least one herd of wild horses that have been around these parts for more'n 75 years."

They reached another crossroads, turned north and passed a brightly painted white wooden schoolhouse that seemed to be defining the northeast boundary of the town. Just outside of the town's limits they came to a Y in the road, marked with a large wooden sign in the intersection. Inside the top part of the sign an arrow pointed northwest toward a gravel road and reading "Highway 79."

The bottom half of the sign's space was marked with a second arrow pointing northeast toward a mixed gravel and dirt road and labeled "Fairburn Agate Fields." Frank had taken the northeast fork and followed the road as it dipped down into a little gully and then gradually headed uphill for just over a mile before reaching a second "Agate Fields" sign. That one was at the entrance to the all-dirt, pot-holed and mostly frozen road that they had followed for another dozen miles before arriving at their entry location.

Chapter Twenty-Seven

"Okay," Maria said aloud to herself as she puffed ahead. "Even if we don't find any 'rock piles' out here, it still should be an interesting walk. And I can write about it when I do my story on the agate fields," she added, giving herself a verbal pat on the back for having yet another good idea.

She looked over to see Frank's car lights reappear moving southeast away from her along the fence line. Then, swinging her arms back-and-forth again to increase her circulation she resumed her movement out across the shadowy grassland. Her breath was now clearly visible in the cold dawn's growing light.

With sunrise fast approaching, she figured the temperature might be all the way up in the low 20s by now. Luckily, not much snow. She gritted her teeth and pulled her scarf tighter around her throat and chin, checking to make sure all the buttons on her wool coat were still fastened.

While the plaid Soo Wool hunting pants she'd borrowed from her neighbor were keeping her upper legs warm, she was regretting her decision to go with style over substance for a covering over her ankles and feet. She had recently bought a pair of Red Wing Tuffys—a high ankle leather shoe-boot into which tapered pant legs could be tucked. They were rugged but not all that warm, at least not the way she was wearing them.

The boots together with these particular pants didn't fit together quite right for the "tuck-in" process, so now there was an area of slightly exposed skin between the tops of her wool socks and the bottom of the pant legs. Her boots might look stylish, she thought, but she felt like her feet and ankles were turning to ice. "Oh well," she said aloud while suddenly longing for the old pair of fur-lined snow boots she'd left sitting by her front door because she thought they'd be way too clunky for an excursion such as this.

She stopped and rapidly jumped up-and-down again. Pulling her gloves off, she loosened the boot's laces and tried re-tucking the pant legs into them. With her fingers quickly turning numb, she re-tied the laces tighter and hurried to get her fingers re-covered with her gloves. "Mmmm, that's better." She was pleased by the sudden warmth created from both her jumping action and the "sealing off" she'd created by tightening the laces. Little things to be grateful for, she thought.

"Okay," she said aloud, double checking her gloves. She jumped a few more times and moved forward at a faster pace. No sign of any "rock pile" as far as she could see, but then she wasn't sure she was even at the actual agate field yet. After she met up with Frank again, she'd convince him to walk back closer to the path she was taking so they could take a second look, especially if he didn't find anything on his own trail. So far, if there were supposed to be any special rock formations or "rock piles" around, she hadn't seen any sign of them. It was just mostly flat, partially snow-covered ground interspersed with clumps of spiny yucca plants.

One of those yucca spines stabbed into her left leg, and she dodged to her right to avoid it. "Ow! What the fu . . .!" The force of her movement away from the yucca's spines had carried her straight into something else in the process. Something even sharper and way more solid. A searing pain coursed through her right leg and she hopped to her left and grasped at it.

"Geez Louise!" she half-sobbed. "Damn it!" Tears came to her eyes and she sank down onto her left knee and grabbed at her lower right leg, keeping it stretched out before her. She had definitely collided with something hard and sharp in the semi-darkness, but she wasn't sure what it could be. Whatever it was it wasn't a rock outcropping because she had felt it move slightly when she ran into it.

She turned back toward the offending object where the growing brightness from the coming sunrise answered her question. A nondescript, close-to-the-ground, hard-edged metal sign with a hand-painted arrow pointing east greeted her gaze. It simply read: "Agate Field." Maria rubbed at her shin and pulled up her pant leg to check the damage. The pain was coming from a nasty looking, bloody gouge about an inch long and half-inch deep.

"Damn, damn, damnit! Ow!" she said again as the exposure to the cold air added to her discomfort. She reached out and scooped up a handful of the dusty snow and rubbed it onto the wound, inhaling sharply at the combination of cold and pain. Glaring at the offending sign, she pushed the pant leg back into position inside her boot top, stood up and resumed walking, now limping a bit from the collision.

At least she now knew she was headed in the right direction. She turned back toward the sign. "Thanks for the directions!" she called toward it, and gave it the finger as her leg continued to throb.

Hobbling along on a 20-degree decline for about another hundred yards, she reached a short flat stretch and started climbing up on a smaller hill she hadn't even seen from her previous position. This landscape was deceiving. Where it had first appeared to be stretched out flat, she could now make out a series of low mesas, interspersed with ditch-like rises and falls just like the one that she had just crossed.

She reached the top of her next short climb, then stopped and gasped at the rugged beauty of the landscape stretching out before her. Maria stared in awe at the geographic features unfolding before her as the daylight gradually increased with the top edge of the rising sun. What had been just a shadowy expanse before was now turning into a series of hills and dales that undulated around her and out toward the horizon.

Suddenly, the top curve of the sun popped up inside the reddish glow, peeking out over the broad flat hilltops ahead of her. Only just barely above the tops of the hills, it appeared to be pushing up against the bottom edge of a bumpy line of dark clouds that were running from south to north parallel to the ground below them.

As the sunlight's intensity continued to grow, changing from red to yellow, she saw that the white ground in front of her wasn't caused by snow cover. Instead, it was mostly created from a permanent white coating. It was on much of the open ground as well as on large parts of the surrounding whitish-gray mesas.

Interspersed between those mesas were dozens of shiny, mostly foliage-free and extremely white mounds, reminding her of the tops of ice cream sundaes, but minus any toppings. The mounds were dotting much of the open land that stretched out between her and the slowly rising sun.

"Oh my goodness!" she reverently whispered at the beauty of the scene. "Oh my!" If she could imagine what it might look like walking around on the moon, she thought, this might have been it.

The mounds appeared to start about seventy to a hundred yards ahead of her before stretching out from west to east in clusters of 8 to 10. Scattered in between them were small clumps of bedraggled dried grasses and more yucca plants stabbing sharply upward through whatever ground was veneered by any the small skiffs of new-fallen snow. But, still no "rock piles" or formations of any kind.

"Well would you look at that," she muttered at a sudden movement interrupting the tranquil scene. About two hundred yards out and munching peacefully on some of those grassy patches were three young mule deer. Could these be the same trio she and Marshal Twocrow had nearly collided with on the road outside of Fairburn the day before? She absently touched at her forehead in reaction.

Dropping onto her left knee while keeping her injured leg up as a sort-of shelf, she snapped open her binoculars case and retrieved the glasses. Easing them slowly toward her face, she pulled her right-hand glove off with her teeth and slipped the glasses' strap around her neck. Balancing her arms on top of her right leg, she focused on the three deer.

She watched as snow puffed up, swirled and resettled as a sudden gust of wind whipped between the first two sets of the white-topped mounds. The disturbance seemed to turn the deer into statues as they jerked their heads upright in unison to stare in her direction. Appearing satisfied that it was only the wind, the one closest to her resumed eating before a faint low growling noise interrupted. The young buck's head popped back up, returning him to full alert. Then, as if on cue, all three animals turned, leaped to the south and bounded off into a small arroyo that pushed up against the largest of the white buttes on the south end of the field.

Maria swiveled the binoculars to follow the animals' flight, re-focusing on the area toward where they were running. As all three dropped out of sight behind a second small rise, she was startled to see the figure of someone cresting the same rise and advancing along its far side just below the mesa's flat top. He appeared to be walking steadily in her direction.

Re-balancing her right arm on top of her right knee, Maria kept the binoculars trained on the man who had appeared on the horizon. He looked familiar, but why? She pulled the glasses down toward her chest. "Maria, don't be an idiot," she said aloud. "That's got to be Frank."

She breathed a sigh of relief as she said his name then scrunched up her face. She looked again. "Doesn't it?" she asked aloud as she continued watching him walk. Maybe this guy was too heavy to be Frank, but then again who else would be out here walking around so early on a cold winter morning?

She started to stand to wave toward him, but thought better of it and sank back down, a nagging doubt forming in her mind. She pulled the binoculars up a third time and re-focused once more, studying the figure as it steadily climbed to reach the flat surface of the mesa. Now she wasn't nearly so sure that it had to be Frank. Not only was he walking from the wrong direction and closer he looked taller and much heavier.

She watched as the figure moved slowly across the top of the flat rise and turned around and stood staring away from her toward the east. Why did he look so familiar?

The growling noise coming from the man's direction seemed to grow louder. What was that anyway? She swung her gaze there and pulled up the binoculars again, this time focusing back toward where the sun had both continued to rise and—at the same time—disappear behind the horizontal line of clouds. With the sound attached it was almost like an unseen engine had been started and was being used to raise the sun up to the point where those clouds had formed. And from there, the engine was continuing to pull the sun back up behind them.

She shaded her eyes against the glare until the bottom of the yellow orb disappeared completely behind the cloud line. Now, she was positive that the growling sound had turned into the sound of an engine. She edged her way several feet back down the slope to her rear in order to decrease her body image, knelt again and cupped both hands around her eyes, letting the binoculars hang free beneath her chin.

Within seconds an image popped up between the horizon and the bottom layer of the clouds. Flying directly toward her from the spot where the sun had disappeared was a single engine airplane. She looked back toward the person standing on the hilltop and watched as he raised a large red flag and waved it back and forth in the plane's direction.

"What the hell? What's that all about?" She muttered the questions to herself as she flipped the binoculars over to her back and flattened her body closer to the ground. She skittered to her left to take advantage of a bit of shelter provided by a small rock overhang and pulled the binoculars back around to take another look. Continuing to watch the horizon, she did a quick focus straight out toward the bottom of the next mesa before slowly elevating the binoculars until she had the plane fully in view.

As far as she could see the sleek plane with subdued red and white colors, had no markings except for a tail number. That ruled out either military, law enforcement or other government agencies, she thought. She adjusted the glasses slightly and used her free hand to scratch the tail number into a patch of dust-covered snow at her side. N-1213-B. Might be just a local rancher out checking his stock, although from everything she'd learned since moving here, that didn't usually happen at dawn. Especially in the dead of winter. Besides, why would someone on the ground be signaling toward it?

The pilot maintained the plane's course on a direct line toward the man on the mesa, seemingly unaware of Maria's presence. If the plane stayed on that track it would soon pass the flag man and continue heading toward her. She'd have to hide. She pushed the glasses back into their case and hunkered down even closer to the rocks, trying to make herself as small as possible as the plane's engine noise grew steadily louder. Now she wished she wasn't wearing the bright red coat, no matter how warm it might be.

The plane passed the first mesa over which she had been watching the sunrise, and the man with the red flag suddenly swung it wildly and angled it to the north. As if on cue, the plane banked off to the north, made a wide loop and started heading back in the direction from which it had come. In less than a minute it had disappeared again below the horizon as the engine's noise steadily softened and then returned to the same low growl she had heard before.

"That's too weird," she muttered, getting back onto her left knee and crabwalking to the top of her own small hilltop. She was hoping to catch a glimpse of where the plane might've gone and also get another look at the man with the flag. She stopped with an audible gasp. "Where?" She asked aloud. Just like that, the man had disappeared.

Chapter Twenty-Eight

Groaning at the reminder of the pain in her right leg, now renewed by her crabwalking maneuver, Maria struggled back up onto her feet. Moving stiffly she walked over and climbed on top of the rocks in front of the spot where she had been hiding. Gaining several feet of elevation, she pulled out the glasses once again and scanned the eastern horizon, slowly sweeping from north to south. Nothing. It was if the plane and the flag man had both dropped off the face of the earth.

"What kind of shit is going on out here?" she asked aloud, not caring who or what heard her or might object to her swearing.

She pulled the glasses back up and looked again, this time emitting a loud yelp of surprise as she swung around to the southeast and clearly saw Frank's image filling up her view. He was standing atop the mesa near where she thought the plane had made its last sharp turn. She took a few steps gingerly toward him, and spotting her, he gave her a little wave.

Maria waved in return and decided to wait where she was until he arrived. Her leg was hurting more than it had before and seemed to be stiffer. But maybe if she moved around a bit it would loosen up? She took another couple steps, grimaced and stopped. She probably hadn't done herself any favors by crawling up and down on that hillside, she thought as she waved again.

Frank increased his own pace and half-jogged down the mesa toward her, picking up his speed even further when he saw that she was favoring her leg.

"Hey!" she greeted him with both a shout and yet another wave and he reciprocated while pointing toward the leg where a red stain from the wound had now appeared.

"Hey yourself. What happened? Why you limping?"

"Collided with the wrong part of a metal sign," she shrugged as he gave her a quizzical look. "Don't worry, I'll be okay, just a little gouge above my ankle. There were like two places on that sign that I could hit to make a hole in my leg, so naturally I ran directly into one of them. Story of my life." She shrugged again and pointed toward the northeast. "You see that plane?"

"Yeah. It's some sort of Piper airplane. Super Cub, I think. I saw one out at the Hot Springs airport last fall. They're pretty cool."

"And he was getting signals from that guy with the flag?"

"Huh? What guy with the flag?"

"Oh come on! You must've seen him? On that hill near where you just came across? Some big guy was up there with a red flag like he was signaling to that plane. You know, like he was directing him somewhere."

She waved her arms back and forth as if that would help clarify her explanation. "He swung the flag and then pointed it there." She pointed toward an area northeast of where the plane had disappeared. "And the pilot must've been watching him because the plane made a sharp turn in that direction and then went back around and down." She took a couple steps that way and pointed again. "Kind of there."

"Yeah, I saw the plane turn, but I didn't see why it turned." He pointed at the letters and numbers—N-1213-B—that she had scratched into the skiff of snow just off the top of the ridge. "What're those letters and numbers? Did you do them too?"

"Yeah," she nodded. "It's the tail number on that airplane."

"Tail number? What's that?"

"It's kind of a fingerprint or serial number for a plane," she answered, pulling her ever-present notepad out of the inside pocket of her coat and quickly scratching the numbers onto it. She had meant to do that before and this was her chance. She rebuttoned her coat, moved forward and swiped the writing off the ground with the toe of her boot. "Every plane has its own number and you can track it that way if you need to." She shrugged. "I dunno if it'll be something we need, but you never know."

"Okay, sure?" he seemed less than convinced but not in the mood to question her further. He held out his hand and pointed at the binoculars hanging around her neck. "Okay if I take a look through your BI-nocs?" He accented the first syllable as the word "buy."

She slipped them off and handed them over to him. He fiddled with them and focused out in the direction she had indicated earlier. "I don't see anything except the hillsides," he said after several more seconds of the process. "Maybe it was a local rancher's plane. He could be landing on any of those flat grassy areas out over near the Cheyenne River. One of the ranches by Red Shirt has a private strip. Or, I suppose he could be heading on up to the Prairie City airport. But a guy with a red flag is a little weird."

"Prairie City? You mean like the place where all those cops supposedly are from? The ones that said they 'found' your friend's body and then came down to Hot Springs yesterday?"

"Um, yeah, I guess." Frank stopped talking as he thought further about that. "As a matter of fact, exactly like that." He pulled the binoculars back up and re-scanned the horizon, this time looking more toward the spot where the sun had risen before disappearing behind the clouds.

"See anything?"

"Naw, just . . . wait a sec." He moved his fingers slowly to fine tune the focus and exhaled sharply. He handed the glasses back over to Maria. "Right there. Look." He pointed and she zoomed in on the spot. "Can you see anything or am I imagining a pickup truck?"

"Not sure. Definitely something kicking up a little dust. Hey! You're right. I think it IS a pickup. Kind of looks like that one we saw earlier in Fairburn. It's got that cool split rail siding around the back. Same color too."

He frowned. "How do you know that? It was too dark to see the color when we came through town."

"Well . . . it seems the same," she said firmly trying to reinforce her statement. She bent down on her good left knee and once again propped her arm on the shelf created by the top of her right thigh, focusing with her right hand as closely as she could to follow the pickup as it slowly climbed up to the top of the hill. Suddenly, the vehicle dropped down out of sight. "Damn it!" She swore at losing sight of it. But before she could complain further, the small truck came up again, now moving south to north along the horizon.

Dust swirled around it briefly as it came to a stop and a man got out and walked around to the back. Grabbing onto the wooden siding he quickly pulled himself up into the back. He stood there holding something up to his ear as if having a conversation, and then bent down and stood up again holding the same red flag Maria had seen earlier. She kept the glasses trained on him as he rapidly waved the flag back-and-forth. As if on cue the red and white plane reappeared, now flying on a south to north line that was taking it directly over the truck.

"Here, look!" she said excitedly, passing the binoculars back to Frank, who dropped onto his belly and used both arms to stabilize himself as he re-focused the glasses for his own eyes. "Can you see him?" Maria edged forward alongside him and put a hand on his back. "He's waving that red flag I told you about and . . ."

"Yeah, yeah, I got him. I see him now," Frank interrupted. He moved the glasses to follow the plane as it passed over the pickup and dropped over the northeast horizon, then disappeared. Swinging the binoculars back around to refocus on the pickup truck, he watched as the man standing there put down the flag, turned and started to climb down. Frank gasped. "Holy crap. It's . . .!"

"What? What . . . who do you see? Who is it?" She interrupted and held out a hand for the glasses.

Frank lowered the binoculars and held himself on his right elbow as he handed them back up to her. "That guy and that truck. Now that I can see it clearer, I'm pretty sure it's the same pickup truck I saw up by the Sandman Elevators two nights ago, and I'd bet anything he's the same guy who was shooting at me up there, too." He gave Maria an urgent look. "And even if that's not him or his truck, he's definitely the same guy who was with that Prairie City cop yesterday. That's the guy that I told you about by the Vesta Café. He was in Hot Springs yesterday."

Maria focused in on the man and made a little gasp of recognition of her own. "Yes, you're right. That's definitely the same guy. I saw him yesterday, too," she said in explanation as Frank gave her a quizzical look. "He WAS with the Prairie City policeman and they were talking to Marshal Twocrow when I went down to the Cop Shop in the morning. I'd recognize that patch of bright white hair anywhere."

She watched as the big man picked up the device he had been talking into before and seemed to be talking again. "He's got a walkie-talkie or some kind of two-way radio," she said. "He's talking to somebody. Maybe the pilot of the plane." The man waved an arm in their general direction and turned, hooking the walkie-talkie onto the top of his coat before climbing out of the back of the truck. He stood facing them and Maria exhaled sharply. "Oh my god! I think he might've seen us. He said something into the walkie-talkie and now he's looking right at us."

She ducked down and pulled at Frank's arm to join her as the man appeared to be moving a few steps toward them while continuing to stare off in their direction. "Do you think he can see us?"

Frank held out his hand for the glasses again and slid down around the edge of the rock outcropping for a quick look. "I dunno. Maybe? It's hard to say." He watched as the man moved quickly toward the cab of his truck, reached in and took something out. The man turned back around and pulled up a pair of binoculars of his own, this time definitely looking right at them. After about 30 seconds, he put the binoculars back inside his pickup's cab and once again unhooked the walkie-talkie from his coat.

"Now he's got some binocs, too! And he's talking to somebody again." Frank scrunched down next to Maria and tugged at her to wiggle backward down the little knoll on which they had been sitting. "Come on! We gotta get back to the main gate and head out of here." He gave Maria a long look. "Your coat's kinda hard to miss, though. Pretty bright. It's possible he might've seen that." He shrugged. "Hopefully, even if he saw us, he didn't have time to get a good enough look before we moved to figure out who we are."

"You think he's worried about us seeing him?" she asked.

"Yeah, I do," he replied. "I'm sure he's trying to figure out WHO it is that's been watching him doing whatever the hell it is that he's been trying to do."

Chapter Twenty-Nine

Prairie City's streets were just starting to come to life on the bright but cold winter morning when Police Chief Al Tollefson wheeled his new police cruiser past the town's Main Street and Clover Avenue intersection and up to his usual parking spot in front of the police station.

"Morning Chief," one of his deputies came out the door, pulling on his gloves as he walked. "Glad you're here, 'cause Hillman's on the horn and he said he was gonna hold until you arrived. Must be something urgent."

"Thanks Ralph." He tapped the brim of his hat and hurried inside.

"Oh, Chief!" Pauletta Zachman, his front desk manager greeted him with both urgency and relief in her voice. "Batch is . . ."

"Yeah, Ralph caught me outside. So I know. Send the call through to my office." He gave her a beleaguered smile and hurried into his office, firmly closing the door and grabbing for the phone without taking off his coat. "Batch? What's going on? Why you calling?"

"We might have a problem down at Fairburn," Hillman began, skipping even a "hello" as he replied. "Pete just radioed me that there were a couple people across the agate field who he thinks spotted him directing the plane down my way. He took a look at them through his binocs, and while he couldn't be positive, he thought one of them was a girl reporter he and I met yesterday in Hot Springs.

"He's driving around to that northside gravel crossing so he can try'n get ahead of where they might have to drive out to get to the main road. But he's not sure if he can get over there before they do since he has to go about 10 miles north before he can cut over." He paused. "Might be nothin' but he said he was pretty sure it was the same girl we met yesterday, and she was watching him through some binoculars of her own. That doesn't sound so good. What d'ya think?"

Tollefson moved around the desk to his chair and sank down while undoing his coat's top button and exhaling slowly. "What do I think? I think why in hell were you talking to a Hot Springs newspaper reporter in the first place?"

"We weren't. I mean, in the first place. She showed up when we were talking to that Marshal out front of the Hot Springs P D, and she just started asking a lot of questions, that's all. We didn't hang around after that, but we did meet her, so it's possible she could've recognized Pete."

The chief gave a noncommittal grunt in response before continuing. "And why do you think she'd be out there so early?" Before Batch could answer, he added, "You said there were a couple of people out there. Any idea who might've been with her?"

"Might'a been an Indian?"

"What?"

"Yeah. Delaney said it looked like a young guy and he was pretty sure he was Indian. If so, that might be one of Darveaux's friends or maybe even a relative of his."

"Shit! It might even be THE Indian friend of Darveaux's, that Silver Shore character. What the hell would he be doing out there and why bring a reporter? That doesn't make any sense unless . . ."

He paused and Hillman filled in the silence. "Unless what?"

"Did either you or Pete tell anyone that you were going to be taking the shipment down to Fairburn once you got it the other night? Did you say something in front of Darveaux?"

The silence in response was almost deafening and Tollefson nearly exploded out of the desk with the phone clamped tightly against his head. "You dumb shits! If you said something to Darveaux that would've tipped him off, he could'a told Silver Shore about it before he died. Goddamnit all to hell!"

"Listen, Sarge, I don't think we said anything. Maybe the girl and the Indian were just out there, you know? Hiking or something . . . maybe?"

"Just OUT THERE hiking or something at dawn on a freezing cold morning. Sure, that makes so much fuckin' sense, don't it," he paused. "How close is the plane to you?"

"Not far, probably halfway, but . . ."

"Just get on the horn to them and tell them we need them to loop back and scare the beejeezus out of whoever the hell is out there. Across from where they saw the guy with the flag. Tell 'em we need 'em to buzz them; even take a couple shots at them if they have too. Do whatever it takes to keep them from leaving the area for a while longer and give Pete some more time to get over there to cut them off."

"Sure boss . . ."

"Now! Goddammit, do it now!" he shouted. There was a rap at the door and then it was pushed open. Pauletta leaned in, a concerned look on her face.

"Everything okay in here Chief?"

He clapped his palm over the phone and waved her away. "No! But it's not anything you or anyone here did. Just Stupid Ass Batch screwing things up again! Sorry." He waved for her to go on back to her desk. "Don't worry, I'll take care of it."

She nodded and gently re-shut the door, almost as if she were afraid that closing it too hard would re-start the police chief's tirade.

"Now, listen, get your ass in gear and get on this Batch," he hissed into the receiver. "Get your ass on up to Fairburn and help Pete take care of whatever this damn mess is that the two of you have gotten yourselves into! And don't let that reporter and that kid, or whoever the hell it is, get back to Hot Springs. Whatever you do, you stop them. You got that?

"I'm tired of worrying about some Indian kid screwing up our whole operation. So whatever you need to do to get this taken care of, you do it. And I mean whatever. You understand?"

"Yes," Batch's response was an almost whisper, his voice hoarse with fear. "But what about the plane, Boss? Once they come back this way, whose gonna land them and get the drugs?"

"All right, wait there to get the plane landed and off-loaded into Fitz's storage shed. Once you pay the pilot, get your ass down to Fairburn. I'll come out and pick up the shipment and meet you there later."

"Okay," Hillman answered.

"You THINK you can handle your end of that plan okay"

Seeming to miss the sarcasm in Tollefson's voice, Hillman responded with a brighter tone to his own voice. "Don't worry boss, I've got it. We'll take care of it. We won't let you down. They won't get out of Fairburn." Hillman hung up and Tollefson glared at the phone before dropping the receiver back onto the phone cradle.

"You dumb bastard," the Police Chief muttered. "For your sake, you better hope like hell that they don't."

Chapter Thirty

"We have to get back into Hot Springs and get in touch with the Marshal," Maria said. "Tell him what we saw. You jog over to get your car and I'll walk back on the route I followed coming in here and meet you by that gate."

"You sure you want to walk alone?"

"Positive. You can pick me up at the gate so we don't waste any time getting started back into town. Besides," she added quickly, "I need to find a place to go pee, and I really don't want you around while I'm doing that, okay?"

"Yeah, uh, that definitely would be for the best," Frank agreed, his face turning a deep crimson with embarrassment. "I'm sure there are lots of spots behind some of those bigger yucca plants up ahead, and I promise not to look. Plus," he added trying to get the subject changed, "it will be a shorter walk for you, especially since you're dealing with that bum leg." He waved. "I'll see you at the main gate."

He started off at an angle to the southwest. "Oh!" he exclaimed and turned back. "I forgot to ask, did you see anything that might've looked like it could be a rock pile? Any type of formation at all?"

"No, not a thing. You?"

He shook his head as he walked back toward her. "You know, while I was walking, I was thinking more about it, and it just doesn't seem like Gene would've come all the way down here before going back up to where I found him. Especially in the shape he was in. That just doesn't make much sense. I'm betting that he stopped somewhere north of here, probably a lot closer to the Railway Café and Sandman complex. I think we probably wasted our time looking around here. Sorry. I guess coming out here was a stupid idea in the first place."

"No it wasn't! Really." she moved closer toward him until they were standing face-to-face. "And he didn't say he had hidden it that night, did he? Maybe it was something he hid before he got into all that trouble. So checking all these possible hiding spots is still a good idea.

"And, listen, if we hadn't come out here this morning we wouldn't have seen that guy or that plane. It seems to me like they both might have something to do with your friend's death. So, while we may not have found whatever it was Gene hid by his so-called rock pile, we did see something strange going on that we can talk to the Marshal about when we get back into town. Right?"

She gave him a firm nod of reassurance. "And that really might help him with his investigation." She laid her hand along the top of his arm and gave him a second reassuring nod while adding a sympathetic look in the process.

"Yeah, well, okay," he said. "Hope so . . ." he hung his head slightly and let his response trail off. Maria suddenly moved her arm around him and gave him an intense hug. Frank seemed startled by her reaction. He took half a step away as if unsure what to do next before leaning back in and hugging her in return. "Thanks," he whispered. "That helps."

"Me, too." She reached up to her neck and pulled the binoculars over her head and handed them to him. And I forgot I had these until that hug." She touched the area just below her neck. "Hugging with binoculars kind of smarts! You can put 'em back in the car." Maria grinned, reached out and squeezed his arm, then pointed in the direction that he needed to go. "Okay, you should get a move on to retrieve your car and I'll find a spot for my potty break and then start gimping my way back over toward the main gate. See you there soon."

"Yeah . . . right," he stammered, holding the binoculars awkwardly in both hands while looking embarrassed again, both by her reference to the potty break and by how he had responded to her hug. "Okay, then I-

I'll see you over by the gate." He looked down at her leg. "You sure you'll be all right walking? I can put the gate down and drive in to get you, even if it IS against the law."

"No, don't do that. It hurts but it's not gonna slow me down that much. Probably better to keep moving anyway or it'll just stiffen up." She waved him away and he took off at a brisk pace leaving her to navigate back toward where she had first started out in the dark. She looked around toward where they had been watching the plane and the man on the far hillside but could not see or hear anything further.

"Probably nothing." She shrugged.

She turned and started walking. Her leg was still sore but definitely not hindering her pace. And, just as she had thought, the movement was actually helping loosen it up so she could walk faster. Despite the cold, she was feeling okay but as she hurried along, she was growing more anxious to find a spot to make her bathroom stop before Frank came around with the car.

"Stupid weak bladder," she muttered.

The top of a now orange colored sun emerged from above the dark line of clouds and a wave of light and shadows suddenly started filling up the spaces stretching out in front of her. And, while it may have been psychological, she also thought she could feel an immediate rise in the temperature. As she hurried along she kept an eye out for anything looking like either a rock formation or rock pile, but nothing seemed to fit.

She drew closer to where the gate was located and was surprised to see that on her earlier trek going out toward the agate beds she had walked almost directly through a large prairie dog town. The holes, some mounded, others mostly flat, were all around her and she was glad she hadn't accidentally stepped into one of them on her first pass through.

"Tripping and falling over a prairie dog hole; that would've definitely added insult to injury," she muttered to herself.

A couple of the brown furry rodents had emerged from their dens and were exchanging a series of shrill chirps with each other as a warning of Maria's approach. She warily maneuvered her way around them and headed on a new line toward the gate which now lay about 75 yards ahead. She stopped and looked around one more time, carefully checking as far out as she could see in each direction. As she rotated back past the sunrise and shifted her gaze to the right of where the sun was now filling the sky, she paused.

A mounded formation of some sort was jutting out haphazardly on the north. To its south side, a depression stretched out between two rows of the larger spiky yucca plants. She could definitely have some privacy down among the rows of those sharp-spined yucca plants.

She made her potty stop a quick one and a couple gusts of icy wind made her grateful she wasn't living in pioneer days and having to "go" by "going outside" all the time, either out in the open like this or inside a rickety outhouse. "I salute you Grandma Laura and Great-Aunt Minnie," she exclaimed as she stood and pulled up her quilted pants. "The pioneer life is definitely not the life for me."

She stared out at the mound again. From this backside angle she noticed something different. This little mound now looked more like a small tower, only visible because of the backlighting from the rising sun's rays. "Damn Frank. You were right about those early morning shadows."

She moved closer to the tower-shaped mound that was emitting a long narrow shadow stretching out for several yards in her direction. Instead of being a mound it now had more of a "tower" shape. Maybe even like a rock pile.

"Is THAT a rock pile?" she asked herself aloud. She took several paces toward it but couldn't tell if it was a tower built from stones, was a natural formation, or was just dirt that had somehow been molded into its tower-like shape by either animals or the wind. Wishing she'd kept the binoculars, she cupped her hands around her eyes to see if that would help.

As if Mother Nature was suddenly intervening and re-encouraging her to "move along," another gust of wind whipped past the tower and into the depression where she was still standing. The wind's force caused something along the base of the formation to make a fluttery movement. Maria's heart rate increased. "What is that thing?" Could it be a bag of some sort? If a bag had been haphazardly stuffed alongside the little formation in the middle of the night, it might now be partly exposed by the wind's blowing the surrounding dirt away for the past two days.

She pushed up on her toes and craned her neck toward it. Whatever this little tower was—whether rocks or dirt—wasn't clear. And, it might just be an elaborate version of the many prairie dog holes dotting the grounds around it. And yet, the way the little tower seemed to be formed, it definitely could be something more.

"All right, if you ask me, that's definitely something someone might call a rock pile," she said aloud, encouraging herself to check it out. Besides, she thought, this was close enough to the gate that it wouldn't have been difficult for an injured Gene to go into it, stash the bag, and then get back out of there in a short time. This made sense! She thought excitedly. There was another movement at its base as the swirling wind gusted again.

"Hah!" she exclaimed, forgetting her sore leg and starting to jog toward the formation. This might be exactly what they'd been seeking. She came up near the edge of the depression laughing aloud at her good luck when suddenly the ground erupted in an explosion of dirt, snow and feathers. Maria screamed, but her voice was drowned out by an unearthly shrieking noise created by something brown and white and beating the air directly in front of her.

"What the hell?" Maria yelled, leaping back in shock and surprise as a fury of feathers and talons topped by a large pair of bright yellow eyes and a sharp yellow beak whirled in the air then turned and flew back directly at her head.

She ducked as the bird swooped past her face, emitting a blood curdling screech as it went by. Maria stumbled backward a few feet further and turned to her right just as whatever this thing was came straight back at her again, it's talons now extended as if intent upon making a full-force attack.

Maria half fell and stumbled sideways in fear while emitting a matching screech of her own. But unlike the bird's war cry, hers was a screech of sheer terror. The small but deadly looking brown and white bird continued trying to get at her head, its wings extended and flapping wildly as it screeched again and again.

"Oh my god!" she screamed while instinctively pulling her hands toward her face for protection as the bird veered past and flew on, hitting her right shoulder with a talon and screeching another warning as it went by. Through her half-closed fingers she could see Frank's car pull up next to the gate as she looked around to see where her attacker had gone.

The robin-sized dynamo whipped around, landed on top of a large rock about 20 yards to her right and gave yet another deafening screech. It started to extend its wings again, and then suddenly RAN full speed toward her for several yards as if launching itself into a new takeoff to re-attack. The bird' maneuver also served as a warning for her to leave now if she knew what was good for her!

"Don't worry, you crazy ass bird, I'm going! Just leave me the hell alone!" she yelled at her defiant attacker as she threw caution aside and started running full speed toward where Frank had now exited from his car and was re-opening the wire gate. He stood holding the gate's anchor post in one hand and looking totally amazed by the confrontation between Maria and the little bird as it swooped back at her for a third time. Once more it clawed at her shoulder as it flew past landing this time atop one of the fence posts about three fence sections away.

"What the hell IS that thing!?" She was yelling the words in rapid gasps as she ran up to his side. Grabbing at his free arm she stood hiding behind him while pointing accusingly past his shoulder in the bird's direction. "That's some kind of devil bird and it's trying to kill me!" Maria's adrenalin level was spiking and her whole upper body was shaking. She stood gulping for air as she tried to calm herself down now that she had Frank standing there between her and the bird.

"Relax, don't worry. It's just warning you to get away from its home," he said. "It's one of them underground ahls. Lakota people call it Hinhan Makhotila." He pronounced it Heen-hahn Macho-TEA-lah while cautiously eyeing the angry bird as he spoke. He firmly pulled the barbed wire gate back into place and gave it a reassuring pat, as if the strands of spiky wire would provide a sufficient barrier to prevent the bird from continuing its attack—if it decided to do so. "You must-a got too close to its burrow."

The bird rose up and flew to another of the wooden posts, now just two fence lengths away. It perched there for a few seconds before extending its wings out to their full two-and-a-half-foot expanse and emitting another full-throated scream in Maria and Frank' direction. Seemingly satisfied that it had driven the terrible intruders away, the little bird lifted off the fence post, flapped twice and gave them one more screech as it turned east and flew back in the direction of the prairie dog town.

"A what?" Maria was still shaking as she watched the bird go. "A Macho what?"

"A Hinhan Makhotila (now he pronounced it MACHO teelah). Um." He paused. "It lives in prairie dog or badger holes. In the abandoned burrows. Local ranchers call it a Bur-row-ing Ahl," he said slowly, emphasizing each syllable. "Because it LIVES out there in the ground. It usually lives in a burrow."

"It LIVES in a burrow?" She stared out at the bird's disappearing form as it settled back near the spot where it had first attacked her. "So, it's a killer bird that comes out of the ground? I was right. It's a devil bird all right! Did you see that damn thing's claws? They were huge! What kind of bird has claws?"

"Those are his talons," Frank said patiently. "You must've accidentally stumbled onto its home. Like I said, it's probably living in one of them old prairie dog burrows on the edge of their town. Anyway, it's an ahl. An ahl that lives in the ground. That's why it's called a bur-rowing ahl."

Registering the blank look still on her face, he stopped explaining, pretended to flap his arms like wings and emitted a loud, "Hoo! Hoo! Ahl. Get it? It's an ahl!"

Maria stepped away from him, finally recording a glint of understanding. "You mean it's an OWL?"

"That's what I've been saying." He nodded vigorously, double-checked the gate hook and turned back to face her. "Yes! Hoo! Hoo! It's an ahl . . . owl?" He slowly enunciated the name to correct the way he'd been saying it. "It's one of them kind that usually lives around prairie dog towns in an abandoned prairie dog burrow."

"An owl that lives in the ground and flies out to attack people?" She looked defeated at the image she was creating in her mind's eye. "Who'd believe something like that?"

Again he gave her a vigorous nod of assent as if that reaction could break through her obvious fog. "Yep. THAT's what I've been sayin'. That's why it's called a Bur-row-ing Ahl . . . owl," he self corrected again. It's probably already started getting its nest ready down inside the burrow—to raise its chicks as soon as the weather turns." He started to move toward his car while Maria fearfully looked again toward where the bird had now disappeared.

Chapter Thirty-One

She turned and started after him. "Wow, a burrowing owl. I guess I've heard of them but never figured I'd see one." Forgetting about the ache in her leg she hurried to catch up to him. "I was taken by surprise because I didn't know they attacked people, that's all. You saw that damn thing. It was definitely trying to kill me!"

"Yeah?" he looked skeptical. "I doubt it. I'm sure it wasn't TRYING to kill you; just scare you away. Like I said, they're just real protective." Now he gave her a sympathetic look. "I'm sorry that I didn't warn you that you might run across one of them when you were walking out there. Even in the off-season like this they still can be real fierce when they guard their nests."

"Ya think?" she said sarcastically as she gave one more wary look in the owl's direction as if expecting a renewed attack any second. "How in the world was I supposed to know that other things live in prairie dog burrows besides prairie dogs?"

He shrugged. "You know you're lucky it's winter or you might'a had a snake come out of one instead." He grinned as she shuddered at the thought. "How'd you get on top of that ahl's . . . that owl's burrow in the first place?" He stopped and gave her a pained look. "You weren't going . . .?"

"No! I wasn't peeing on the devil owl's nest!" she interjected, giving a little gasp of disbelief like she couldn't believe he would even ask. Quickly, she explained what had transpired as he stood there looking out toward where the owl had retreated, nodding knowingly as she spoke. "But obviously that stuff that he had built up around the burrow's entrance wasn't any kind of rock pile, was it?" she concluded, a contrite sound in her voice.

"Nope. Sorry. It's kind of a territorial thing for them. Like building a private entrance or something." He pointed out past the front end of the car as she leaned back on the hood. "Listen we better get going." He walked over and pulled open the passenger side door, holding it back for her as he spoke. She walked over beside him and put a hand on his shoulder. "I'm sorry if I acted so scared and crazy. It wasn't your fault I turned her into a killer bird."

She looked glumly back toward the agate fields. "Guess that owl's just one more thing to add to my long list of things that are P.O.-ed at Maria Tager. That damn list is getting bigger by the day! It goes hand-in-hand with the list I've been putting together called, 'Things I've Learned The Hard Way.' Now THAT'S a long list!"

"Well, that little owl was just trying to protect itself from you because of how you look. You know?" Frank gave another little shrug as he spoke.

"What?"

"I told you when we got here that you looked like a big fluffy red bird with that old puffy red coat." He gave her a little grin. "That poor little bird was probably the one who thought SHE was being attacked by a giant killer red . . . what kind of killer red bird would you like to be?"

Maria gave him an incredulous look and then a little shove as he laughed at her response and jumped back out of her way, bumping the car door shut again in the process. They both laughed, and then stopped short as a growling noise interrupted their fun.

"What's that?" A look of fear came over Maria's face as she pointed past his shoulder. Frank spun around to see what was causing the unwelcome intrusion. He stared out ahead of the car and gasped in surprise. Rising up from the northeast horizon and coming directly toward them, just barely above the ground, was the same Piper Super

Cub that they had seen flying past the man with the flag on the far side of the agate field.

They both ducked as the plane roared past them, its wheels barely clearing their heads and the top of Frank's car in the process. They could clearly see the pilot and a passenger studying them as he guided the aircraft back up and around to the west before veering sharply off to the north.

But instead of flying back away, the plane suddenly started to climb again before banking hard to the east and looping back around in their direction. Now the pilot turned the nose of the aircraft down and started to dive, seeming to be aiming the plane directly at them. Frank gasped again as the plane began picking up speed.

"What the hell? That crazy bastard's coming right for us. He's going to try to hit us with his wheels! Quick! Get in!" Maria scrambled into her side of the car and Frank raced around to his as the plane continued its rapid descent straight at them. He fumbled with the engine key, got it inserted and fired up the engine but not before the plane loomed directly in front of them, its wheels coming straight at the car's windshield.

"Holy Moley! He's gonna hit us. Quick! Get back out!" He jerked on the hand brake, leaving the engine idling and pushed open his door, pointing desperately at Maria's door as if she didn't know what she needed to do to get out. "Get out! Get out! Jump out and roll toward the ditch!"

He dived down and out of his own door and half rolled, half crab-walked sideways as Maria did the same. They both slid down into the ditches on either side of the narrow road while the plane whooshed on past them, missing the car by a couple feet but stirring up a huge cloud of dust as it roared by. As it started to climb, gunshots rang out and

Maria cried out in disbelief as the bullets kicked up the dirt beside the car before one clanged into the car's roof.

The shooting was coming from the plane's passenger side.

"Oh my God! Now they're trying to shoot us. Maria!" Frank shouted across to her as the plane looped around behind them and took another bead on them, this time swooping in toward them from behind. "Quick, get under the car's running boards for protection!" he commanded. "Run back toward the car and roll up under before he comes back. Scrunch down in front of the rear wheel!"

Following his own instructions, he jumped up and raced toward his side of the car. Adrenaline pumping, Maria duplicated the move on her side, diving straight at the rear wheel and grateful for the cushioning provided by her heavily padded coat as she once again slammed into the ground.

They both slid on their bellies under the car's running boards and rolled up as tight as they could in the space between the tires while listening to the plane's engine and another round of gunfire filling the air.

"Oh my God!" Maria said as they heard at least two more bullets strike the car's roof above them followed by a sharp clang as one hit the hood. The whole car shook violently from the downdraft caused by the plane's dropping almost on top of it once more. Then the Piper aircraft headed back up, its engine growling yet again in protest to the pilot's hard climbing maneuver. Meanwhile, Frank's car continued to hum, its own engine still running smoothly despite the intrusion.

Slip sliding their bodies closer together, they struggled to work on leaving as little of themselves as possible exposed to yet another air assault. "Ow!" Frank reached a hand up toward his face. "This muffler's getting hot on my side. Be careful or you'll get burned." He edged partly back out from the running board's protection, preparing to push his body completely out and rush back toward the ditch and whatever protection that might offer.

But this time the plane banked back off in the direction from which it had first appeared and flew away. Maria and Frank lay there panting, the only sounds coming from the old car's motor and their heavy breathing as they listened to the plane's engine noise dissipate.

"Geez," Maria was shaking as she spoke. "Do you suppose they think that we saw something out there that we shouldn't have? That guy with the white hair must've sent his plane buddy over to find us and put the fear into us about telling anybody about what we saw. Either that or they just wanted to kill us and get it over with."

"Yeah, you think?" Frank looked over at her and she could see how thoroughly frightened he also looked. "I don't know about you," he said, "but their flying and shooting at us definitely worked on me. In fact it scared the shit out of me! We need to get the hell out of here before that white haired guy comes after us, too. He's probably already on his way, although he'll have to go quite a few miles further north before he can take that dirt road that goes across the open prairie. But once he takes that across he can get on the main north-south road and head back down in this direction."

She nodded, listened carefully for any more plane engine sounds and then, satisfied that there were none, skooched out from under the car. Pulling herself to her feet, she looked over at Frank who was staring in disbelief at the row of bullet holes that were now tattooed along the roof and hood of his car.

Rainbow Rock

Chapter Thirty-Two

Twocrow awoke with his heart racing, startled out of the deeply intense dream he had been having. He had been trapped on the center of the big wooden train trestle that had once crossed the Fall River Canyon, staring in terror as an old-fashioned steam locomotive bore down on his position. As he had been desperately trying to scramble to safety the train, instead of blowing its whistle, kept ringing an annoying bell as its warning as it rumbled full bore toward him.

Cocooned tightly in his bed sheets, he thrashed about to break free before finally rolling sideways, his heart still beating wildly. His first thought was he must be having a heart attack. Then the jangling of the bell came again and he realized the sound he had been dreaming about was just the unfamiliar ringing coming from a new desk style telephone he had had installed just a few days earlier.

"Ah, shit!" he exclaimed as he struggled against the sheets, bumping the back of his head against the bedpost in the process. "Wait Damnit! Just wait!" he commanded, but the phone kept insistently clanging away from the next room. Finally able to extract his old body from his self-inflicted mummification, he threw the sheets aside and stood up.

Stumbling across the room he grabbed for the phone's receiver but instead knocked the whole of it off the front of the end table where it was sitting. He lurched on toward it trying to stop the phone's fall and in the process promptly cracked his funny bone on the little table's front corner. He reached for his elbow and growled in pain.

The phone continued its fall to the floor and its receiver came free, which promptly stopped the ringing. It was replaced by a muffled and confused voice saying, "Hello? Hello? Anybody there?"

"Ow! Dammit! Shit! Twocrow you dummy!" he howled, cradling his throbbing elbow and snagging the phone receiver at the same time. "Dammit, anyway!" he roared as the intense radiating pain coursed through his arm from where he'd struck the sensitive spot on his elbow.

"Uh ... what? I'm ... uh ... Um, Marshal Twocrow, are you okay to talk?" A woman's voice on the other end of the line sounded stunned by the angry, upset response she was hearing. "Isn't this . . . I mean, IS this Marshal Al Twocrow?"

"No, not dammit to you!" he stammered, embarrassed by his reaction. "And I mean YES! Yes, it's me. This is Twocrow, the Marshal!" He paused, realizing he must be coming across as if he were some sort of blooming idiot. "Sorry. I'm so sorry," he quickly apologized. "I just cracked my funny bone on the way over to pick up the phone, and now my elbow hurts like hell in a hand basket!"

He rubbed at it again hoping the stinging pain would dissipate. "My apologies. I didn't mean to swear, and my words weren't aimed at you. Very sorry."

He glanced at a large circular clock he had mounted on the wall directly across from where he was standing. It read 7:03 a.m. "Your call woke me up so I'm still a bit disoriented," he added, hoping that might help with his explanation. "I'm usually up and at 'em way before this time of the day, but I stayed up later than usual last night—sort-of waiting on a call."

Then he paused, putting his response together with the fact that he was now ON a call. "Who's this I'm talkin' too, by the way?"

"You were probably waiting on a call that was supposed to come from my office," the woman said apologetically. "This is assistant medical examiner Valerie Walker. Calling from the Pennington County Morgue," she added. "And, I know how much hitting your funny bone can hurt. It's weird that it's called that, isn't it? Funny bone? Definitely not a laughing matter when it happens." She ended her response with a small chuckle, almost as if hoping that might help calm Twocrow down a bit and lighten the mood.

"Anyhow, I had your phone number on my desk from Doctor Cosgrove. He said you were anxious to get a readout on that body that you had brought in here yesterday by the Sheriff's Office. You know, the victim that was found down at the Sandman Elevator Complex," she hurried to add, obviously hoping there wouldn't be any more outbursts from the Marshal or that he'd be confused about which body she might be referring to.

"I think he thought I was going to be coming in to work again last night and not so early this morning." She rushed on with her explanation when he didn't immediately reply. "And," she continued, "his note said he tried reaching you about 6:30 last night but he didn't get through before he had to leave. So he left me a note to give you a call AS SOON as I got in—all CAPS and underlined twice—as soon as I got in. So I thought since I missed it last night . . . well, sorry, I probably called you too early. I'm so sorry to wake you up like this, especially since it caused you to get hurt."

"No, no, no it's fine. I'm glad you called," the Marshal interrupted. "And, again, it's me should be apologizing for being so discombobulated when you rang me. I don't know why the hell I was in such a deep sleep this morning? Like I said, I'm usually up and at 'em way before this. Don't apologize. I'm truly glad you called."

He stopped, realizing how lame this must be sounding and hoping that she'd just get on with it. "So you have something to share with me?"

"Yes, yes, I do," she continued. "The doctor left me a copy of his initial report, which pretty much verifies what the police report stated when they brought the body in. It looks like the young man's death was caused by trauma from multiple gunshot wounds and loss of blood."

"Mmmm," Twocrow muttered, gingerly rotating his sore arm to further loosen it up as he responded. "And what about his booze levels?"

"Booze levels?" she seemed put off by the question.

"Alcohol in his bloodstream? I told the Sheriff's Office I needed to have a tox screen done too. Figured they'd just pass that request on to the doc."

"Oh, that!" She paused. "Booze levels. That's a new one," she mumbled with a semi-disgusted add-on tone to her voice. "Okay. So, no, there's nothing I can see here," she said more firmly.

"You mean the doc didn't do one?" Twocrow responded, the irritation returning to his voice.

"I didn't say that, did I?" It was her turn to sound irritated. "He DID do a tox but there's nothing about any alcohol in the blood so far as I can see in the report." He could hear her rustling the paperwork as if searching through it once more just to reassure herself. "Nope . . ." she stopped. "Well . . . okay . . . so, it says there was a small amount of alcohol found in both his mouth and upper throat. But Doctor Cosgrove wrote that it looked like it was forced in there because there was nothing in his stomach."

He could hear her rustle the papers once more. "And no alcohol in his blood either as far as could be determined. He's got that written down and underlined, too." Now she seemed embarrassed as she spoke. "Sorry I didn't see his note before."

"That's interesting." Twocrow had been talking with the phone cord stretched out and now he picked the phone's base unit off the floor and moved around to the edge of a chair to sit down. Balancing the desk-style base on his lap, he grimaced as he massaged his elbow while grunting in relief that the funny bone's pain was lessening. "Did the doc estimate the time of death, Miss Walker?"

"Mrs.," she answered. "And, yes, he put down that it was sometime between 9 p.m. and midnight on the thirty-first."

"Okay, well . . ."

"Marshal, there's another thing here in the notes that the doctor wanted me to share with you, but he asked that you keep it to yourself until he gets the chance to meet with you in person."

Twocrow slid back further onto the chair and replaced the phone's base set onto the end table while cradling the receiver against his left ear. "O-kay," he slowly answered, trying to keep the wariness out of his voice. "What was that?"

"It's about the bullets that killed this young man," she said. "Looks like he took three of them, one in the upper left forearm and two in his left side. The one in his forearm is kind of weird and that's one for sure that Doctor Cosgrove wants to double-check. But the two in the boy's side came from a .357 Magnum." She paused as Twocrow sucked in sharply at the report.

"No question on that?" he asked before she could say anything further.

"No. Definitely a .357."

Neither one of them spoke for a few seconds before Twocrow finally said what they both were thinking. "So, good chance it might be a Cop's gun, huh?"

"Sort of looks that way, although the shooter could've been using a stolen gun or found some way to get hold of a .357 through the Black Market," she affirmed. "Anyway it was one of those two bullets that was the primary culprit. Ripped through the top of his kidney and lodged just below the heart. Most of his blood loss would've come from that one."

"Mmmmm. You're right about that," Twocrow agreed. He absently drummed his fingers on the top of the end table as he spoke. "You said the other one; the one in the arm, that one was 'weird?' How was it weird?"

She rustled the papers yet again as he waited for her to look at what the doctor had written. "Well, he wrote here that he can't be sure, so he needs to talk to a ballistics expert over at the Sheriff's office before formally writing it in."

"Okay. I understand. But can you at least share with me what his thinking on it might be? Could be a big help in my investigation if I have some idea of what kind of gun I might be looking for."

"I guess that would be okay as long as you promise not to let it out. And he wants you to hold off on sharing anything on the potential of a police officer's weapon being used, too. Is that okay by you?"

"Yes," he answered. "So, do you know when he expects to have something definite to share . . . even with me?"

"Probably no later than noon; and maybe even mid-to-late morning. He wants to know if you can come up and meet with him in person?"

"I'll be there. Tell him 11 or maybe 11:30. But no later."

"You got it. Well, I'll . . ."

"Wait! Wait!" he interrupted as he stood back up. "What about that other gun?"

"Oh, sure," her voice once more took on a flustered tone. "Sorry. Let me get over to that page again." She paused. "Okay, here it is, and I have to admit I've never heard of a gun like this one. It's some sort of German model, a . . ."

"Walther? Walther P-38?" He cut her off with his questions.

"Why . . . yes." He could hear the surprise in her voice. "How did you know that?"

"Tell Doc Cosgrove that I'll be looking forward to my conversation with him later this morning," Twocrow said, ignoring her question. "And, listen, thank you again Mrs. Walker. Despite my erratic behavior when I first picked up the phone, I really AM glad that you called."

*****

After a quick shave and sponging off the upper part of his body with a soapy cloth, Twocrow hurried out and started his car to let it warm up while he plotted his next steps. He'd need to check in with Maria and Frank and let them know what was going on and then get on the road between 10:15 and 10:30, latest, in order to get to downtown Rapid on time. If they wanted to ride with him, he would take them, and maybe on the way back they could check out a couple of the "rock pile" spots Frank might have remembered.

Back inside, he brewed a cup of coffee and made a piece of toast before dialing Maria's home phone number. He chewed thoughtfully as he listened to the ringing go on and on. After a dozen rings with no answer he hung up and washed down the last bite with the last of the coffee, rinsed the cup and left it to dry, then pulled on his coat.

Pushing his hat firmly into place, he tried Maria's number once more, and then dialed the newspaper office number. After two rings, Janeen Wilder, the *Star*'s front desk person, answered.

"Janeen. Hi. Hey, this is Al Twocrow. Is Maria Tager around?"

"No. No she's not in yet," Janeen answered. "Kind of unusual, too. She's usually at her desk way before me. Real go-getter, as I'm sure you know." She laughed as if sharing an inside joke, and Twocrow gave her an obligatory chuckle in return.

"Yeah. Hard to stay ahead of that girl, and well . . ." he paused as if trying to figure out the best way to say what he was going to say. ". . .

well, anyway, she's been riding along with me on this shooting death involving the Hot Springs kid."

"Yes, I know," Janeen answered, a disapproving edge to her tone.

Twocrow ignored it and continued without missing a beat. "So I was just going to let her know today's schedule if she still wants to continue riding along. She leave you any idea when she might be in?"

Once again he could hear Janeen rustling papers on her desk. "Nope, there's nothing here. Let me take a quick look at her calendar." He heard her put the phone down and a few seconds later come back on. "Her calendar's clear, but when I talked to her last she was pretty caught up in having both a story and a couple of pictures from this case of yours in this week. I'm sure she'll be checking in soon to stay ahead of our deadlines."

"Okay, good. Well, if she stops in and she hasn't been in to see me—or hasn't seen me yet in person as far as that goes—can you have her give me a quick call? I should be back over to my office in the next 15 or 20 minutes."

"Will do." Janeen's voice tone changed to one of concern. "Um ... She's okay, right? I mean there's nothing to worry about from last night is there?"

"Why?" Twocrow was on instant alert at her question. "What happened last night?"

"Well, she had some guy staying with her and she wouldn't say anything more than that. Even though I was a little concerned about that, it didn't seem to be a worry for her at all. But now that she's not in and you're asking about her too, well . . . you know?"

The Marshal laughed lightly. "Oh, sure. Of course. But I know about that. In fact, I helped set that up. But how would you have known?" he added quickly. "It's good you're concerned; and good for her to have friends who care. By the way, how did you find out she had someone staying with her?"

"Because she came down here to pick up some of the old clothes we keep in the back shop. The ones the printer and pressman can slip into if they spill something on theirs, that sort of thing. Anyway, she said she had a guy staying with her who could use some clean stuff while they got his things washed up and dried overnight. Just seemed a little unusual because she never talked about a guy friend before. At least not to me." She said it with a tone that indicated that if she didn't know about a guy, then no one else would either.

"Listen, don't you worry. That young man's a good friend of mine and she was giving him a place to sleep overnight at my request. She wouldn't be in any kind of danger from him, you can trust me on that."

"Oh . . . good! Glad for that," she replied. "All right then. Well. Maybe she had to take him somewhere before coming in to work. You don't suppose she went over to your office first, do you?"

"Sure, sure, that might be what happened," he said. "Look, I'll just make a quick stop up at her place and then head on over to my office right after. Dog chasing its tail here," he added, laughing again despite the uneasy feeling in his gut. "Now don't worry. I'll call you if she's not at one place or another, but I'm sure I'll find both her and my young friend in the next half hour. Thanks Janeen. I'll talk to you soon."

He hung up, buttoned up his coat and headed out the door. Even though he believed that what he had just told Janeen sounded right, he still couldn't shake the uneasiness that was permeating his body as he hurried out to his car.

Chapter Thirty-Three

Frank maneuvered his car around one of the big potholes that he had hit on his way into the agate fields, turned west and headed toward the intersection with the primary gravel road that they would have to follow back into Fairburn.

"Wow, no wonder we were bottoming out on the way in," Maria said, looking out the window at the large, semi-frozen depression that they had just avoided. "Somebody ought to get a road grader out this way and fill those things in."

"Yeah, good idea," Frank agreed, "and it probably needs to be somebody like you. I don't think the county officials would pay much attention to somebody like me." He swept a hand in the air to point toward himself as he spoke. "Just sayin'." He tensed up and sucked in a deep breath. "Oh-oh."

"What?"

"See that dust plume coming hell bent down on the gravel from the north?" He pointed out the right front corner of the windshield across in a northwesterly direction. "Still a couple miles away, so that much dust has to be coming off a big car or a pickup truck going fast. Locals don't usually tear down these roads like that, so it might be our guy from out east." He eased over to the side of the road and slipped the car out of gear. "What do you think?"

"About what?" Maria nervously eyed the dust cloud as it grew larger and closer.

"Well, that pilot definitely got a good look at us before he headed back in the direction where we first saw that pickup, so if this is that guy's truck then there's a good chance they've already had a conversation about us and he's coming around to make sure we won't be telling anyone about what we just saw happening out there."

"Which is clear as mud as far as I'm concerned," she said with disgust in her voice.

Frank shrugged. "Yeah, for sure. I'm not sure I saw anything."

"So, what do we do?"

"We've got three choices," he answered. "We can wait here and see if whoever it is goes on by. We can continue on out to the intersection and try to get back into Fairburn ahead of him. Or we can turn around and go back over those hills we just came through and see if we can get out of sight. There's a couple spots behind us that might work for that."

"No way we can go faster than whoever that is," Maria said as she continued watching the dust cloud grow closer and larger. "No offense, but your car's get up and go seems to have already got up and went."

"Yeah, ha, ha, very funny." He shrugged again. "But, you're right. And turning around might just stir up a lot of dust of our own. That would make us an easy target, too. So maybe we should just hunker down and wait here to see if he goes on by."

She nodded her affirmation as Frank looked out toward the dust cloud again. "I guess it could just be a local rancher driving into town. And even if it is our guy, it'll be easier to turn around here and head back if he spots us. My car's not fast, but it handles the open countryside pretty good. We could pull off onto one of those little cattle trails we came past and drive out onto the open prairie. Won't raise as much dust out on that dry grass either. Plus, I've got my snow tires on, so that'll help get up and down on these hillsides, even on the frozen or snowy spots.

"Yeah, and if that IS the fancy pickup we saw over on the east side, I don't know if the guy'd want to risk getting it all banged up trying to chase us down. He'd probably just call in his plane buddy to track us down again. But it would give us a little more time to try to get away."

She pointed toward a cluster of bushes. "Okay, maybe you should pull up ahead to where those shrubs are growing alongside the road and wait there. Plus, with the sun still behind us, that should make it harder for him to see clearly in our direction."

"Yeah, that should work." He shifted into low gear and eased the car ahead, trying not to stir up any dust of his own in the process. He pointed toward the near side of the shrubs as they drew closer.

"I'm going to back in along this side so that we can get the hell out of here in either direction if we have to. Okay?" Not waiting for a response, he pulled up next to them on the road, then backed partway onto the nearly flat ditch with the nose end of his car pointing slightly skyward.

"I think we must be out of any sight lines now because I can't see anything but tree branches and sky from here," Maria complained. "So I hope you can get at least a partial look back toward the main road?"

Frank leaned forward over the steering wheel. "Yeah. Well, sort of," he said. Maria groaned and opened her door. They were parked so close that she could only get the door open half way before it bumped up against the shrubs. "What are you doing?" he asked, startled by her maneuver.

"I'm going to get out and look through the branches out toward the road, that's all. You just stay behind the wheel and be ready to roll." She picked up the binoculars, edged her way through the narrow opening and on back to where a little gap in the branches gave her a clearer view out toward the intersection.

After looking at that spot, she swung the binoculars to her right and focused toward the dust cloud created by the oncoming vehicle as it came swirling in their direction from the north. The dust seemed to sweep forward like a giant wave as the vehicle suddenly slid to a stop at the center of the intersection where their little dirt road connected. As the dust settled and the air cleared the sun lit up a dark pickup with a split-rail box around its back side.

"Oh hell!" she exclaimed. "That's definitely our pickup guy."

"Is he turning down this way?" Frank revved the engine slightly, a bead of perspiration forming above his right eye.

Maria looked back into the binoculars. "No. But he's getting out of the cab and looking over in this direction." She kept trained on him and nodded. "I was right, he has to shield his eyes to see anything down here, so just stay cool."

She watched as the man pulled a walkie-talkie up to his ear and seemed to be carrying on a conversation with someone. Then, as if responding to something he was hearing, he reached back into his truck's cab and pulled out his own pair of binoculars to take another look down their road. Seemingly satisfied there was nothing down their way, he turned the glasses toward the front of his truck and looked down the roadway toward Fairburn. At that point he waved his arm skyward as he said something else into the walkie-talkie.

Maria swung her glasses skyward expecting the small plane to suddenly reappear but the air above them remained clear and quiet.

She turned her binoculars back toward him and watched as he continued to have an animated conversation while now pointing off toward Fairburn.

"Can YOU see anything down to the south?" she leaned partway into the door to ask Frank the question. "He keeps pointing straight ahead of him like there's something happening down that way."

"Here, give me the glasses," Frank responded. He slipped the gear stick over to neutral and pulled on the hand brake to keep the car from rolling. She handed the binoculars across to him and he opened his door and got out. Standing with the door half open, he leaned against it and focused south.

"There's dust of some sort down that way. It's probably somebody local coming out of town to connect onto the Highway 79 northwest access road. He must be seeing it too. Maybe he thinks it's us? He might think we're ahead of him and trying to head back out to the main highway. You know, like maybe we're trying to drive up to Rapid?"

Maria looked back through the tree branches and was surprised to see the pickup start to move. "Hey, you're right. He's on the move. Must be going to find out who's down there." She scrunched her way through the door's narrow opening and plopped down onto her side of the seat. Frank quickly scrambled back behind the wheel, handed over the binoculars and released the hand brake before shifting into gear.

"What's the plan?" Maria asked.

"By the time he gets down there, that car should already be up a ways on that northwest road. Just guessing, but I'll bet it'll be up there by at least a mile; maybe even all the way out to 79. So if he thinks it's us, he'll probably follow. That should give us a chance to get back through town and drive over to the southwest entrance road; the way we came into town this morning. But we'll have to get moving now before he realizes his mistake and backtracks. Even though we're slower we should have enough time to get through town and out ahead of him."

He turned halfway in his seat and gave her an inquiring look. "Okay?"

"Do we have any other options?" she asked as he pulled away from behind the bushes and back onto the dirt road heading west toward the intersection where the pickup had been stopped.

"Well, we could turn north here at this intersection and drive back the way the pickup just came from. I've never been up on that road, so I don't know if my car can handle it. And if he's working with someone else, we might just end up getting ourselves trapped between his pickup and whoever might be up in that direction. So, I think going into Fairburn is a better choice. Plus the southwest access road is a quicker route out to the main highway. Back through the town and out into more traffic on Highway 79. Safety in numbers."

"Okay. Let's do that. I trust your instincts." She reached out and patted him on the shoulder. Facing forward she exhaled sharply. "Okay. I've always wanted to say this so now's my chance."

"Say what?"

"Let's roll!"

*****

It was just over a mile until they reached the "Y" intersection where their road connected with the gravel access road coming in toward Fairburn from the northwest. Here, just as Frank had remembered, the choices were to turn right and head out toward Highway 79 on that northwest route into Rapid City, or turn left and go straight into Fairburn. He nodded right toward the empty road as if to reaffirm what he'd told Maria earlier and then turned left.

Now that the morning sun was lighting up the little town, it definitely reflected its reputation as a "Semi Ghost Town," except for the big well kept white school building perched at the northeast corner entrance to the community. Several kids were traipsing toward the school's front entrance, books and lunch boxes in hand, while others were disembarking from cars and pickup trucks that had pulled up next to the building's west side.

Maria was surprised to see two kids—a boy and a girl about 10 or 11 years old—ride up on horses, jump down and tie their reins to an old-fashioned hitching post alongside a little storage shed near the school's back door.

"Wow, going to school by horseback," Maria exclaimed. "The longer we're on this trip the more story ideas I get. Did you know that kids out here go to school on horseback?"

"Oh sure. They're probably from some of the Lakota families living out between here and Red Shirt," Frank replied. "Some of those families out there don't even have a car. But everybody has a horse."

She unzipped the top of her jacket and reached into the inside pocket to retrieve her little notepad, beginning to make a few more notes as they made their way past the school's intersection. They turned west toward the old hotel that they had driven past in the dark a few hours before. Frank sucked in sharply after making the turn and Maria pulled her pencil back from the notepad and looked up at his reaction.

"What?" She was on instant alert.

"It's that pickup truck," he replied, pointing kitty-corner past her right shoulder. Coming in hard and fast on a dirt street that entered into the town from the north, the pickup was kicking up a big plume of dust in its wake. Frank stepped on the gas, and then hit the brakes sharply as two more children hustled across the street ahead of him. Meanwhile the pickup had nearly reached the intersection they were approaching and would easily intercept them there.

"Gotta try another way," he said. He cranked the steering wheel hard left and turned into an open dead-weed covered lot between two houses. One house had smoke wafting from its chimney while the other had broken windows and a ramshackle open door barely hanging onto its hinges in the frigid early morning breeze.

Maria turned to see if the pickup's driver had seen them and watched as it pulled to a stop at the intersection before slowly advancing across the street, moving along parallel to where they were driving on the rocky weed-covered lot a half-block to the east.

"He's there!" She pointed straight out her window toward a house on that side of the car. "He's on the street on the other side of that house," she clarified. "He's driving the same direction we are!" She pointed ahead. "When we get up to the end of this lot, he'll see us for sure if he looks over our way!"

Frank hit the brakes again, shifted into reverse and started backward. Cranking the wheel around, he put the rear end of his car into the north side yard of the vacant house and then pulled back into the empty lot, headed the other direction, heading back toward the street they had just left behind them. Maria joined him in looking anxiously to the left across his shoulders and past the side of the house as they eased forward. But there was no sign of the pickup as they returned to the main road.

"What do you think? What should we do?"

"We gotta try getting back out of town the way we came in this morning," he replied. "If we turn back toward where we just came from we'll be driving out in front of the school again. With all those kids arriving, somebody else might get hurt." He tapped the steering wheel. "Simple. We can't go that way. Only one choice."

She nodded. "Yeah. You're right. Do you think that guy's looking for us, or just on his way back to where we saw his truck parked earlier—you know, over across from that old hotel—by that camper? Maybe he's just on his way home. Back to where he lives."

She had barely finished the sentence when the back window of the car made a huge cracking sound. Maria screamed and Frank turned halfway around in his seat to see the pickup barreling toward them through the open lot, the driver leaning out the window and shooting in their direction.

Chapter Thirty-Four

"Maria! Get down!" Frank shouted. He pulled Maria halfway down to put the back of the seat between her and the shooter. "Hang on. This is going to be crazy." He jerked the steering wheel hard left and tromped down on the gas, spinning the car's wheels in the slick grass. The car leaped forward in a series of sharp bumps as he got it started back onto the hard-surface street and headed west, and the car's tires squealed in protest at his maneuver.

"Frank! Look out!" Maria shouted the warning as a middle-aged man standing several feet into the next intersection leaped back out of their way, dropping a handful of papers and envelopes in the process.

Frank swerved to the street's center and glanced in the rearview mirror watching the man shake his fist and drop to his knees to begin gathering up the papers scattered during their near miss. A blare from the horn of the pickup caused him to leap back again as the truck came barreling through the intersection behind them.

Frank turned his gaze down toward Maria's terrified face. "Gotta hope and pray that no one else comes out into the street because we sure as hell ain't slowing down again!" As if to accent his reasoning, the car's back window made a second loud cracking sound as yet another bullet connected.

Frank hit the intersection and turned hard right, passing by the corner where the camper was parked. Racing west alongside the old hotel he gunned his car up and over the nearby railroad tracks. As he bounced down on the other side of the tracks, Maria bounced upward in response, nearly hitting the roof from the reaction.

"Ow! Holy hell Frank!"

"Would you rather get shot or just get banged around?" he shouted back at her. "Just hang on, okay?" He started out of town and up the incline leading west but just as soon as they began to climb the car groaned and the engine started winding down. Frank shifted all the way down to low, but his car kept decelerating. He banged on the steering wheel with his open hand. "Oh hell," he exclaimed. "The engine is going out! That bullet that hit our hood earlier must've knocked something loose. Crap! We're going to stop!"

He looked into the mirror again and saw the sunlight reflecting off the top of the pickup as it came up over the tracks behind them.

"Frank! Look out!" He snapped his gaze back to the front in time to see a black and white police cruiser swing across the road and effectively block off the top of the hill. The cop who was driving leaped out and moved to the front of the car.

"Yeah, yeah, all right, there's some help," Frank's voice was filled with relief.

But the policeman dropped down into a crouch in front of his car, aimed the gun in their direction and fired a shot. Then he stood, continuing to point the gun at them and began waving for them to stop.

"What's happening? Is that cop shooting at US?"

"Frank, I think that's the cop from Prairie City," Maria answered. It looks like that officer who was poking around in Hot Springs yesterday. He's NOT going to help us, he's gotta be here to help that big goon behind us. That's his buddy." She looked back through the badly damaged rear window at the pickup still bearing down on them as Frank's car continued to decelerate. "What're we gonna do? I'm scared!" Maria shrank back, a panicked expression on her face.

"Hang on!" he ordered and suddenly cranked the steering wheel hard right and down into the ditch. They bumped to a stop just short of the double row split rail fence that was separating the road from an upslope area on the north as the pickup kept advancing. At the top of the hill, seeing what Frank was doing, the police officer slapped the hood and hurried to get back into his car. He slid in behind the wheel and started turning the cruiser downhill toward them.

Frank gave Maria a desperate look. "Okay, quick! Get out now and get through that fence. Then run like hell straight up the hill ahead of us. There's that old abandoned mine way up there, just past that big rock at the top. Maybe we can get inside and hide, or escape."

He opened his door and she followed suit on her side as the pickup came racing up behind the spot where they had turned and pulled to stop. He ran across to where she was standing, trembling, grabbed her hand and put something into it. "This will protect you. Don't worry."

She opened her hand to see his brightly colored Fairburn Agate.

"No, Frank. Not your rainbow rock. I can't!"

"Yes you can! Just take it and quit arguing. Come on! We gotta run!"

Chapter Thirty-Five

Twocrow parked and hurried into the Law Enforcement Center's offices, rattling the glass in the top half of their office door harder than he expected as he jerked it open. He grimaced and stopped to carefully re-shut it as the young Sheriff's deputy Jim Dolan, and veteran police officer Paul Ramsay looked up from their desks with startled expressions.

"Sorry. Just me. Don't worry, nothing's broken." He tried to put a reassuring sound into his voice, but they both looked slightly skeptical.

He gave the room the once over, assured himself that neither Maria nor Frank were present and then paced on over to his desk. He looked up at the clock. Already 8:20. "Better check in with Janeen," he said, more to himself than the others, who nonetheless looked up again as he spoke.

He gave them a wave. "Just talkin' to myself," he said. "Can't remember where I put a phone number." He reached out and snagged the local phone book off the corner of his desk and opened it to the business listings in the front. Locating the *Hot Springs Star*'s number, he dialed and waited. Janeen answered on the first ring and it was clear from her tone that she was as worried as he was when he told her he hadn't located Maria yet.

"Do me a favor," he said. "Just take a quick look at her desktop for me and see if she might've written down any notes or phone numbers related to this case? Anything you think is a possibility that I can check out. And if there is, give me a quick call back. Otherwise just stay in touch if you hear anything." He gave her his office phone number and re-cradled the receiver. He flipped the phone book shut and the wind created by his action sent several papers flying off his desk. Grumbling, he retrieved them and opened his desk drawer to put them inside.

The brightly painted, carved wooden box lay there in the center of the top drawer where he had left it from the day before. Putting the papers alongside it, he pulled the box out. He held it up to look it over again just as Deputy Dolan came from across the room, a cup of coffee in one hand and a folded note in the other. The Marshal's name was written in large block letters across the folded over part of the paper.

"What's that?" Dolan asked, pointing with the paper toward the box. "Looks pretty cool whatever it is?"

"Well, I'm not sure, but apparently it's some sort of secret treasure box. My young Indian visitor yesterday morning left it with me but I haven't got a clue as to how to open it to check it out."

"Then how do you know it's a treasure box?" Dolan replied. "Might just be a nice decorated box." He shrugged and held out the note in front of the Marshal while gesturing toward the box with the coffee mug he was balancing in his other hand. "Trade ya. I've got a message that was called in for you earlier this morning, and I'm curious to take a closer look at that box if that's okay? Like I said, treasure box or not it's cool!"

Twocrow hesitated and then placed the box onto the young deputy's hand while taking the note in exchange. "Oh!" he exclaimed as he opened it and eyed the time posted at the top. "Is this right? The note says the call came in at 4:45 a.m.?"

"Guess so? If that's what it says. It was folded up like that when I picked it up from the corner of the counter when I came in about half hour ago." He was holding the painted box aloft and moving it around as he talked. "How'd you learn this thing might be a secret treasure box, anyway?"

"Maria Tager." Twocrow muttered.

"Oh, sure, when she was in here with you yest . . ."

"No, no. I mean the note. This message was called in by Maria Tager. I'm just surprised to see that that's who it was made the call, especially at that time of day" the Marshal said. "But . . . yes," he nodded at the box, "now that you mention it, she IS the one who told me that box probably was a treasure box of some kind. She said her grand-mother had a similar one when she was a young girl."

Dolan rolled the small box around in his fingers, studying all the intricate details of its carvings while Twocrow read through the note a second time. The young Sheriff's deputy stopped his actions and pointed with the box toward the note. "That's not trouble, I hope? I'd hate to see anything bad happen to Maria."

"Oh, it's Maria now, is it?" Twocrow glanced up at the deputy with a twinkle in his eye. "Are you two an item?"

Dolan reddened. "Naw. It's just . . ." he paused as if looking for the right words. "Well, I do think she's kind-a cute, and I was thinkin' of maybe askin' her out one of these days. You think she'd go out with me Marshal?" He looked anxiously at the older man as he asked.

Twocrow chuckled. "Dolan, we're not in Junior High here. How would I know?" He gave him a quick up-and-down look as if evaluating him. "I guess you're not too ugly, so she'd probably give you a chance if you asked her proper like."

"Gee, thanks," Dolan said drily. "Glad I'm not askin' YOU out." He set his coffee cup down and held the box out in front of his face again, this time slowly moving his fingertips around on the various carvings and ridges along its outer edges. He paused on a fox's head and moved it over under Twocrow's desk lamp, holding at an angle in order to study it closer. "You got a paper clip?"

"Sure." Twocrow opened the center desk drawer and moved things around before retrieving one and handing it up to Dolan as he finished reading the note. "Maria says here that she and Frank Silver Shore were heading out to the agate fields east of Fairburn to look over the landscape at sunrise." He glanced up at the wall clock. "Probably already on their way back by now."

"Agate fields? What for?" Dolan was pulling apart the paper clip but stopped to give Twocrow a quizzical look. "You mean those rocks with the colored circles inside them?"

"Yes, but they're a lot more than rocks with colored circles . . ." he stopped as he saw Dolan had quit listening and was once again concentrating on poking at the fox's head with the end of the opened paper clip. "Whatcha doing?"

The deputy pushed harder and emitted an exasperated snort. "Nothin' I guess. Just seemed like there were some small scratches around the fox's head and that maybe . . ." He pulled back the clip and glared at the box. "Probably just my imagination." He shrugged and tossed the box toward the Marshal, but Twocrow was swiveling his chair back toward the desk and missed the deputy's action.

"Marshal, the box!"

Twocrow swiveled back just in time to see the little box strike the front edge of the desk, bounce up slightly and then plummet toward the floor. He swiped at it trying to stop the fall, missed and watched helplessly as it fell the rest of the way to the wooden floor. It made a small "crack!" sound as it hit.

"Oh damn it!" the deputy dropped to his knees and moved toward the box. "I'm so sorry. I shouldn't have tossed it like that. Shit Marshal I think I broke it." He picked up the box to show one end protruding outward.

"No, look!" He pointed. "It's not broken. That's an opening and there's something inside." Twocrow reached for it and held it up. "Here, hand me that paper clip you were messing around with." Dolan sat back on his haunches and passed the clip over to him, watching intently as the Marshal dug the pointed end inside the protrusion and finally pried out a folded piece of paper. As it popped out a second piece of paper slid toward him and he reinserted the clip and pried that one out too.

"What are they?" The deputy watched intently as Twocrow set the box down on top of the desk and started to unfold them. The Marshal scanned the first small paper, then the second before looking up at Dolan.

"You didn't break anything. You hit the Jackpot!" he answered, giving the deputy a big smile.

*****

"This phone number might've been from someone that Gene Darveaux was either calling or hearing from on a regular basis," Twocrow said, pointing at the smaller piece of paper. "And see, he's written that it's connected to somebody called Sarge."

Paul Ramsay, the police officer who was on duty, had joined them at the desk as they reviewed the two small notes and tried to figure them out. The one that had come out of the box first was dated two days ago, the day Darveaux had been killed. The other paper had just the words, "Contact Phone," the number itself, and "Sarge" scrawled on it. The phone number listed appeared to be from outside their county.

"We should call it," Dolan said. "Might not be anything, but you never know?"

Ramsay nodded his agreement. "Yeah, I mean, nothing ventured, right?"

"All right, let's do it," Twocrow said. He was interrupted by the main office phone starting to ring. He nodded toward the police officer's desk. "Paul, you better go get that. If that's Janeen down at the

Star, tell her I'll call her back soon unless she has something urgent. Jim and I can make this call."

Paul looked disappointed at having to miss whatever excitement might be generated from Twocrow's phone call. Seeing the expression on his face, Twocrow said, "Don't worry Ramsay, I'll keep you in the loop on this one, too."

He picked up the receiver and dialed the operator. Giving her the number off the sheet, he waited patiently while she checked a couple of sources and then announced, "It's located in rural Pennington County. Okay, I'm connecting you," and left the call after it began ringing. After several buzzes indicating that it was ringing at the other end, a staticky connection clicked on. "Hello?" The responding voice was tentative as if surprised that someone was calling.

"Yes, hello," Twocrow replied. "This is Deputy U.S. Marshal Al Twocrow from the Southern Hills Marshal's Office . . . down in Hot Springs. Who am I talking to?"

"Uh. Hello Marshal. Uh, well, this here's Rod Huseth," the man answered, clearly flustered. "I'm, uh, well I'm not sure I should'a even been answerin' this phone. Hell, didn't even know it was out here. I was just cleanin' up the warehouse when I heard it ringing, so I thought maybe it was something important. Otherwise . . ."

"Yes, okay Mister Huseth," Twocrow cut him off as he wrote down the man's name. "Do you mind tellin' me WHAT warehouse you're talking about, and WHERE you're located? I just found this number and that's why I'm calling it. I wasn't even sure who it might be?"

Huseth hesitated before continuing. "Well, sure. I'm in a warehouse out by the Prairie City Airfield. Like I said, I didn't even know there was a phone in here. I do a lot of the cleanin' up, sortin' and stackin', things like that," Huseth said.

"So you don't know who might have access to the phone?"

"No, not for sure. I usually get my regular work schedule from Pete Delaney, but he ain't been around here yet today. So, since I hadn't been out to the field for almost a month I thought I'd just check the warehouses and at least sweep each of them up. Little surprise for the big man." He chuckled as he said it. "You must know how the dust can settle in around here this time of year, right?"

"Yes, yes, I DO understand that," Twocrow agreed, shrugging in Dolan's direction and giving him an "I'm not sure about this?" look as he spoke. "Well, listen, I don't need to keep you from your work Mister Huseth. Can you tell me what the warehouse building number is there, in case I need to check on something further?"

"Don't know if anyone would hear the phone unless they were actually in here, and there ain't no regular numbers on the warehouses. This is the one we all call the Double Yellow shed. If you come on up here, just ask for that one and anyone can tell you. There's only the one. Two-toned yellow color. It's out on the west side of the airfield."

"Okay, thanks much . . . Rod, was it?"

"Yep, Rod Huseth. Glad to help."

Twocrow started to say goodbye and then saw Dolan pointing frantically at the note with the phone number. "Oh, Mister Huseth, one more thing!" He heard the man on the other end say "What's that?"

"One more thing. Do you know if anyone working out there goes by the name of Sarge?"

"Sarge?"

"Yes, Sarge. Just wondering if . . ."

"Well, there's the Chief."

"Chief?" Twocrow conjured up an image of one of his forebears as he spoke, wishing people wouldn't always call Indians by the nickname.

"Yeah, that'd be our Chief of Police. Tollefson. Al Tollefson. He's the head guy around here. The guy I work for, Pete . . . Pete Delaney . . .

sometimes I hear him callin' Chief Tollefson 'the old Sarge.' So, I 'spose it could maybe be him?"

"Yeah," Twocrow said, stroking at his chin. "I guess it just might be. Well, thanks again." He hung up and told Dolan what the man had said.

The young deputy looked excitedly toward the Marshal as Twocrow sat staring thoughtfully at the phone. "Could you hear?" he asked.

"Yeah. You think the Police Chief in Prairie City had something to do with all this?" he responded, picking up the note with the phone number on it as he spoke. Before Twocrow could answer, Ramsay came hurrying across the room.

"Was that Janeen?" Twocrow asked as the police officer approached. "Did she find out anything about our girl?"

"It wasn't her," Ramsay answered. "It was something really strange, though. That was the Postmaster out at Fairburn and he said that as he was walking across from the postal pickup box back to the post office with an armload of mail, he heard gunshots. And then an old beater of a car came racing past him and almost hit him. And then a big pickup truck that he thought was owned by a local guy named Pete Delaney came barrelin' after it. He figured Delaney was chasing that old car. He said it looked like the car's back window had a couple of bullet holes—but he wasn't sure if they were caused by Delaney, but thought they might. He figured he'd better call it in."

"Well, maybe he should be calling that in to the Custer County Sheriff's office, not here," Dolan said.

"Yeah, he said he DID call it in to them, but they were all tied up with some disturbance going on out by Custer State Park Headquarters and they advised him to call us and see if we could handle it."

"Fairburn . . ." Dolan started, then stopped and looked over at Twocrow. "That's where Maria said they were headed, right?"

Twocrow nodded. “Yep, and Delaney’s the name of the guy that runs those warehouses up by Prairie City, at least according to the guy I was just talking to on the phone. On top of that, I’m pretty sure Delaney was the big guy who was here yesterday with that cop I told you about—the one who came down from Prairie City investigating the shooting. I remember he made a big deal out of the fact that he lives out in Fairburn, although I don’t know what kind of vehicle he might be driving. What about the other car? Anything more on that or whose it might be?”

“Well, that’s just it,” Ramsay answered. “He said it looked like that old beater was being driven by a couple of kids. Older teenagers maybe. A boy and a girl and that they looked scared shitless. He said they made a quick turn and drove like hell out toward the west entrance into the town with the pickup hot on their tail. That’d be the southwest gravel entrance road coming into town off of Highway 79.”

“That’s gotta be Maria and my young friend Frank,” Twocrow replied, sliding his chair out from the desk and jumping to his feet. “Dolan, I’m going out there. You up for riding along?”

“You bet, let’s go!” The deputy hurried over to the coat rack to grab his hat and coat while the Marshal began putting on his own. Twocrow turned back to Ramsay as he buttoned up his jacket. “Okay, listen, if Janeen calls from the *Star*, give us a buzz on the two-way with whatever she has to say. Meanwhile, I’d appreciate it if you’d call the sheriff and let him know where we’re headed. You got my call sign?”

Ramsay gave him a little nod and salute in response, looking glum at being left behind.

“Oh,” Twocrow added as he reached the door. “Tell him in case we get into some sort of shootout, I’d be much obliged if he could see fit to send anyone else who might be in the vicinity over there to give us a hand.” He glanced over at Dolan who seemed startled at Twocrow’s declaration. “You know?” Twocrow said. “Just in case.”

Rainbow Rock

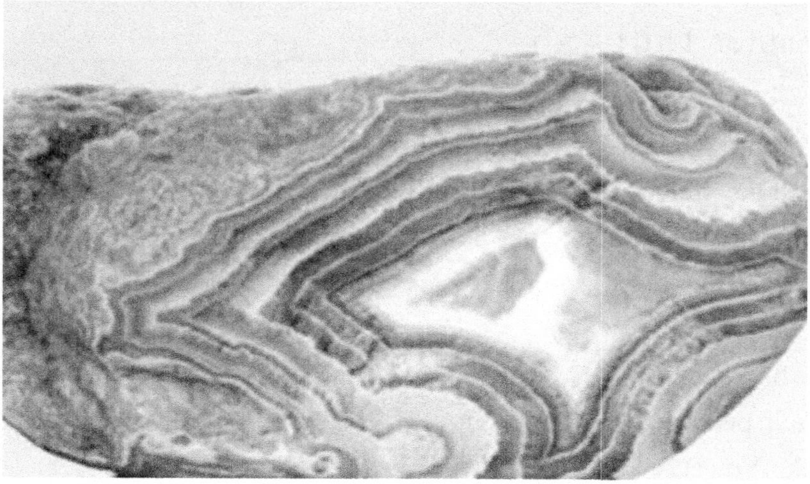

Chapter Thirty-Six

Maria cringed from a sharp pain radiating through her right leg and thrust the rainbow colored rock into her coat pocket before scrambling up the ditch's embankment. Frank already was frantically making his way through the split rail fence and she dropped down onto her hands and knees to follow him.

"It's up there!" Frank gasped. He swung around and reached back to help pull her under the bottom rail. "We need to get to that big granite rock. You sure you can make it? Your leg?"

"I'll make it! Don't worry about me," she shouted back as she cleared the fence, and trying to ignore the tears of pain created by her movements. "Just get on up there yourself so you're safe! Go! I'll be right behind you!"

An immediate second dropoff greeted them just beyond the fence. They scrambled down into it and then resumed their upward trek, now through a wide-open field alternatively covered with yucca plants and dead grass. After about 40 or 50 yards, they reached a fully grass-covered mesa that overlooked a second slope before cutting sharply back upward toward the large rock outcropping crowning the cap of the hill.

Maria glanced back over her shoulder and saw the big man getting out of the far side of his pickup and lumbering toward the front end of the hood, a gun raised as he hustled forward. The police car was still coming down the hill toward him but hadn't yet reached the point where the truck was stopped. "No way somebody his size is going to catch us on foot!" she yelled to Frank. "But when that cop gets there, that'll probably be another story. Let's go!"

She felt an adrenaline surge and the pain in her leg seemed to dissipate in the process. They struggled together up the hillside as shots rang out behind them and dirt began kicking up to their right.

"I don't think he can get a good angle on us while we're moving uphill!" Frank panted, "Especially the higher up we go. Plus he has a pistol."

Maria was gasping for breath but staying close behind him. She pointed toward a shelf-like rock overhang that started just below the bigger rock on the crest of the hill and appeared to wrap around to the hill's back side. "Is that it? Is that where we need to go?"

"Yes! And over on the other side is an opening into that old mine I was telling you about."

"Wait a minute. You mean the one filled with hibernating snakes?" She started to stop, but jumped forward again as a bullet whined overhead and knocked loose a small rock just up the hillside to her left.

"Well . . . yeah. Maybe." He ducked in behind a boulder and waited for her, dragging her in beside him as a second bullet ricocheted off the front side of their temporary shelter.

"What do you mean, maybe?" she was gasping for each breath now as she pushed up tightly against him to gain the full protection afforded by their rock shelter. "Before we even think about going in there, you gotta tell me. Are there snakes in there or not?"

"Well, that's the story I've heard," he gulped. "But I've never met anyone who's actually gone inside in the winter to see if it's true. Maybe it's just a story the owners tell to keep intruders or partyers from trying to go in. Besides," he reasoned, "even if there are snakes in there, they SHOULD be hibernating. That means sleeping, doesn't it?"

Another shot struck the rock and she scrunched in tighter against him and looked up toward the overhang. It was still about 20 to 25 yards beyond where they were sheltering.

"Well hell," she answered as she turned onto her knees. "So our choices are getting shot by some maniac cops or getting bitten by poisonous snakes? I gotta tell you Frank, you sure know how to show a girl a great time." Before he could respond, she pushed herself up and ran up to the top, diving across the crest of the hill for cover. She lay there panting and looking wildly about, waiting as Frank started moving up behind her to renewed gunfire, this time coming from two shooters.

She looked over at the spot where the mine's entrance was supposedly located. From the northwest, the angle toward which the mine was facing, the small entrance was barely visible and completely overhung with dead grass and weeds, tangled tumbleweeds, and two scraggly shrubs stretching out from either side toward the middle as if desperately seeking a way to embrace. The prairie had grown up to reclaim much of the entrance area during the many years that it had remained unused, and unless you were almost on top of it like she now was, it probably just looked like another grass-covered hilltop.

She looked back toward the road. The cop was still shooting from alongside his car and both he and the bulky white-haired man were focusing on Frank and ignoring her. Both men's shots were either going high or wide as Frank dodged and ducked his way to the top of the hill. From the two shooters' location she thought that the mine entrance must be nearly invisible.

"Move around to your right to make sure you're completely out of their sight line," Frank commanded as he reached her side. "I'm going to go ahead and see what's down below us and whether we can try to go further." He jumped up and ran past the front of the mine and half-slid, half-crab walked down the hillside in front of it. Maria knelt, watching him while taking in long, deep gulps of air to try to rejuvenate her oxygen levels following their steep climb.

Frank skidded on down and Maria moved to her right while keeping him in sight. It looked like he was intentionally making deep tracks and gouges in the hillside as he moved. Finally reaching a flat area, he signaled for Maria to stay down just as another bullet ricocheted off a nearby rock protrusion. She scrunched lower, gave him a little wave of assurance and slowly crawled forward.

Jumping down just a couple more feet, she hit the ground hard and half-rolled, half-crawled about seven or eight more feet beyond the crest of the hill. Here she was engulfed in deep shadows as the rocky hillside blocked off the sun, which was still low in the eastern sky and creating a sort-of halo effect above the hill's top edge.

Frank walked out onto the second small ledge and took three huge steps onto it as far as he could to stand directly facing the top end of a ponderosa pine tree. The top quarter of the soaring tree, which stretched up nearly 100 feet, was poking just beyond the ledge, its branches nearly touching the flat rock. He turned around at that spot and rapidly climbed back to where Maria sat waiting.

"Have you heard anything further, any more sounds from those two guys down below?" Frank moved in toward her as he waited for her response and listened intently. She shook her head "no."

"I'll check on their location," he half-whispered. She shook her head "no" again, this time more adamantly, but he gave her a dismissive wave and edged himself up to see if he could spot their assailants. As he moved up above the ridgeline another shot rang out. "Aaghh!" He gasped, grabbing at his left shoulder and falling back, rolling past her before stopping on his side propped up by a yucca plant in another shady area below the hilltop.

"Frank!" She anxiously called to him and quickly skittered over the rocks to where he had fallen and was lying moaning and clutching at his shoulder, his hand bloody from a hole in his jacket. "Frank," she repeated and pulled him away from the spiky plant and onto his back while quickly ripping open the coat. Blood was oozing from the wound and she pulled her scarf off, wadded it up and pressed it down hard on the wound site with both hands.

"Well, that was dumb," he muttered, looking back at the hilltop where he had been shot. He stopped talking as they heard voices and then the sounds of someone starting to climb up the hill toward them. "Oh, hell, they're coming up after us." He pointed back down the steep incline in front of them. "Maria, you gotta get out of here."

Instead, she gestured toward the tangle of brush over the mine's entrance. "Why don't we just go into the mine? I'll get the branches and weeds out of the way. Hang on! Here," she grabbed his right hand and put it on top of her wadded scarf to help stem the bleeding. He started to protest but she was already moving forward and clawing at the underbrush.

"Be careful. If there are snakes, you don't want any of them striking at you when you dig." He had a pleading sound in his voice and when she looked back at him she could see a look of desperation in his eyes.

"Don't worry, I'll be careful." Now eyeing it more warily, she grabbed gingerly at the tangle, wrapped her arms firmly around some of the brush and pulled, nearly falling over backward as the branches came away. "Oh hell! Oh no!" she swore as she ended up on her backside. "Oh my god! No, no, no!"

"What? What? Did you get bit? Maria! Talk to me!"

He quickly stopped talking as they heard the voices growing louder on the other side of the hilltop, one voice telling the other to move carefully and to cover each other as they continued up the hill.

Maria shook her head, tears welling in the corners of her eyes as she listened to the men's approach. "No, it's not that," she replied. She got to her feet and went back to the mine's entrance, pulling back on the nearest branch. Frank groaned, not from his wound but from what he saw. The mine's entrance was covered with boards and huge rocks were piled in front of the boards to hold them in place. Someone had sealed off what might have been their last best route to escape.

*****

Twocrow's two-way radio crackled and a scratchy sounding "Base to Red Menace, over" came across. Dolan stared at it then reached over to respond as Twocrow waved toward him to answer.

Giving the Marshal a questioning look as he pulled the mic free from its holder, he asked, "WHAT's your call sign? Red what?"

"Red Menace," Twocrow answered.

"You're shitting me?"

"No. Really. Why not? When I heard that whacko McCarthy using it all the time at those Congressional hearings, I thought, 'Hell yes! I'M the Red Menace'." He smiled. "Ask anyone who's ever made me angry. They'll clearly know."

The deputy shook his head. "O-kay." He mashed down on the mic's button. "This is Red Menace, over. Go ahead Base."

Paul Ramsay's voice came through more clearly. "Yeah, I got another call from the Custer Sheriff, and he says there's a pair of motorcycle cops—one up from Chadron and the other down from Rapid—who've been coffee-ing out at Maverick Café. He said they're willing to head right over to Fairburn and have a look-see until you arrive if you want them?"

"Tell him I said 'Damn right I want them'," Twocrow responded with a wave toward the radio. "Pass my call sign on to them and have 'em check in with me as soon as they get there." Dolan nodded and quickly relayed the response as the Marshal swung out of one of the tightest parts of the Fall River Canyon road and started to pick up speed as he headed toward the Highway 79 intersection.

The radio crackled again and Ramsay replied that the motorcycle cops were on their way.

"They'll get there way faster than we can," he assured his passenger, "plus we can use their help."

"Sure," the deputy agreed. "You know, I'd like to have some training as a bike cop. That might make for a good time, don't you think?"

"If you've got a death wish," Twocrow said gruffly. "And if you're going out with Maria, I don't think she'd be too keen on the idea."

Dolan chuckled at the thought. "I'm definitely gonna ask her out. We'll see how it goes before I commit to motorcycling."

The radio crackled again. "Twocrow!" Ramsay's voice had an intense sense of urgency and he ignored using the Marshal's call sigh. "Any way you can pick up your pace? Those bike cops are getting closer and the one from Rapid just checked in. He said they're slowing down and approaching with caution because it sounds like World War Three is going on over there." There was a slight pause and then Ramsay added, "Over."

Twocrow grabbed the mic from Dolan's hand and ferociously mashed down the button as he flipped on the overhead emergency light and made a sharp left turn onto Highway 79. "Paul, call 'em right back and tell 'em to approach with extreme caution. They might be dealing with ex-military sharpshooters so no sense taking any chances.

"Got that? Over."

"Yeah, got it," Ramsay replied, not bothering to add "Over."

Chapter Thirty-Seven

Maria continued to listen intently but the only sound she was hearing now was the far-off cawing of a crow. She shook her head. If the white-haired man and police officer were still coming after them, they were doing it very quietly. She crawled back to Frank's side. "If they're still coming, they must be waiting to see if we're going to make any sort of a move that will put ourselves back into their line of fire first," she whispered.

Frank nodded, continuing to hold down tightly on the scarf to stop any more blood loss. "I'm sorry about that," he said, nodding toward the mine's sealed off entrance. "That was a big surprise."

"Well, nothing we can do about it. We can either wait them out or figure out another way out of here," she responded under her breath. "Not any other options, are there?"

Frank pointed toward the protruding top of the ponderosa pine. "There's one other option. Go climb down that tree."

"Down the . . . are you out of your mind. I'm not going to try to climb down that tree." She stood and looked to the left. "Maybe I can just make my way around the west side of that hill."

"No, listen, they'll see you there for sure and they'll either shoot you or go back and take a car around and cut you off by the time you get to the bottom. Just crawl down the tree instead," he said. "Make your way down to that ledge and then go out across it and reach out to that pine tree. It's almost touching the ledge already, so you just have to grab a branch and get out onto it. Once you do, you can climb down in 10 or 15 minutes, easy.

"When you get to the bottom, go back toward Fairburn. It'll be to the east around the hillside. It should lead right back over to that old train depot and warehouse location. From there you can find someone around there or in the town to help us." He grabbed her arm. "Maria, it's really our only chance."

He pointed toward the marks he'd made before when he first went down to the small ledge. "With all that mess I made going up and down before it'll look like you went down in that direction and then took off walking way around the northwest side, like you were just suggesting . . . but earlier. By the time whoever's chasing us figures out you're not going that way, you should already be at the bottom and heading into Fairburn for help."

"Frank, I don't want to leave you here alone. What if they shoot you?"

"Yeah, and what if you're here and they just shoot us both? Then what?"

She shuddered. "Cripes, Frank. Either idea is shit and you know it."

"Then try to make the best out of two really bad choices," he said. He pulled her scarf away from his wound, gave it a quick look, and pushed it back into place. "No way I'm going anywhere, anyway, so please just try my plan. Okay?"

She leaned in and gave him a quick hug, pulling back again as he sucked in his breath and grimaced. "Okay. I'll try." She started sliding away from him but when she was about five feet further down the hill, she stopped and crawled back. Grabbing his right hand, she pushed the Fairburn agate into it. "You'll need this more than me."

Before he could object, she rolled away and resumed her skidding, crouching descent. He watched, tears forming at the corners of his eyes as she changed from a crouch to finally standing back up and walking forward.

Maneuvering past two granite outcroppings that seemed to be erupting from the hillside for absolutely no reason, she stepped out onto the small ledge. Carefully making her way across, she reached the point where the rock outcropping was nearly touching the top branches of the pine tree.

The branches there were only about two-to-three inches in diameter, but they seemed sturdy. Below them, in ever widening circles, were other larger branches descending down to a longer, branch-free open trunk space that extended the final 12 to 15 feet from the bottom branches to the ground.

Maria figured if she could get that close, she'd find one way or another to either shimmy or jump on down to the ground. She turned and waved at Frank to signal her intention to give it a try and stretched out her arm until she could latch her fingers onto the closest branch.

But just as she grabbed ahold her feet slipped away from the outer edge of the ledge and she skidded forward, half falling and half jumping toward the tree in the process. As the branches there swallowed her up, one poked into her shoulder and side and another one scraped across the corner of her face, barely missing her left eye as she desperately stretched out and wildly flailed at the other branches for support.

She fell several feet emitting a small scream before clamping her mouth shut and hoping no one but Frank had heard her. Now partially flattened tight against the trunk amidst the unruly branches she struggled to locate one that she could rest her feet on as she figured out the best way down. Within seconds she'd succeeded, firmly securing each foot onto separate spots. Taking another deep breath to calm herself down, she turned and feebly waved toward Frank to let him know that she was okay and on the tree, ready to start down.

She felt something warm trickle down the side of her face and tasted blood as it ran from the deep scratch and into the corner of her mouth.

"Well, crap, there goes my last hope of getting Jim Dolan to go out with me," she muttered under her breath. "Or probably any guy as far as that's concerned," she added, picturing herself with a disfigured face that would surely be a permanent deterrent for any guy who seemed like he might be interested. "Oh, what the hell?" She looked skyward with resignation in her voice. "Guess it'll just have to be the solitary writer's life for me."

She sighed and carefully started making her way down, stopping just before moving below the final line of sight that stretched out over the ledge in Frank's direction. She was glad to see him wave and then give a heartening smile and thumbs up.

"Okay, see you at the bottom, one way or another," she softly said in his direction before resuming her descent. After several more branches, she stopped and looked down. The interlaced branches made it a slow go. It was still more than 50 or 60 feet to the bottom row of branches and it seemed like it might be a very long and hard fall if she didn't do it right.

As she balanced and contemplated her options she heard another gunshot. And, despite the tree's needle-laden branches and the top of the ledge muffling most sounds, she could make out a loud exchange of men's shouted voices coming from the area where she had left Frank. Then she thought she heard someone frantically yelling her name. "Frank!" she answered. "Frank! Is that you?"

A handsome man's face popped out over the edge of the ledge and stared down at her. "Nope," he called down. He leaned out further and waggled a gun toward her. "Definitely not Frank. And if you don't wanna get him or yourself shot, you better start climbing back up here right now."

*****

"Red Menace, this is Rapid Cycle One. Do you copy, over?"

Dolan grabbed the mic. "This is Red Menace. Go ahead Cycle One, over."

"Yeah, Marshal, this is Officer Willis Foster. We're down below a hill about three-fourths of a mile in from 79. What's your E-T-A?"

"Soon," Dolan answered, skipping the formalities. "Just turning onto your road, so hang tight until we join you." He looked at Twocrow to make sure he was not saying something out of place, but the Marshal nodded his approval as he cranked the wheel right and headed down the gravel road. He snapped off the car's overhead flasher and concentrated on the road. After crossing two small hilltops, he dropped into a steeper depression leading up to a much larger third hill. The two motorcycle cops were stopped at the bigger hill's base.

A big man in heavy leather riding gear embellished with a Rapid City badge left his motorcycle alongside the other rider and made his way toward Twocrow's vehicle, pulling off a helmet as he walked. Twocrow and Dolan exited their car and moved to meet him, accepting the cop's quick handshake and greeting.

"Willis Foster," the Rapid officer said. "That's James Star back there, coming out of Chadron. We like to meet over at Maverick once a week for coffee and just generally catch up on the latest in motorcycle policing, if you know what I mean?"

Twocrow nodded. "Sure. Shop Talk. Glad to have your help Foster."

Dolan took a few more steps and waved in Star's direction. "Your name is James?" he asked with surprise in his voice. "Hey, great to meet you. My name's James, too. I'm Dolan with the Fall River Sheriff's office. But I go by Jim."

"Well, actually, I usually do too," Star answered, leaving the bikes and walking quickly over to warmly shake Dolan's hand. "Good to meet you." He gave Twocrow a little wave of acknowledgement. "Marshal."

A barrage of gunshots from beyond the hilltop interrupted.

"Look, like I said, I'm glad you boys are here to give us a hand, but if we can wrap up this social aid meeting, I'd like to get the hell going over this ridge and try and save a couple of kids' lives, okay? Have you taken a look at what might be going on over there?"

"Sure Marshal. Sorry." Star said apologetically. "There's 3 vehicles parked in the road below—one's a pickup truck, one a police cruiser and one's an old Plymouth that's sitting nose first against the split rail fence on the north side of the road. We could see two shooters advancing slowly toward the crest of the hill and it looked like one was a cop. But after we had your warning, we thought we better pull back and not approach them, even if they might be 'friendlies.' Was that right?"

"Yeah," Twocrow said. "They may be on a legitimate stop here, but we're thinking not. We think that they're chasing a couple of young people out of Hot Springs who might have some key information about a shooting we're investigating from two days back."

"You mean that Indian kid killed up north of Hermosa?" Foster asked.

"Yes, the same. You didn't happen to get a look at the insignia on the police cruiser, did you?"

"Couldn't see it clearly from where we stopped," Star answered.

Twocrow nodded. "Okay. Well, I'm worried they're going to take out these young people before we can get in there, especially if we come barreling up over the hill and spook them." He pointed at the fence and the hillside to their north. "Can those bikes of yours handle that terrain over there okay? Maybe we can come up on them from the back side?"

The motorcycle cops exchanged a quick look and a grin. "Of course. Piece of cake. But what about the fence?" Foster responded.

"Pull it down."

"Yeah?" He looked from Twocrow to Dolan but neither said anything more. "Sure thing. Once we pull it apart and get in there, it shouldn't take more than a minute or two to get up to where we saw those shooters." Foster said. He pointed to the open area northeast of the fence. "We can cross down into those little ravines and hillclimb on up the backside of the hill that they're going up on foot on their side. Hopefully we'll get up there before anyone gets shot."

"Yeah," Twocrow agreed. "Hopefully."

"Come on, no time to waste," Dolan said, hurrying toward the split rail fence and starting to push at the top rail. The motorcycle officers crossed the shallow ditch and put their shoulders into the rail on either side of him. In less than a minute, the rail cracked and then fell into two long pieces. The Fall River deputy immediately switched his focus to the bottom rail, this time jumping on top of it and trying to force it down.

Twocrow joined them. "Maybe those cops aren't out to cause any harm to our young friends. But if I'm right, they're shooting at a young man named Frank Silver Shore and a female reporter from Hot Springs named Maria Tager who's with him," he panted as he struggled to help. "If I'm wrong, then our pulling in up there will be a way for us to help out some fellow officers with whatever they're trying to do. But, again, if I'm right then we can put a stop to something bad going down. A 'win-win,' right?"

"Sure," Foster agreed, dropping onto his backside and kicking violently at the fence with both of his heavy leather boots. With a loud crack, the rail gave way and splintered into two parts.

"Okay, go get your bikes and we'll get these rails pulled further apart," Twocrow said, reaching down to take one end of the cracked rail. Star was already on the move and Foster leapt to his feet and raced after him. Dolan moved up next to Twocrow and began pulling the wooden rails further apart, creating a path for the motorcycles to get through.

In less than a minute the bike cops had fired up their machines and sped over to the fence, carefully easing their way through the hole and out onto the prairie. "We're going with you," Twocrow said, putting a hand on Foster's back to encourage him to slide forward. "Dolan, you climb on here with Foster and I'll hitch with Star." He gingerly made his way over to Star's bike as he was speaking.

Star gave the old lawman a dubious look. "You sure you just don't want to drive down to where their cars are parked and wait for us there Marshal?" the Chadron officer interjected. "Not that you're not welcome, but I'm just sayin' it could get pretty bumpy on the ride up that hill."

"Don't worry about me. I've been bumping across these prairies for almost 80 years and most of the rides were probably a hell of a lot tougher than the one you're about to give me." He pushed Star's body slightly forward on the seat and started to get on behind him as Dolan and Foster smirked at the exchange.

Struggling to swing his leg up across the seat, Twocrow finally signaled for Dolan to join him. "Give me a little boost up, would you Dolan? Like I just told Star here, I'm not worried about the ride. But I could use a little help getting it started."

Chapter Thirty-Eight

The motorcycles bounced their way through the two small arroyos and on across the rock-strewn and yucca-covered landscape before grinding steadily upward. They paused just before reaching the final ridgeline leading up toward a long-closed entrance to the old abandoned mine.

"You ready? You still hanging in there okay?" Star asked, lifting up the visor of his helmet and looking back over his shoulder at Twocrow. Twocrow had removed his revolver and was holding it with his right hand while gripping firmly onto the back of Star's seat with his left. The Marshal checked that his weapon was ready for action and nodded.

"You know the first lawman I ever really knew around these parts used to ride a horse called Star. And if I'm rememberin' right, that ride was a lot like yours, especially when Star was feeling a bit feisty." He grinned at the motorcycle cop. "Let's do this."

Star grinned back and signaled to Foster, snapped his visor back down and gunned the engine. The bike jumped forward but the Marshal held on like he was riding a bucking bronco and they crested the hilltop and sped head-on at the old mine.

Off to their left, standing on a small ledge, a uniformed police officer brandishing a gun was gesturing vehemently at someone perched on the top branches of an adjacent pine tree.

"That's Maria!" Dolan yelled. He tapped Foster's shoulder and pointed. Then he pointed toward the hillside jutting out over the boarded up entrance to the abandoned mine. "Marshal, look!"

A bulky man with a bright white patch of hair sticking out beneath his cowboy hat was moving, gun in hand, toward a body on the ground.

"It's Delaney," Twocrow called back. "We'll take him, you go to Maria." The two motorcycles split apart with a roar and Twocrow held out his revolver and fired into the air. The big man on the hilltop paused and turned his weapon in their direction as the motorcycle bore down on the mine's entrance. The body on the ground stirred and started to sit up, once again drawing Delaney's attention. The big man returned his gaze to what they could now see was a young man on the ground.

"That's my young friend Frank," Twocrow said, leaning in close to Star's right ear to make himself heard. "Frank!" he called out seeing Delaney stepping closer toward the young man now propped partway up on his left elbow. "Look out above you!" Star gunned the motorcycle's engine and spun to his left guiding his bike directly at Delaney.

"Frank! Get down!"

Looking wild-eyed in their direction then back toward the big man advancing at him with a gun, Frank ducked and rolled to his right just as the top edge of the rising sun came up over the hilltop behind him. Frank raised his right hand as if to fend off the big man pointing the gun and a flash of light reflected off an object in his hand directly at Delaney. Surprised by the sudden light hitting his face, Delaney jerked back slightly and fired a shot wildly over the younger man's head.

Twocrow gripped Star's shoulder like a vice to steady himself, aimed for Delaney's legs and fired. The big man cried out in pain and dropped his hand to his right knee, a look of disbelief on his face as he turned back to face the oncoming motorcycle. The Chadron cop responded with one more slight gunning of his engine, bumping into Delaney's left leg and knocking the big man off his feet before skidding the bike to stop.

"All yours Marshal." Star flipped the visor up again and nodded as he pulled his own weapon free from his side holster. "I've got him. You go check on your friend." He straddled the bike to keep it level, then snapped down the kickstand and leaned it slightly to the left. Twocrow slid off to that side, grabbing onto Star's now outstretched left hand to maintain his balance as Delaney cowered before them.

Back on solid ground, Twocrow stood still for a few seconds to regain his land legs. Feeling settled, he cautiously started toward Frank who had rolled onto his back and was holding down on a wadded up scarf at the corner of his shoulder.

"Hello Marshal Twocrow," Frank said with a small smile. "Really glad you could join us up here." But before Twocrow could respond they were interrupted by a gunshot, followed by a scream from Maria.

*****

Maria had struggled back up to the treetop grateful to still be wearing her heavy coat and padded pants to protect against the sharp points of the tangle of smaller branches that seemed to be collaborating to impede her efforts. Blood was still running down the side of her face from the earlier wound and she really didn't want any more.

Climbing the final few feet, she stopped and stared across the small divide that separated the treetop from the edge of the rock ledge. The spot where she had first jumped toward the tree was now occupied by the handsome police officer pointing his service weapon straight at her head. He waggled the gun. "Come on. Over here. And don't try anything or MY friend over there is going to put a bullet in the head of YOUR friend. Understand?"

He gestured back at the mine's entrance just as a roaring sound interrupted and two motorcycles came barreling up over the ridgeline to the northwest and slid to a stop.

"What in hell?" the officer said. In response the bikes both roared again as one veered off to the right toward the mine and the second one headed directly toward them. Almost immediately they heard a shot, followed by a loud exchange of voices, and then another shot coming from the mine entrance area. The man holding the gun in her direction swung around to see what might be happening, and then snapped his attention back at Maria.

"Hey, I know you," Maria said as he waggled the gun toward her. "You're Hillman from the Prairie City Police. You need to let me go."

Hillman glared. "Shut up and come on! Now!" Maria hesitated and he fired a shot above her, clipping off the corner of a small branch above her head. She screamed and held up her right hand.

"Okay. I'm coming, I'm coming! Don't shoot me!"

The motorcycle racing toward them skidded up to the edge of the extended rock ledge and pulled to a sharp stop. A passenger behind the bike's driver fired a shot into the air before aiming the weapon in Hillman's direction.

"Fall River Sheriff!" the man yelled. "Put your gun down and back away!" Maria instantly recognized Dolan's voice.

"Jim!" Maria called to him from the tree. "He's police from Prairie City. Name's Hillman. He and that other guy are trying to kill us!"

The Rapid City motorcycle officer leaned ahead to balance his big bike and nodded to Dolan to dismount as he drew his weapon and aimed it in Hillman's direction, using his windscreen as a partial block around which he was zeroing in on the Prairie City cop. "Let her go Hillman, or we're going to shoot," the bike cop ordered, cutting the engine on his bike. In the sudden dead quiet created by the engine's stoppage they all could hear him cocking the service weapon that he had pointed at Hillman.

Slowly raising his left hand, the Prairie City officer leaned forward with his right arm and placed his gun on the ground. Then with both hands raised Hillman backed away as Dolan tapped the other cop on his left shoulder. "You keep him covered and I'll go over." The Rapid City policeman nodded, saying nothing more as Dolan walked across to where Maria was precariously balancing on the nearby branches.

"Be careful Maria," he said. "We got you. The Marshal's over by your friend. Are you okay?" She nodded and he holstered his gun and inched out to the ledge's rim, extending his hand in her direction. "You'll be safe. Just reach out, take my hand, and come on across." Maria leaned ahead, straddled the space between the ledge and her tree branch and half-jumped, half-fell into Dolan's outstretched arms. The force of her jump caused them both to stumble partway up the hillside before stopping in a tight embrace.

"Thank you! Thank you!" she half-sobbed as he pulled her even closer. "I thought I was going to die."

"I'm so glad you're okay," he answered. "So glad!" She gave him a warm smile and stepped back, giving a little wave of thanks to Foster as well. As they turned to stabilize themselves Dolan's feet suddenly slid sideways and he fell, jerking Maria off balance with him in the process. She struggled to stay on her feet stumbling backward toward where Hillman was standing, her body now shielding the Prairie City cop from Foster's line of fire. Seeing his chance, Hillman jumped forward and grabbed her around the neck.

Holding Maria as a shield, he leaned out and retrieved his gun and then swung it back and forth toward the semi-prone Dolan and the Rapid City officer. "Both of you throw your guns over here." Foster hesitated and Hillman fired into the air eliciting a scream from Maria in the process. "If you don't want her hurt, throw me those guns." He pointed to Foster.˙ "And toss me your bike keys then move on over by your buddy! Do it now!"

Foster and Dolan tossed their guns out onto the ledge and Foster removed the keys from his bike and threw them in Hillman's direction.

Then watching Hillman's every move, he cautiously crossed over to Dolan's side and helped him to his feet. Maria slowly held out her left hand and gestured toward them. "I'll be all right."

She glanced over her shoulder at Hillman. "Leave them alone and I'll go with you back to your car. Okay?"

He loosened his grip slightly and waggled the gun toward the keys. "Go pick up those keys, hold them out where I can see them, and back up to me again." She stepped ahead and he stopped her. "Do it slowly."

Trembling, Maria stepped forward and picked them up, then slowly backed up to where he could grab her left arm and pull her back in toward him. "Now put 'em in your pocket and then we're going to my car." She hesitated and he twisted her left arm, causing her to cry out in pain. "Do it! And you two stay the hell out of my way!" he added to the police officers as they reacted to Maria's cry.

She slipped the keys into her coat pocket, brushing her hand across her notepad and pencil in the process. "Come on, let's go!" He jerked on her arm and roughly started pulling her away from the ledge. Maria suddenly screamed, leaned back and ripped the pencil out of her pocket. Swinging wildly around she stabbed it down into the top of his hand.

Hillman yelled in surprise and pain, and she responded by stomping down on his right foot. Then dropping to the ground, she rolled back toward the center of the ledge as he bent partway over in response to her actions.

"Aaghh! You bitch!" Hillman started to straighten up, raising his gun hand toward her.

A shot rang out and Hillman cried out again, this time from the pain of a bullet hitting his right arm. He jerked backward from the impact, dropping his gun in the process. Dolan sprang forward and leaped at the wounded officer, tackling him to the ground and kicking the gun away as he wrestled him away from where Maria lay sprawled.

Foster raced ahead to help as Dolan and Hillman rolled across the flat rock surface and directly into another of the bordering yucca plants. Hillman yelled in pain again, this time as the yucca spines jabbed into his backside. "Stop!" he gasped as Dolan shoved him harder into the spines. He held his hands out to his sides. "Stop. I give up."

Dolan pushed away from him and lay panting as Marshal Twocrow walked toward them with his weapon extended. "Your shooting Marshal?" Dolan asked as he gestured toward Hillman's wounded right arm.

Twocrow nodded, a glint in his eye.

"Not bad for an old fart like yourself," the deputy grinned. "You know, you really ARE the Red Menace. You give lessons?"

Hillman groaned and resignedly leaned back away from the yucca plant while holding his left hand on top of his wounded right arm and glaring at Twocrow.

Maria scrambled to her feet, picked up Hillman's gun and walked over to Dolan, reaching down to give him a helping hand up and squeezing tightly against Dolan's outstretched left arm as she carefully handed him the gun. "Here," she said. "You got that?" He nodded and signaled for Foster to come and help. "Yeah," he said softly, taking the gun with his right hand. "Got it."

He wrapped his left arm around her shoulders and gently guided her away as Foster moved in to handcuff Hillman under Twocrow's watchful gaze. "And if you don't mind," he added as they started walking back uphill toward the mine's entrance, "I got you, too."

Chapter Thirty-Nine

Saturday, Feb. 5, 1955
The 6th Day

Frank came out of the kitchen into Elizabeth's living room, carrying two cups of hot tea and handed one to Elizabeth. He started to give the second one to Maria, but she waved him away from the small rocking chair where she was seated. The left side of her face was heavily bandaged from where she had struck the tree branch trying to get off the hilltop.

"No, none for me," she groaned. "But I think another round of pain-killers might be in order, if you wouldn't mind grabbing the bottle out of my coat pocket?" She gestured toward her coat hanging on the coat rack by the door.

"Sure. Hold this." He handed her the second cup and walked over to retrieve her medicine.

Handing her the bottle and taking back the cup he turned toward the couch where Elizabeth was holding up a medicine bottle of her own, reading the label. He sat down halfway between the two women as Maria took out two pills, swallowed them with some water, and gingerly leaned back in the chair with another little groan.

"I'm still achy after all that banging around out there," Maria said. "But at least the doctor says I shouldn't have any long-lasting scarring once this heals. He used some of those new smaller polyester stitches. Said I could be his guineau pig if I didn't mind. It'll give me another story topic, I suppose." She looked over to Frank and gestured toward his shoulder, also swathed in bandages. "How are you holding up?"

"I'm good. Still can't believe I got shot and can walk around here like nothing much happened. Guess I'm lucky the bullet didn't go all the way through or your scarf might not have stopped the bleeding." He smiled and reached into his pocket, pulling out both the spent bullet and his rainbow rock. "And now I've got this cool souvenir to keep alongside my lucky protective agate. Two lucky charms, huh?"

Maria gave him a dubious stare and then shrugged. "Okay sure."

"Well, the rainbow rock's a protective charm for sure," he said, slipping the bullet back into his pocket and holding up the agate. "Marshal Twocrow swears it reflected the sun into Delaney's eyes just as he was shooting at me and that blinded him just enough to keep him from hitting me." He turned it over in his hands. "My rainbow rock."

"But it didn't stop you from getting shot in the first place, right?" she said with a skeptical tone to her voice.

"That's because you didn't give it back to me until after I got shot," he said indignantly. He tapped the rock with his other hand and returned it to his pocket.

"I was holding it in my hand when the big goon was trying to shoot me, and when I rolled away the morning sun flashed off of it right into Delaney's eyes. Blinded him for just enough time to cause him to miss me and help the Marshal get him instead. Say what you want, but I'm a firm believer in my rainbow rock's protective powers."

She laughed. "Okay. Then I'll be a believer, too." She looked across the room at Elizabeth. "And what about you? What's your latest?"

"Now that I'm taking these antibiotics I feel a hundred percent better," Elizabeth said, taking her own next dose with a big gulp of the tea as she snuggled down into the couch's corner and pulled the blanket up tighter around her neck and shoulders. "Those days spent in the Medical Center were a lifesaver, too," she paused and gestured around the apartment. "In more ways than one, I guess. I'm really glad we weren't around here when those guys broke in and ransacked the place."

She sighed and settled back in her corner of the couch. "I'm grateful for your offer to stay at your house Maria, but I want to be here, even if they tore the place apart and it's going to take a few days to get everything back in order." She stared intently around the room. "What a mess!"

Frank absently pushed aside some of the books and papers scattered on the top of the end table between himself and Maria to make a place for his cup of tea. Liz's large photo album that had been lying open and serving as a sort-of paperweight for everything else tumbled to the floor and popped open. In semi-slow motion, the papers that had been lying underneath it started sliding after, first a few, then as a cascade.

The papers scattered over and around the book and Frank groaned as he eyed the additional mess he'd just created. He eased down onto his knees and started picking everything up.

"Just leave it for now," Elizabeth said. "Sit back down and relax. Drink your tea. Marshal Twocrow will be proud." She lightly laughed, took another sip of her own tea and pointed to her throat with a smile. "I know it's silly, but it feels great to be able to laugh again without coughing."

Frank put a handful of the papers up on the corner of the end table and reached down to pick up the photo album. "Nice album," Maria said as Frank laid it over on top of the papers.

"I had it out for the Marshal so he could get a picture of Gene," Liz answered. "He said that Prairie City cop took some too." She pointed. "It was from the next page, I think."

Frank flipped over the page exposing the blank spots where three of the four photos were missing. He nodded his affirmation and started to shut it. Suddenly he stopped and looked again at the other photo still mounted on that page. “Hey!” He sat up straighter on his knees and pulled the album closer toward him while pointing at the photo. “I know this spot.”

Frank removed it from the album and held it out toward the two women. The photo pictured Elizabeth, Gene and their parents standing on a flat rock overlooking a small river below. A rainbow caused by the rising mist arced off the water behind them, both filling the low sky and seeming to embrace them within its brightly colored bands.

Elizabeth smiled. “Yeah, that’s where Gene and my Dad used to go fishing and swimming sometimes. Mom and I went along just that one time ’cause it was their spot, not ours. Took me 15 minutes to set up the camera so we could all be in the picture. The missing ones were just of Gene and me. Hopefully they’ll be returned.”

She stopped as a tear trickled from the corner of her eye. She took a moment to compose herself and then continued. “Now with Gene gone, too, I’m the only one left.” She sniffed and wiped her eye. “Those photos were taken just before Mom and Dad’s car accident.

“It’s a spot out northeast of Hermosa. I hadn’t been there before. There were all kinds of cool little rainbows forming in the spray along the creek below. They looked like they were coming down at the base of the rock. I guess from the reflections of the afternoon sunlight bouncing off the water. Little rainbows arcing everywhere.”

“Isn’t that Spring Creek? The one that runs up north of the agate fields?” Frank was getting more excited as he spoke, running his thumb across the photo as he asked the questions.

“Well . . . sure. How’d you know?”

“ ’Cause I went there a couple times with Gene, too. Just the two of us. We skipped out on school the last time and spent an afternoon fishing, swimming and just lying around.”

He turned to the next page in the album, then turned it toward Elizabeth and pointed at one of the photos there. It showed a big cottonwood tree nearby. "We sat in the shade right about there. Just out front of that big tree; that cottonwood tree. Nagi Wagaca, he called it. The Cottonwood's Shadow."

"Wag what?" Maria said.

"Not wag, like a dog's tail. Wahg," Frank said it slower, emphasizing the WAH part of the word. "He made me learn to say it before we could leave to come back home. NAH ghee WAHG-hah chah. Took me like half an hour to pronounce it right, so now I always remember."

He paused and moved his hand off the photo to one side, a shocked expression on his face. Then he drew an imaginary spot in the air. "And . . . and right over here, just to the side of the cottonwood tree was a giant rock formation. He said during part of the day it was marked by the cottonwood's shadow. Did he tell you about it too? About the rock pile?" He turned to Elizabeth with the question.

Now it was Elizabeth's who had a shocked look on her face as she slowly nodded in return. "You remember now too, don't you?" Frank said as he watched her expression. "And your dad, he called that spot by the tree the rock pile. Gene did tell you about it, didn't he? You know?"

"Frank. I'm so sorry. I was so sick I wasn't thinking straight about it before. I think this is it. And Gene and I called it Rainbow Rock."

Maria made an audible gasp, reached over and grabbed the photo book, starting to stand as she spoke. "You mean Rainbow Rock and what he might've been calling the rock pile, they were both on this spot?"

Frank grinned at the two women. "Yes!" He pointed emphatically at the album. "Gene said your dad loved the crazy rock formations there, especially the big one in the shadow of that twisted old cottonwood tree. The rock pile."

He took the album back from Maria and held it triumphantly above his head. "We gotta get ahold of Marshal Twocrow right away."

Chapter Forty

"Well, I can report that things are coming together," Twocrow said as he gingerly cradled the hot mug of tea Frank had immediately offered him on his arrival. He blew across the top of the mug, took a drink and smiled. "Good job on the tea, Frank. You're a quick learner." Frank gave him a little "aw shucks" dismissive wave in response as Maria reached out and patted him on the shoulder.

He nodded toward Jim Dolan, who was still standing near the door. "Dolan and I just came from a meeting with the sheriffs from all three counties—Custer, Pennington and Fall River—and even though we don't fully have everything in order yet, we do have enough now from the ballistics and what they've told us to charge both Delaney and Hillman with Gene's death. Plus there's an attempted murder charge for shooting at the two of you.

"And there's a lot about an illicit drug operation that not only involves them but also may have led to Gene's death in the first place."

He sipped the tea again and sat down in the chair that Maria had abandoned on their arrival. "We've also charged the police chief in Prairie City, Al Tollefson, with conspiracy in Gene's shooting, and the Pennington Sheriff thinks he can probably tie him into the drug operation as well," Twocrow continued. "Now, we just have to track him down because he's on the run."

"The Marshal and I were just coming back into town from that meeting up in Custer when we got the call on the two-way that you wanted him to come over immediately," Dolan added, trying not to appear ill at ease. "So, I hope you don't mind my just 'dropping in' too, without a formal invite, I mean?" He gave Maria a shy smile as he spoke.

"Well, I for one am really glad to have you here, just like I was especially glad you were along with the Marshal when you came to Frank and my rescue out at Fairburn," Maria responded, self-consciously moving her left hand up to the bandage on her face. "Hope you can put up with my grotesque appearance," she added. "I'll probably be running around with this thing on my face for the next couple of weeks."

He gave her another smile in return. "Don't worry, that bandage can't hide your natural beauty. I'm just happy you could get it fixed and that you'll be back to yourself soon. Maybe we can go out somewhere to celebrate . . . you know, when it's time to get the bandage off. And . . . and, uh, for everything else." He turned red with embarrassment as he looked around at the others in the room, realizing they were all caught up in the exchange between him and Maria. "S-Sorry," he stammered. "Hope I'm not being too forward?"

"No-no, it's fine," she hurried to cover his embarrassment, turning slightly red in the face herself at her own reaction. She looked around the room. "You're all enjoying this, aren't you?" They all laughed as she looked back at Dolan. "Yes!" she emphatically added. "I'd LOVE to go out with you . . . just to celebrate me, of course!"

"Good," he chuckled. "It'll be a date then."

"If you two are done with all this puppy love exchange, can we get back down to business?" Twocrow spoke gruffly but Maria could see a twinkle in his eye as he looked in her direction before giving a little nod of affirmation to Dolan.

The Marshal edged forward on his chair as he spoke. "Delaney seems like he might be ready to talk more, or at least negotiate, so we're going to keep working on him. Hopefully he'll come clean about the drugs and about why they shot Gene in the first place. Looks like they've got quite the drug network in place and drug deliveries have not only been made throughout the three counties but even wider. Maybe even into surrounding states. If so, that'll involve the FBI."

"As will that plane, I'm sure." He gestured toward Maria. "Delaney said that plane was bringing in a big shipment for them. That satchel of money that Gene told Frank about may have been payment for that. Anyway, your writing down that plane's tail number is opening up a wider investigation, too.

"That plane came out of Kansas City and Delaney admitted that he and Hillman were supposed to meet it and pick up a drug shipment. They were directing it to a grass runway out near Red Shirt, up along the Cheyenne River. But when he spotted the two of you they got worried that you knew more than you did, so he says they never actually off-loaded the plane once it landed.

"We're thinking that's where Tollefson came in and he's got the shipment." He took another sip. "On top of that we have your report of someone shooting at you from that plane. Lots of good stuff for our investigators to work with."

"My 'reporter mode' kicking in," she answered. "Just can't help myself. Plus it really helped with our coverage in the paper. Got all kinds of stories about all this, not to mention my 'first person' account of nearly getting killed."

"Well, with all you found out," the Marshal replied. "I might have to deputize you."

"I'll second that," Dolan chipped in. "All three sheriffs said to pass along their compliments to you for your quick thinking . . . and your bravery." He quickly turned toward Frank. "And to you, too, Silver Shore. Hell of a thing you did out there. Really great!"

Frank nodded his acknowledgement while Maria shook her head slowly. "I think it'd be a huge conflict of interest to be a deputy and write about it, too," she said with a grin. "But thanks for the vote of confidence."

She touched her face again and pointed down to her left leg. "Can you come in and say something to my editor so I can take some time off and rest up my injured leg—not to mention my aching face? I think Janeen and I spent an extra 10 hours getting all the stories done and put together with my photos. He's always telling me how lucky I am to be getting all this great experience, but I really don't want to drop dead from exhaustion before age 25."

"Yeah, I couldn't believe when I heard he was having you get the paper ready even after all you went through," Dolan agreed. "I've heard before that your boss is a real taskmaster, but wasn't that a little above and beyond?"

"Actually," she admitted, "I really wanted to do the stories, plus I was pretty proud of the photos I had taken earlier, so wanted to get them done, too. I complain now, but I probably would've complained even more if I hadn't had the chance to put this edition to bed." She picked up a copy of the 24-page special edition they had published and held it out, a big photo of Twocrow walking away from the shooting site with a story and smaller shots of Gene, Hillman and Delaney below it. All the others applauded and she did a mock bow.

"Probably why so many small town newspaper people don't have any kind of social life, huh?"

"We definitely gotta change that?" Dolan interjected, then joined the others in another laugh after first blushing an even deeper red than before. "Gotta keep our social lives out of meetings like this, too," he added. He walked over and squeezed Maria's shoulder then took the paper and stepped back to look through it. "Hey!" he said, blushing again. "There's a picture of me in here, too."

"So you believe Gene's death was all about the drugs then?" Elizabeth asked, pulling the blanket up tighter around her neck and shoulders. "I just can't imagine how he got himself involved in all that mess in the first place?"

"I have to believe he didn't know that's what he was getting himself into until it was too late," Twocrow said. "And then when he tried to get out of it, well, that's when he got into so much more trouble. I think he ended up getting killed because he knew he couldn't keep doing what he was doing. But, I guess we'll find out more as the investigation continues, especially if we can track down that bag of money that he told Frank about. You really think that so-called rock pile is at this spot?"

The old Marshal held up the photo Frank had found of Elizabeth, Gene and their parents pictured at the top of Rainbow Rock and tapped it lightly. "I definitely know about this place along Spring Creek, but I've never heard it called Rainbow Rock or the rock pile before." He handed it over to Frank. "Glad you remembered."

Frank studied it again, looking at the rainbow formed from Spring Creek's rising mist. He re-placed the photo on the table, tracing his finger along the red band along the rainbow's top edge. Arced neatly beneath it were the other traditional colors—orange, yellow, green, blue, indigo and violet.

"Colors of the rainbow; ROY-G-BIV," Maria said as she watched his actions.

"Is that another one of those Peter Pan things?"

"Peter Pan things?" Elizabeth interrupted. "What are you talking about?"

"No," Maria hurried to respond. She looked over to Elizabeth. "I'll fill you in later about the 'Peter Pan thing.' Anyway, ROY-G-BIV comes from the first letters of the traditional seven colors of a rainbow, as seen in order from top to bottom. Red, orange, yellow, green, blue, indigo and violet. Saying ROY-G-BIV is how we memorized the colors for school quizzes."

"Wow. That's cool." He eyed it again. "I wonder why a rainbow has just seven colors?" he mused.

"Well that's kind of the weird thing, too," Maria answered. "In my physics class the professor said that those are just the seven colors we can see. He said there could really be up to a million colors of the rainbow. It's just that we humans can't see them with our puny eyes."

"Seriously? A million? Come on."

"No, truth. I'm being serious. On top of that he said every person sees a rainbow just a little different from what everyone or anyone else sees it. So each person sees his or her own individual rainbow according to their particular angle, the light, and how each person's eyes interpret color. All those variables."

"Wow," Frank said again. "That is so weird, but kind of cool, too." He sat down and stared closer at the photo.

"Have you ever wondered why a rainbow doesn't have a shadow?" he asked, holding the photo up again and turning it toward Maria. "Because no matter how hard you look, you can't see a rainbow's shadow, can you? I'll bet finding a pot of gold at the end of a rainbow would be easier than trying to figure out where a rainbow's shadow begins or ends."

"There aren't any shadows because I think rainbows are just a type of mirage. A mirage doesn't have a shadow either," Maria answered.

"What? But how can rainbows be mirages? You really can see them . . . can't you?"

"People swear that you can see mirages, too," Twocrow jumped in on the conversation. "I've heard that, haven't you? But rainbows and mirages, either one, are nothing more than illusions. Or visions, I suppose. And when you try to get closer to either one of them, they just either move farther away or disappear completely don't they?"

Frank sighed and tossed the photo back down on top of the album cover.

"They're kind of like the things Gene and I hoped would be true about our lives someday," Elizabeth added with a sigh of her own. "You keep chasing after them and never catch up. Nothing more than illusions, huh?"

"No," Maria answered. "Your dreams, those things you're looking for, are a lot more than that, because you can still catch up with those things and make them come true. Don't ever give up on your dreams or Gene's. He needs to be remembered and honored."

She stood and walked over to the coat rack and Dolan tossed the paper onto the end table and hurried over to help her with her coat. Maria pointed over at the photo. "Let's get started."

Afterword

This is a work of fiction, but it includes a blend of real and fictional places and people, with factual references to people who lived and worked in the Black Hills and its surrounding communities in the mid-1950s. Here's a look at more of "the facts" and "the fiction."

The Drug Problem:

In the mid-to-late 1950s in many regions of the United States, an illegal drug trade connected to the distribution of methamphetamines, morphine and heroine—a growing enterprise for organized crime as well as localized criminal elements—was underway in many parts of the U.S.

This story imagines one part of this illegal trade occurring in the greater Black Hills region encompassing the Dakotas, northwestern Nebraska, and eastern Wyoming.

Unfortunately—as often seems to occur in cases of such abuse—the mis-use of these drugs and the criminal trade that began with them grew out of their earlier legitimate medical usages. This was particularly true with both amphetamines and methamphetamines, which had first been distributed as popular treatments for a wide range of maladies, beginning in the late 19-teens and throughout the 1920s.

The drugs had been developed to stimulate the central nervous system, raise blood pressure, and enlarge nasal and bronchial passages. By 1932, an amphetamine product was even being marketed as an over-the-counter inhaler, and it was often regularly recommended as treatment for nasal congestion or hay fever and even as treatment for the common cold.

Produced under various prescription names in the 1930s, methamphetamine use was greatly expanded when the drugs were widely distributed to soldiers, sailors and marines during both World War II and the Korean War. This drug distribution was touted as a way to help overcome combat fatigue or to improve endurance and mood. But after their combat tours were over, many Vets—who had developed a reliance on the drugs—continued to seek methamphetamines as a way to combat what eventually would become known as PTSD. Simultaneously, these drugs also grew in popularity among the non-Veteran population, earning a reputation as "wonder" treatment for everything from weight control to depression.

However, as the drugs' addictive qualities became better known, medical professionals grew wary of continuing to provide such meth prescriptions, a move that created the opportunity for a growing black market trade for the popular drugs. While many "customers" continued to be former military users, others were just ordinary people who truly looked upon "meth" as a so-called "miracle drug," able to help them with everything from staying alert on the job or during long-distance drives, to enhancing athletic performances or serving as a "study aid" for students cramming for exams.

This black market trade grew exponentially thanks to a network of local and regional distributors. Either operating independently or under the larger umbrella of organized crime, these new "providers" took illegal drugs into even the most remote corners of the nation. What once was thought of as a big city law enforcement problem also became a problem for rural communities, Indian Reservations, remote ranching regions, and even in the shadow of the Mount Rushmore National Monument.

*****

Ellsworth Air Force Base is a real military facility located along I-90 (and in the 1950s along Hwy. 16) east of Rapid City. During World War II it operated as an Army Air Base. It was not called Ellsworth until the mid-1950s, when it was named for one-time base commander **Brigadier General Richard Ellsworth**, who—along with 22 other airmen—died in a crash of their B-36 aircraft on a 1953 training mission.

*****

Fairburn is a real town—also often referred to as a "Semi-Ghost Town"—located just outside the southeast corner of the Black Hills. It can be found east of Highway 79. It is south of Rapid City and Hermosa and north of Buffalo Gap and the "Gap road" leading west toward Wind Cave National Park. The one-time "boom" town was founded in 1879. Its name comes from combining "Fair" (or pleasant) with the Scottish term "Burn" for a stream or brook, since it was located on the banks of a pleasant small river called French Creek running along the south edge of the town.

*****

Hermosa also is a real town. Rapidly growing today but very small then, the town is located southeast of Rapid City along Highway 79. The story's nearby **Railway Café and Sandman Grain Complex** are fictitious but based on many similar small cafés and grain collection and distribution sites built throughout the region and often served by the railroad to transport grain to key ports along the Missouri River.

*****

Hot Springs is the County Seat of Fall River County in the Southern Black Hills. City, county and federal law enforcement agencies often worked side-by-side out of the Fall River Courthouse, an elegant stone building that still stands on the north end of River Street. It is located about a block from Evans Plunge, a warm (not "hot" despite the town's name) mineral springs that features both indoor and outdoor pools, water slides and spas. The Plunge, in operation continuously since 1890, was named for Fred Evans, an early Hot Springs community leader who also constructed the Evans Hotel in the heart of the city.

*****

Marshal Alvin Twocrow is based on a Lakota man and friend of the author named Albert Twocrow. As a character, he was first introduced as a young ranger (for what would eventually become Wind Cave National Park) in the book *And The Wind Whispered.* His close friends **Laura and Minnie Thompson**—young reporters and sisters who also were introduced in that book and are referenced further here—were based on the real Thompson sisters whose family owned and published ***The Buffalo Gap News*** in the 1890s and on into the early1900s.

Laura Thompson moved to the East Coast area to become a newspaper reporter in Connecticut and New York. **Minnie Thompson** worked as a reporter in the Black Hills and was friends with **Carrie Ingalls Swanzey**, sister of journalist and author **Laura Ingalls Wilder**. Carrie was a newspaper writer and editor in the community of Keystone, which is located at the base of Mount Rushmore.

*****

Frank Silver Shore and his friends, brother and sister **Gene and Elizabeth Darveaux,** are fictional but also are based on real people whose lives were affected in a similar fashion as theirs at the time of this mid-1950s story.

*****

Reporter **Maria Tager** is fictional, but her character is based on real female reporters who worked at ***The Hot Springs Star.*** The ***Star*** was the longtime weekly newspaper for both the Hot Springs community and the Southern Black Hills region. First founded in the 1880s, the ***Star*** merged with the Edgemont-based ***Fall River County Herald*** in 2019 to become the ***Fall River County Herald Star.***

The Rapid City Journal is the largest newspaper in the Black Hills and the second largest daily in South Dakota. ***The Black Hills News*** is a fictional newspaper based on several smaller newspapers of the time.

*****

Prairie City and its airfield are fictional, imagined by the author and located "somewhere" to the south of Ellsworth AFB and east of the communities of Hermosa and Fairburn. Likewise, the **Prairie City Police Department** and its officers—**Al "Sarge" Tollefson, Glen "Batch" Hillman, and Pete Delaney**—are fictional, also a creation of the author.

While the **Sandman Elevator** complex and the **Railway Café** are fictional, the **CBQ** Railroad Company and its rail line running north from Chadron, Neb., up past Buffalo Gap, Fairburn and Hermosa and on to Rapid City, S.D., was real at the time. Much of that rail line remains, but under new ownership.

*****

Agates . . . exist in a wide range of shapes and usually are identified by "banded" patterns and colors inside. They are found all around the world.

Many people—not only in the Black Hills but also in various regions of the world where agates are found—believe agates possess mystical powers. Among those so-called powers: the ability to help an agate bearer distinguish between honest and false friends; the ability to help young people, especially children, stay safe; the ability to help mothers-to-be avert miscarriages; and the ability to keep violent weather out of an agate bearer's path.

An agate also supposedly provides its bearer with the ability to adhere to his or her core spiritual beliefs and values when confronted with adversity.

The Fairburn Agate

As its name implies, this particular agate was first "discovered" by white explorers and settlers in and around the community of **Fairburn**, although they were known by the Native Americans for generations. Often called "rainbow rocks," they are identified by bright, tightly banded, concentric inner rings of many and varied colors, including black, white and pink, colors not normally found among the 7 traditional ROY-G-BIV rainbow colors—red, orange, yellow, green, blue, indigo and violet.

Designated by the South Dakota State Legislature as its official state gemstone, the Fairburn Agate took on its name after early finds of the stone in rocky fields 15 to 20 miles east of Fairburn—although a number of the agates often were (and continue to be) found in Teepee Canyon, located west of the Southern Black Hills town of **Custer**. It is because it is unique to this region that is mostly located in South Dakota, that the S.D. State Legislature designated it as the state gemstone in 1966.

The primary Fairburn Agate "Fields" or "Beds" are located near the **Kern Ranch** out along French Creek en route to that waterway's confluence (or dumping off point as the locals say) with the Cheyenne River. Some fields also are located just across the Cheyenne River from the tiny Oglala Lakota village of **Red Shirt** on the Pine Ridge Reservation.

Fairburn Agates are typically found east of Highway 79 and as far out as **The Badlands National Monument**. Fairburn agates of any size are highly valued and often sell for hundreds or even thousands of dollars.

*****

The Piper "Cub" aircraft was first built in the early 1930s and was the most popular, utilitarian aircraft of its day. In the late 1940s, a variation known as "**Super Cub**" began production, built for comfort, long range and cargo possibilities.

This latter design would lead Piper in a new direction, away from the utilitarian Cub towards comfortable, social, longer distance air travel—while still following the construction methods that had made the Piper Cub affordable, durable and practical.

This **"Super Cub"** became a legendary force in "bush flying"—around the world—operating from remote areas to open fields and clearings, or even on floats in wilderness lakes and rivers. They also were adapted for use on skis for landing anywhere a flat patch of snow could be found. They can land on almost any size airfield, including grass runways and rocky ground.

*****

The story's general premise began with meetings I had with a Lakota woman whose mid-1950s family experiences were similar to those depicted, including the death of her younger brother after she and her family had moved to the Southern Black Hills from the Pine Ridge Reservation.

At the time of those meetings in the 1970s—when I was writing for the Black Hills newspaper *The Hot Springs Star*—she shared recollections and also introduced me to the Fairburn Agate and the Fairburn Agate Fields where the rocks can be found. She said that many Lakota consider the agate a "protector stone."

She also told me about a place overlooking a small river where her family would swim and fish and where rainbows could be viewed in the mists created by the river's rapids. Her father called that place The Rock Pile. But because of the rainbows in the mists, she and her brother gave it a more fanciful name. They called it **Rainbow Rock**.

Acknowledgements

Thank you to my wife Susan for her expert reading/reviewing eye and her patience during my "writing time." Thanks to Joe & Karen Muller and Earnestine Colgan for their help in tracking down information about locations and businesses in Hot Springs and the Southern Hills area during the 1950s. Thanks to Dave and Cathy Sorenson and Carolyn Amiet for their manuscript review. Thanks to many Lakota friends and writers who provided assistance with historical and language details, and to Mary Brandt Kistler for the Chapter 32 photo. Finally, thanks to the Fall River Historical Society, the Hot Springs Library, and *The Hot Springs Star*, whose archives provided valuable background information.

About the Author

A native of Minnesota, Dan Jorgensen grew up on a South Dakota farm, attending a one-room country school and becoming the first member of his family to attend college. After earning both his bachelor's and master's degrees from South Dakota State University, he studied creative writing and film at Colorado State University where he wrote his first book *Killer Blizzard.*

He has won awards for both his creative writing and newspaper feature writing and for his work in educational public relations.

In addition to writing many hundreds of news and sports articles and feature stories, both as a journalist and in public relations, he also is the author of 9 books, including the award-winning bestsellers And The *Wind Whispered* and *Killer Blizzard.* He also has written 3 songs, a one-act play; contributed to 2 anthologies, and is a frequent presenter on the topics "Storytelling—From Journalism to Creative Writing" and "The Writing Life." He also writes the blog "A Writer's Moment."

Among the professional organizations with which he has been affiliated are the Council for Advancement & Support of Education (CASE); The National Association of Science Writers; Kappa Tau Alpha (the national journalism honorary); Sigma Delta Chi; Veterans of Foreign Wars; Rotary International; Historical Writers of America; and The Historical Novel Society.

Dan and his wife Susan live in Milliken, Colorado.

On Sale Now!

Three teenaged budding reporters stumble onto a murder…

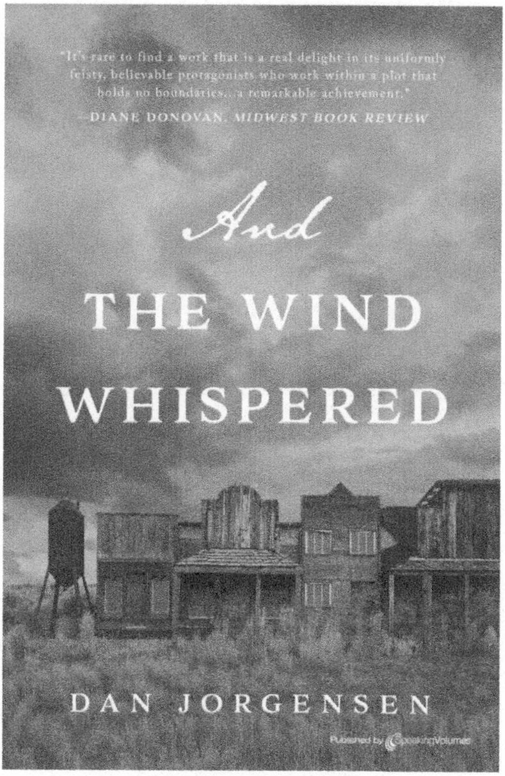

For more information
visit: www.SpeakingVolumes.us

On Sale Now!

A story that could have come out of today's headlines…

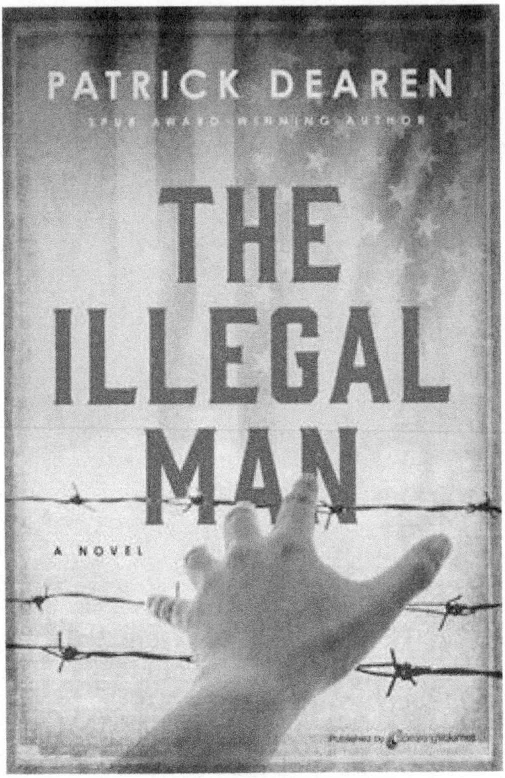

For more information

visit: www.SpeakingVolumes.us

On Sale Now!

PEACEMAKER AWARD WINNER

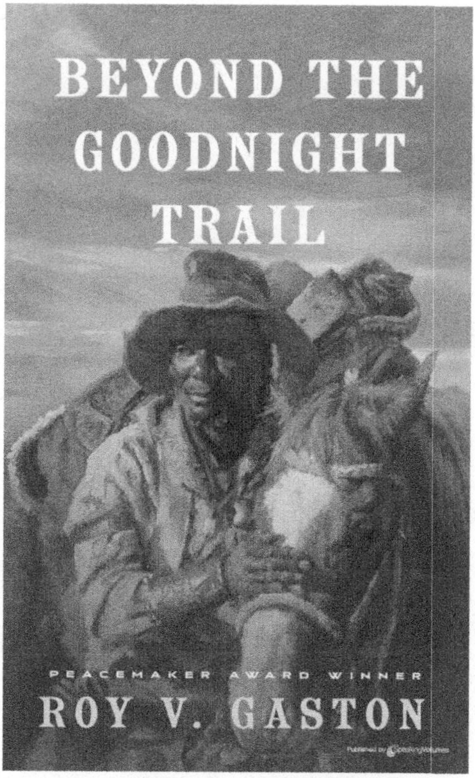

For more information
visit: www.SpeakingVolumes.us

On Sale Now!

SPUR AWARD-WINNING AUTHOR
JAMES D. CROWNOVER

FIVE TRAILS WEST SERIES

For more information
visit: www.SpeakingVolumes.us

Made in the USA
Monee, IL
15 July 2022

99794840R00204